# A DIGEST
## OF THE
# BIBLE

THE AUTHORIZED VERSION
CONDENSED FOR EASY READING

ARRANGED AND EDITED BY

*Peter V. Ross*

PRENTICE-HALL, INC.
NEW YORK

# Contents

# CONTENTS

# CONTENTS

# CONTENTS

# Preface

How LONG does it take to read a book? Some people read three or four books a day, after a fashion. Others do well if they read that many in a year.

If you can read fifty interesting pages in the course of an evening, you can, during the evenings of one busy week, read the Bible—here shaped to swiftly moving narrative.

A *Digest of the Bible* is a condensation of the King James Bible. It tells the story in clear unbroken sequence; it preserves the original wherever practical; precept and doctrine it presents without slant or comment.

The reader, with a minimum of effort, acquires a vivid, comprehensive picture of Scripture. Thus equipped, he will be encouraged to carry out his resolution, made more than once, to read the Bible in its entirety.

The translators of the Authorized Version hold out the inducement: "If we be ignorant, the Scriptures will instruct us; if out of the way, they will bring us home; if out of order, they will reform us; if in heaviness, comfort us; if dull, quicken us; if cold, inflame us. Tolle, lege; tolle, lege—Take and read! take and read!"

San Francisco                                        P. V. R.

# Genesis

## Introduction

NEARLY three hundred years before Christ, bands of restless Gauls, crossing the Hellespont, entered Asia Minor. They settled midway between the Black and Mediterranean Seas in a district to which they gave the name Galatia.

Paul visited the region, in his day an important Roman province, twice during his missionary journeys. Afterward, learning that his friends of the churches there were being "bewitched," he wrote that stirring "Epistle to the Galatians" in which occurs the well known statement:

"It is written that Abraham had two sons, the one by a bondmaid, the other by a free woman. But he who was of the bond woman was born after the flesh, but he of the free woman was by promise. Which things are an allegory."

Allegories in the Sacred Scriptures? Yes, and almost every other form of writing; for the Bible is more than a book, it is a library of sixty-six volumes embracing not all of Hebrew literature but much of the best of it. It is the product of many men writing through many centuries. It contains folk-lore, epistles, orations, poetry, philosophy, history—all of surpassing literary charm.

Its supreme value, however, consists not in recording history, or in adorning literature, but rather in teaching ethics and religion. To this end allegory, metaphor, and parable are most effective vehicles, as their frequent use by Jesus abundantly attests. Hence the care of the author to set forth Biblical narratives as found on the sacred pages.

Were there, actually, an Adam and an Eve, someone may ask, brought into being precisely as described in Genesis? Why confuse ourselves with disputation? Is it not enough that there are a thousand million mortals who walk the earth today answering the description of those Biblical characters and exhibiting human nature as it appears in all times and races?

Job is a more definite type—the upright man brought low by sickness. Whether there really was a man in the shadowy land of Uz bearing that name—a question often raised—is not to the point. The undeniable fact is that more than one stricken soul can be found in any community this day wondering, as Job wondered, why the good man should be made to suffer. And are not his friends "miserable comforters all" gathered around to remind him that his troubles must be due to some unconfessed wickedness?

And why argue whether the Red Sea and the Wilderness adventures are authentic history? Is it not self-evident that every nation has its Wilderness and its Red Sea? Every individual has his, for that matter. While

> Daily,with souls that cringe and plot,
> We Sinais climb and know it not.


## Story of Creation, Gen. 1, 2

The Bible opens with an account of the creation of the earth and its inhabitants. The discerning reader soon discovers that there are two narratives quite dissimilar. Originally separate writings, they have been pieced together by an editor now unknown. With the two documents before him, apparently, he built the Book of Genesis by first taking a section out of one document and then out of the other until both were consumed.

The first narrative refers to the Creator as "God." It runs

uninterruptedly to the fourth verse of chapter two of Genesis. Then it gives place, for a time, to the second and probably older narrative, which refers to the Creator as "the Lord God." Rather readily distinguishable at first, the two stories soon become so intimately blended as to be difficult to identify.

"In the beginning God created the heaven and the earth," Genesis starts out. "And the earth was without form, and void; and darkness was upon the face of the deep."

"Let there be light," God said, "let there be a firmament . . . let the dry land appear . . . let the earth bring forth grass . . . let the waters bring forth abundantly the moving creature . . . let the earth bring forth the living creature after his kind . . . let us make man in our image, after our likeness, and let them have dominion . . . over all the earth." It was done.

"And God saw everything that he had made, and behold, it was very good. And the evening and the morning were the sixth day." He rested on the seventh day and blessed and sanctified it. Thus ends, for the moment, the first account of creation.

The second account starts out: "These are the generations of the heavens and of the earth when they were created in the day that the Lord God made the earth and the heavens, and every plant of the field before it was in the earth, and every herb of the field before it grew."

## Adam and Eve, Gen. 2, 3

The Lord God, the narrative proceeds, formed man of the dust of the ground, Adam was his name, and put him in a garden which He planted eastward in Eden, commanding him: "Of every tree of the garden thou mayest freely eat; but of the tree of the knowledge of good and evil thou shalt not eat of it, for in the day that thou eatest thereof thou shalt surely die."

Observing that it is not good that man should be alone, the

Lord God caused a deep sleep to fall upon Adam and took one of his ribs and made a woman, Eve.

Out of the ground the Lord God formed the beasts of the field and the fowls of the air, and brought them to Adam to see what he would call them.

The serpent, more subtle than any beast of the field, beguiled the woman into eating the fruit of the forbidden tree and also giving it to her husband; arguing: "For God doth know that in the day ye eat thereof then your eyes shall be opened and ye shall be as gods, knowing good and evil."

Because of this offense the Lord God cursed the serpent declaring: "Upon thy belly shalt thou go and dust shalt thou eat all the days of thy life." Unto the woman he said, "I will greatly multiply thy sorrow." While to Adam he announced: "In the sweat of thy face shalt thou eat bread till thou return unto the ground; for out of it wast thou taken, for dust thou art and unto dust shalt thou return."

Then, the narrative continues: "Behold, the man is become as one of us, to know good and evil; and now, lest he put forth his hand and take also of the tree of life and eat and live forever, therefore the Lord God sent him forth from the garden of Eden to till the ground from whence he was taken."

### Cain, Abel, and Seth, Gen. 4, 5

Adam and Eve's first child was Cain, a tiller of the ground; the second was Abel, a keeper of sheep. Because the Lord had more respect for Abel's offering from his flock than for Cain's offering from the produce of the soil, Cain one day, while the two were in the field, rose up and slew Abel. When the Lord asked Cain, "Where is Abel thy brother?" Cain answered, "I know not; am I my brother's keeper?"

"Now art thou cursed," pronounced the Lord, "a fugitive and a vagabond shalt thou be in the earth." Then Cain went out from the presence of the Lord and dwelt in the land of Nod on the east of Eden.

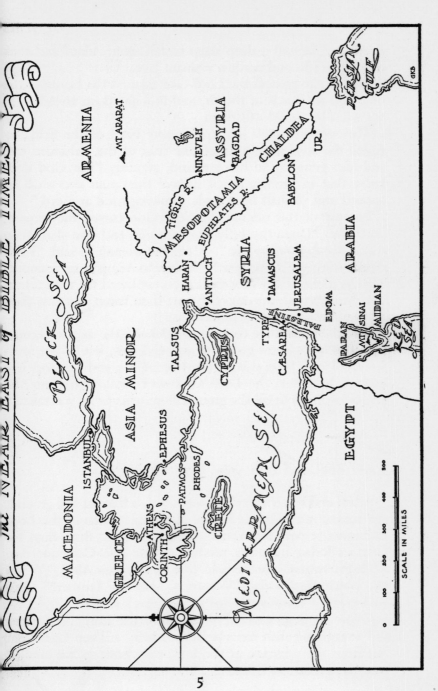

5

Among his descendants were Jabel, the father of those who dwell in tents; Jubal, the father of those who play the harp and organ; and Tubal-cain, the instructor of workers in brass and iron.

Adam and Eve's third son they named Seth.   Among his descendants were Enoch and Noah, both of whom walked with God, Enoch indeed so closely that "he was not, for God took him."

## The Flood, Gen. 6-9

There came a day when the Lord repented that he had made man, because his wickedness was so great.   He therefore resolved to "bring a flood of waters upon the earth and to destroy all flesh wherein is the breath of life."   But remembering Noah, the Lord directed him to make an ark of gopher wood; and take into it his family and a pair of creatures of every kind.   Then "were all the fountains of the great deep broken up and the windows of heaven were opened.   And the rain was upon the earth forty days and forty nights."

The ark went out upon the waters, which covered all the high hills under heaven and destroyed every living creature upon the face of the ground.   After one hundred and fifty days the ark rested upon the mountains of Ararat.   Noah then put forth a dove to see if the water had abated.   Twice the dove came back, but the third time it returned not.

Noah now removed the covering of the ark, and, looking out, found that the ground was dry.   He and his wife, and his sons (Shem, Ham, Japheth) and their wives, went forth, taking with them the creatures that had been saved.

Building an altar, Noah offered a burnt sacrifice.   When the Lord "smelled a sweet savor" he said in his heart: "I will not again curse the ground any more for man's sake, for the imagination of man's heart is evil from his youth; neither will I again smite any more every thing living as I have done.   While the earth remaineth, seedtime and harvest, and cold and heat, and summer and winter, and day and night shall not cease."

In confirmation of this promise the Lord declared: "I do set my bow in the cloud, and it shall be for a token of a covenant between me and the earth.   And it shall come to pass, when I bring a cloud over the earth, that the bow shall be seen in the cloud and I will remember my covenant."

## Tower of Babel, Gen. 11

Noah and his people journeyed from the east until they came to dwell in the land of Shinar.   There they resolved to build a city with a tower whose top should reach unto heaven. They said, "Let us make us a name lest we be scattered abroad upon the face of the whole earth."

The Lord, viewing their adventure with apprehension, exclaimed: "Behold, the people is one and they have all one language; and this they begin to do . . . Now nothing will be restrained from them . . . Let us go down and there confound their language that they may not understand one another's speech."   This done, the people abandoned their purpose and dispersed.   The name of the place was therefore called Babel.

## Abraham and Sarah, Gen. 11-18

Of Noah's three sons—Shem, Ham, Japheth—"was the whole earth overspread."   Ham became the father of the Canaanites.   His people built Nineveh.   Egypt was known as "the land of Ham."   The descendants of Japheth took to "the isles of the Gentiles"—the coasts of the Mediterranean—overflowing eventually into Europe and parts of Asia.   Among Shem's descendants was Terah, who lived in Ur of the Chaldees by the lower Euphrates (2000 B. C.).   He had three sons: Nahor, Haran, Abram.   Haran died in Ur, leaving a son named

Lot. Afterward Terah, Abram, and Lot moved northward "to go into the land of Canaan; and they came unto Haran (in Mesopotamia) and dwelt there. And the days of Terah were two hundred and five years; and Terah died in Haran."

When Abram was seventy-five years old the Lord said to him: "Get thee out of thy country and from thy kindred and from thy father's house unto a land that I will show thee; and I will make of thee a great nation." Responding to the call, Abram became the father of the Hebrew race. Taking his wife Sarai and his nephew Lot, he followed the great highway down through Damascus until he came to Canaan, which lay west of the River Jordan. Continuing southward, he passed through Shechem, where in later years his grandson Jacob located the well which still bears his name, halfway between Nazareth and Jerusalem.

But there was famine in the land, and therefore they journeyed on into Egypt. Abram, fearful that the Egyptians would slay him in order to take Sarai, represented to them that she was his sister. They took her to Pharaoh's house, and, on her account, treated Abram kindly and made him generous gifts.

However, a plague breaking out, they confronted Abram with his duplicity and cried, "Take her and go thy way." Abram then went up out of Egypt into Canaan as far as Bethel where he had been at first, very rich in cattle, in silver, and in gold. Indeed so large were their herds, so great was their substance that the land proved insufficient to sustain both him and Lot.

Trouble thereupon arose between their herdmen. Abram therefore said to Lot: "Let there be no strife, I pray thee, between me and thee, and between my herdmen and thy herdmen, for we be brethren."

So they parted company, Lot going east and choosing the plain of Jordan toward Sodom and Gomorrah, while Abram dwelt in the land of Canaan. And the Lord said to Abram: "All the land which thou seest, to thee will I give it, and to thy seed forever. And I will make thy seed as the dust of the earth."

Abram then removed his tent and dwelt on the plains of Mamre in Hebron in the southern part of what is now Palestine. Learning that Chedorlaomer and other kings had sacked Sodom and Gomorrah and carried off Lot, Abram armed his servants, pursued the victors as far as Dan and Hobah to the north of Damascus, and brought back Lot and his people with all their goods.

As he returned from his victory, Abram was met and blessed by Melchizedek, king of Salem, the priest of the most high God, of whom it is written in the "Epistle to the Hebrews," he was "without father, without mother, without descent, having neither beginning of days nor end of life, but made like unto the Son of God."

While the sun was going down one evening after Abram had made an offering from his flock, a deep sleep fell upon him and a horror of dense darkness. Then said the Lord: "Thy seed shall be a stranger in a land that is not theirs . . . four hundred years . . . That nation whom they shall serve will I judge; and afterward shall they come out with great substance. Thou shalt go to thy fathers in peace . . . but in the fourth generation they shall come hither again." As night came on, a moving torch searched Abram's offering.

That day the Lord made a covenant with Abram, saying: "Unto thy seed have I given this land from the river of Egypt unto the great river, the River Euphrates."

After ten years in Canaan, Abram, having had no children by Sarai, took her Egyptian maid Hagar. Therefore Hagar behaved haughtily toward Sarai, and Sarai dealt so harshly with her that she fled.

The angel of the Lord, finding Hagar in the wilderness by the fountain between Kadesh and Bered on the way to Shur, ordered her to return to her mistress, saying: "I will multiply thy seed exceedingly . . . Thou shalt bear a son and shalt call his name Ishmael . . . And he will be a wild man; his hand will be against every man, and every man's hand against him." Hagar named the Lord, "Thou God that seest me." The child came as was promised and Abram called him Ishmael.

When Abram was ninety-nine years old the Lord appeared to him, saying: "I am the Almighty God; walk before me and be thou perfect, and I will make my covenant between me and thee . . . Neither shall thy name any more be called Abram, but thy name shall be Abraham; for a father of many nations have I made thee . . . As for Sarai thy wife, thou shalt not call her name Sarai but Sarah."

Proceeding, the Lord assured Abraham that Sarah would bear him a son and become the mother of nations. At this Abraham fell on his face and laughed, asking in his heart: "Shall a child be born unto him that is an hundred years old? And shall Sarah, that is ninety years old, bear?" To the Lord he exclaimed, "O that Ishmael might live before thee!" The Lord replied: "Sarah thy wife shall bear thee a son indeed and thou shalt call his name Isaac . . . As for Ishmael, I have heard thee. Behold, I have blessed him and will make him . . . a great nation. But my covenant will I establish with Isaac."

Abraham believed in the Lord; and the Lord counted it to him for righteousness.

While Abraham sat at his tent door one day at noon, the Lord again appeared. As he lifted up his eyes Abraham saw three men standing by him. He hastened to have dinner prepared, and stood by them under the trees while they ate.

"Sarah thy wife shall have a son," remarked the Lord. Sarah, listening behind the door, laughed to herself. "Wherefore did Sarah laugh?" inquired the Lord. She, much alarmed, denied, saying, "I laughed not." But the Lord insisted, "Nay, but thou didst laugh."

## Lot—Sodom and Gomorrah, Gen. 18-20

Then the men rose up and looked toward Sodom, whose sins were grievous. Abraham prayed that the city be spared if there were found fifty or forty or twenty or even ten righteous within the place.    And the Lord answered, "I will not destroy it for ten's sake."

But in the evening two angels appeared to Lot as he sat in the gate of Sodom.    They warned him that the city was to be destroyed, and directed him to escape to the mountain and look not behind.    But Lot's wife, unmindful of the injunction, looked back as they ran, and became a pillar of salt.    Then the Lord rained upon Sodom and Gomorrah brimstone and fire. In after years Lot became the progenitor of the Moabites and Ammonites.

## Isaac and Ishmael, Gen. 21, 22

Abraham next pitched his tent in the south country, in or about Kadesh, Beersheba, and the land of the Philistines.    At the appointed time Sarah bore a son and named him Isaac. When he was weaned, Abraham made a great feast.    Sarah, seeing Hagar's boy mocking, exclaimed to Abraham: "Cast out this bondwoman and her son; for the son of this bondwoman shall not be heir with my son, even with Isaac!"

Though Abraham was much distressed he sent Hagar away with food and water, and she wandered with Ishmael in the wilderness of Beersheba.    When the water was exhausted she laid the boy under a shrub, and sat down a good way off so that she might not witness his death.

The angel of God then called to her out of heaven: "What aileth thee, Hagar?    Fear not, for God hath heard the voice of the lad where he is.    Arise, lift up the lad and hold him in thine hand, for I will make him a great nation."    God now opened her eyes to a well of water and she gave Ishmael a drink.    As he grew up, God was with him.    He became an archer in the wilderness of Paran to the south of Canaan.    His mother procured him a wife from Egypt.

After these things God tempted Abraham by directing him to sacrifice Isaac.    On the journey to the appointed spot, Isaac

said, "Behold the fire and the wood; but where is the lamb?"
Abraham replied, "God will provide himself a lamb for a burnt
offering." Arriving at the place of sacrifice, Abraham built
an altar, laid on the wood, bound Isaac, and stretched forth
his hand to slay him.

At that moment the angel of the Lord called out of heaven,
"Lay not thine hand upon the lad." Abraham, lifting his eyes,
saw a ram caught in the thicket, and offered him instead of
his son. And the angel of the Lord, calling a second time,
blessed Abraham because he had not withheld his only son.


*Rebekah, Gen. 24, 25*

Now Sarah had died at the age of one hundred and twenty-
seven; and Abraham was well-stricken in age. He therefore
said to his oldest servant: "Thou shalt not take a wife unto
my son of the daughters of the Canaanites, among whom I
dwell; but thou shalt go unto my country and to my kindred
and take a wife" for him.

Accordingly his servant journeyed to the city of Nahor in
Mesopotamia. At a well outside the town he met Rebekah,
the granddaughter of Abraham's brother Nahor. She had
come with a pitcher to get water. She gave him a drink and
also drew water for his camels. He gave her a golden earring
and two bracelets.

Running to her mother's house, she told what had happened.
Her brother Laban then ran to the man at the well and said:
"Come in, thou blessed of the Lord; wherefore standest thou
without? for I have prepared the house, and room for the
camels."

Abraham's servant now delivered his message. They ate,
and he tarried all night. In the morning her kindred asked
Rebekah, "Wilt thou go with this man?" She answered,
"I will." So they sent her away with her nurse and Abraham's
servant and his men.

Isaac, going out to meditate in the field at eventide, saw the camels coming. And Rebekah, when she saw Isaac, lighted off her camel and donned her veil. Isaac brought her into his mother Sarah's tent, and she became his wife.

Then Abraham married again. He died at the age of one hundred and seventy-five. His sons Isaac and Ishmael buried him with Sarah in the cave of Machpelah before Mamre in Canaan.

## Esau and Jacob, Gen. 25, 27

When her time came Rebekah gave birth to twins. The elder, "red, all over like an hairy garment," was called Esau; the younger was named Jacob. As the boys grew, Esau became a cunning hunter, a man of the fields; while Jacob became a plain man, dwelling in tents. Isaac loved Esau because he ate of his venison; but Rebekah loved Jacob.

Esau, coming in from the field one day faint with hunger, asked Jacob for food. Jacob, bargaining with him, said, "Sell me this day thy birthright." Accordingly "Jacob gave Esau bread and pottage of lentils; and he did eat and drink, and rose up and went his way: thus Esau despised his birthright."

Isaac, now that he was old and his eyes were dim, called Esau to say: "Take, I pray thee, thy weapons, thy quiver and thy bow, and go out to the field and take me some venison; and make me savory meat, such as I love, and bring it to me that I may eat, that my soul may bless thee before I die."

Rebekah, overhearing the conversation, told Jacob what was afoot and instructed him to fetch her two kids that she might make a tempting dish for him to present to his father and obtain the parental blessing. She took Esau's raiment and put it upon Jacob, and put the skins of kids upon his hands and upon "the smooth of his neck." When Jacob presented the dish to Isaac, he said: "Arise, I pray thee, sit and eat of my venison that thy soul may bless me."

Isaac felt Jacob and declared, "The voice is Jacob's voice, but the hands are the hands of Esau." Scarcely had Jacob received his father's blessing and departed, when Esau entered with his dish of venison. Then Isaac related the deception Jacob had practiced, trembling violently.

Esau "cried with a great and exceeding bitter cry," and asked, "Hast thou not reserved a blessing for me?" Isaac replied: "Behold, thy dwelling shall be the fatness of the earth, and of the dew of heaven from above; and by thy sword shalt thou live, and shalt serve thy brother; and it shall come to pass when thou shalt have the dominion, that thou shalt break his yoke from off thy neck."

Esau now resolved to slay his brother Jacob for thus twice supplanting him. Rebekah, in order to save Jacob, directed him to flee to her brother Laban in Haran, and tarry until Esau's fury abated. At the same time she naïvely hinted to Isaac the danger of Jacob marrying some native girl. So Isaac charged Jacob not to marry a Canaanite but to go to the house of Laban and get a wife.

Esau, when forty years old, had married Judith a Hittite, which grieved his parents greatly. Now, noting his father's displeasure, he took Mahalath the daughter of Ishmael.

On his journey toward Haran Jacob stayed overnight at Luz, which he afterward called Bethel. He gathered stones for his pillow. In his sleep "he dreamed, and behold a ladder set up on the earth, and the top of it reached to heaven; and behold the angels of God ascending and descending on it. And behold, the Lord stood above it and said: I am the Lord God of Abraham thy father and the God of Isaac; the land whereon thou liest, to thee will I give it and to thy seed."

When Jacob awoke in the morning he exclaimed, "Surely the Lord is in this place and I knew it not!"

## Leah and Rachel, Gen. 29

Arriving at his destination, Jacob found shepherds at the well with their flocks. "My brethren," he inquired, "whence be ye?" "Of Haran," they replied. "Know ye Laban the son of Nahor?" he continued. "We know him," they answered, "behold, Rachel his daughter cometh with the sheep." Jacob made himself known to his cousin Rachel; and Laban brought him to his house.

Laban had an older daughter, Leah. She was "tender-eyed" but Rachel was beautiful and well favored. Jacob loved Rachel; and offered to serve Laban seven years for her. But at the end of the time Laban tricked him into accepting Leah. Then Jacob served still another seven years to gain Rachel.

Leah bore Reuben, Simeon, Levi, Judah, Issachar, and Zebulon; and Leah's maid, Zilhah, bore Gad and Asher. Rachel bore Joseph and Benjamin; her maid, Bilhah, bore Dan and Naphtali.

From these sons sprang the original twelve tribes of Israel. The children of Levi lost their geographical identity when appointed to the priesthood and placed among the other tribes. The numerous children of Joseph divided into two branches, Ephraim and Manasseh, though they were generally regarded as comprising one tribe only.

## Return of Jacob to Canaan, Gen. 30-32

After the birth of Joseph, Jacob yearned to return to his own country. Graciously declining wages from his father-in-law, he craftily gained possession of the better part of his flock. And Rachel, while her father was looking after the shearing, appropriated his household idols or gods.

Then Jacob and his family, with all the goods and cattle he had got, secretly departed. On the third day his father-in-law pursued and overtook him at Mount Gilead. "Wherefore," demanded Laban, "didst thou not tell me, that I might have sent thee away with mirth?" "I was afraid," Jacob answered, "for I said, Peradventure thou wouldest take by force thy daughters from me."

Jacob, not knowing Rachel had taken the idols, invited Laban to look for missing goods. But the search proved fruitless, because Rachel had put the idols in her camel's saddle and sat upon them.

Then Jacob was wroth because of the intrusion. Sharp words followed, but presently he and Laban made a covenant of peace. As a witness to the compact they gathered a heap of stones which neither should pass to do the other harm; Laban calling it Mizpah, and saying, "The Lord watch between me and thee when we are absent one from another."

As he continued his journey, Jacob sent messengers to Esau. They returned with the report that Esau was coming with four hundred men. Jacob, greatly alarmed, then sent Esau a generous present from his flocks.

That night, when Jacob was alone, there wrestled with him a man until dawn. "I will not let thee go except thou bless me," cried Jacob. And the man, as he blessed him, said: "Thy name shall be called no more Jacob, but Israel; for as a prince hast thou power with God and with men, and hast prevailed." Jacob named the place Peniel, for, he said, "I have seen God face to face, and my life is preserved."

### Meeting of Esau and Jacob, Gen. 33-36

When Jacob went forward to meet Esau, Esau ran to meet him and embraced him. He accepted Jacob's gift, though rather reluctantly because he insisted that he had ample possessions of his own. Jacob blessed him; and they continued on their journey, Esau going ahead to Mount Seir.

Jacob pitched his tent at Shechem in Canaan. Then said he to his people: "Put away the strange gods that are among you, and be clean and change your garments; and let us arise and go up to Bethel." As they journeyed "the terror of God was upon the cities that were round about them, and they did not pursue after the sons of Jacob."

At Bethel he built an altar, because God had there appeared to him when he fled from the face of his brother. Proceeding southward he came to Ephrath, subsequently called Bethlehem. On the way Rachel died in giving birth to Benjamin. Jacob traveled on until he came to Mamre where dwelt Isaac his father. Not long afterward "Isaac gave up the ghost . . . being old and full of days; and his sons Esau and Jacob buried him."

The flocks of the two brothers were so numerous that the land "wherein they were strangers could not bear them." Hence Esau settled down in Mount Seir, southward toward the Red Sea. The district took on the name of Edom and Esau became the father of the Edomites. Jacob continued to dwell in the land of Canaan.

## *Joseph and His Brothers, Gen.* 37

Now Jacob loved Joseph more than all his children, because he was the son of his old age. Among other acts of favoritism he made him a coat of many colors. For all this his brothers so disliked Joseph that they could not speak peaceably to him.

To make matters worse, Joseph told them his dream: "Behold, we were binding sheaves in the field, and lo, my sheaf arose and also stood upright; and behold, your sheaves stood round about and made obeisance to my sheaf."

Still another dream he told them, "Behold, the sun and the moon and the eleven stars made obeisance to me." The latter dream even roused his father's ire, who asked, "Shall I and thy mother and thy brethren indeed come to bow down ourselves to thee to the earth?"

While the sons were tending their father's flock one season in Shechem, they seized Joseph and sold him to a company of Ishmaelites on their way down to Egypt. They told Jacob that an evil beast had devoured him. Jacob rent his clothes and refused to be comforted, crying, "I will go down into the grave unto my son mourning."

## Joseph in Egypt, Gen. 39-41

In Egypt, one of Pharaoh's officers, Potiphar by name, bought Joseph from the Ishmaelites. The Lord was with Joseph and he became a prosperous man. Moreover he found grace in the sight of his master, who made him overseer of his house and put all that he had in his hands. From that time the Lord blessed the Egyptian's house for Joseph's sake.

All was well until one day Potiphar's wife, furious because Joseph repelled her advances, complained of him to Potiphar. Joseph was promptly put in jail.

After two years Pharaoh dreamed that there came up out of the river seven well-favored kine, and seven ill-favored and lean-fleshed, and the latter ate up the well-favored and fat kine.

Again he slept and dreamed that seven ears of corn came out upon one stalk full and ripe, and seven thin and blasted ears sprang up after that, and the seven thin ears devoured the seven full ones.

In the morning, troubled in spirit, he sent for the magicians and wise men. But none could interpret the dreams. Then the chief butler, whose dream Joseph had interpreted while the two were in prison together, reminded Pharaoh of Joseph.

Pharaoh hastily brought Joseph out of the dungeon and propounded his dream to him. "There come seven years of great plenty throughout all the land of Egypt," said Joseph, "and there shall arise after them seven years of famine, and all the plenty shall be forgotten."

And Joseph advised Pharaoh to appoint officers to lay up corn against the years of want that were to come. The plan commending itself to Pharaoh, he observed to Joseph: "There is none so discreet and wise as thou art; thou shalt be over my house, and according unto thy word shall all my people be ruled; only in the throne will I be greater than thou."

Departing from the presence of Pharaoh, Joseph went throughout Egypt and gathered food of the seven plenteous years and laid it up in the cities. When the famine came, Joseph opened up the storehouses and sold to the Egyptians. And all countries came unto Egypt to Joseph to buy corn, because the famine was widespread.

Pharaoh married Joseph to Asenath the daughter of Poti-pherah, priest of On. Their firstborn was named Manasseh; the second, Ephraim.

## Trip to Egypt for Grain, Gen. 42, 43

When the famine touched Canaan, Jacob sent his ten sons to Egypt to buy corn, retaining Benjamin lest some mischief befall him.

Joseph recognized his brethren on their arrival, but made himself strange to them and spoke roughly, demanding whence they came and who they were. When they told him, he ingeniously insisted that they were spies, and that they should prove their good faith by bringing to him their youngest brother, Benjamin.

Nevertheless Joseph had their sacks filled with corn, and into each sack restored the purchase money. Then he sent them on their way, holding Simeon as a hostage. On their return to Jacob they related to him their experience; and when they opened their sacks, every man found his bundle of money. Then were they all alarmed.

"Joseph is not and Simeon is not," wailed Jacob, "and ye will take Benjamin away; all these things are against me. . . If mischief befall him by the way in the which ye go, then shall ye bring down my gray hairs with sorrow to the grave." But after much persuasion, the corn being nearly exhausted, Jacob allowed Benjamin to go with them on their second excursion, Reuben promising to be surety for his safety.

So Jacob instructed his sons to take tempting presents to Joseph, and double money, for he said: "The money that was brought again in the mouth of your sacks, carry it again in your hand; peradventure it was an oversight."

When they stood before Joseph, and he saw Benjamin with them, he entered into his chamber and wept. Controlling himself he came out and said, "Set on bread." Benjamin's portion was five times as much as any of the others. They drank and were merry.

Again Joseph commanded their sacks to be filled, and to put every man's money in his sack's mouth. In Benjamin's sack was put Joseph's silver cup.

When they were gone out of the city Joseph said to his servants: "Up, follow after the men; and when thou dost overtake them, say unto them, Wherefore have ye rewarded evil for good?" Accordingly they were overtaken and searched; and the money and the cup were found in Benjamin's sack. Then they rent their clothes, loaded their donkeys, and returned to the city.

## Reunion of Brothers, Gen. 44, 45

When they came to Joseph's house he declared, "The man in whose hand the cup is found, he shall be my servant." Then Judah interceded for Benjamin, pleading: "We have a father, an old man, and a child of his old age, a little one and his brother is dead, and he alone is left of his mother, and his father loveth him. And thou saidst unto thy servants, Bring him down unto me that I may set mine eyes upon him."

Then Judah offered himself in place of Benjamin, praying: "Let thy servant abide instead of the lad a bondman to my lord; and let the lad go up with his brethren. For how shall I go up to my father, and the lad be not with me?"

Joseph, unable to refrain longer, made himself known to his brothers. "I am Joseph," he said, "doth my father yet live?" His brothers could not answer him, for they were troubled in his presence. He repeated: "I am Joseph your brother, whom ye sold into Egypt. Now therefore be not

rieved, nor angry with yourselves, that ye sold me hither;
or God did send me before you to preserve life."

With these words of comfort he urged them to hasten
ack and fetch their father down to dwell close by in the
nd of Goshen, east of the Nile, not far from its mouth, for
here were yet five years of famine.

When the brothers returned and told Jacob that Joseph
as yet alive and governor in Egypt, his heart fainted for he
ould not believe them.   But when they delivered Joseph's
message, and when he saw the wagons Joseph had sent to
arry him, his spirit revived and he said: "It is enough; Jo-
eph my son is yet alive; I will go and see him."

## Hebrews Emigrate to Egypt, Gen. 46

On their journey they came to Beersheba, where Jacob
ffered sacrifices; and God spoke to him in the visions of the
ight, saying: "I will go down with thee into Egypt; and I
ill also surely bring thee up again."

Joseph made ready his chariot and went up to Goshen to
resent himself to his father; "and he fell on his neck and
ept."

Pharaoh, pleased at the arrival of Joseph's brothers, asked
em their occupation.   They answered, "Thy servants are
hepherds, both we and also our fathers."

And Pharaoh said to Joseph: "The land of Egypt is before
ee; in the best of the land make thy father and brethren to
well; in the land of Goshen let them dwell; and if thou
nowest any men of activity among them, then make them
lers over my cattle."

Joseph, in exchange for the food he gave out in the seven
ears' famine, came into possession of all the money and
ocks and land in Egypt for Pharaoh.

## End of Jacob and Joseph, Gen. 47-50

After seventeen years in Egypt, Jacob, fast nearing his end
called Joseph and his two sons Ephraim and Manasseh to
bless them. Joseph, noting that his father laid his right
hand upon the head of Ephraim, the younger, removed his
hand to Manasseh, saying: "Not so, my father, for this is the
firstborn; put thy right hand upon his head."

But Jacob refused and said: "I know it, my son, I know
it; he also shall become a people, and he also shall be great
but truly his younger brother shall be greater than he, and
his seed shall become a multitude of nations."

Jacob next called all his sons, and said: "Gather yourselves
together, that I may tell you that which shall befall you in
the last days." He then proceeded to outline their futures
Of Judah he said: "Thou art he whom thy brethren shall
praise . . . The scepter shall not depart from Judah, nor a
lawgiver from between his feet, until Shiloh come; and unto
him shall the gathering of the people be . . . Joseph is a fruit
ful bough, even a fruitful bough by a well, whose branches run
over the wall." Centuries later Moses, in blessing the twelve
tribes, said to Asher: "The eternal God is thy refuge, and
underneath are the everlasting arms."

When Jacob had made an end of commanding his sons, he
yielded up the ghost. Joseph ordered the physicians to em
balm him. His sons carried him into Canaan, as he had
directed, and buried him in the cave of the field of Machpe
lah, which Abraham had bought.

The brothers, on their return to Egypt, distrusted Joseph
now that their father was gone, but Joseph assured them
"Fear ye not; I will nourish you and your little ones."

As his end drew nigh Joseph said to his brethren: "God
will surely visit you, and bring you out of this land unto the
land which he sware to Abraham, to Isaac, and to Jacob
. . . And ye shall carry up my bones from hence." So Jo
seph died, an hundred and ten years old.

# Exodus

## Oppression in Egypt, Ex. 1

Centuries rolled by. The children of Israel, only seventy in number when they entered Egypt, multiplied and increased in power greatly, until there arose a king who "knew not Joseph." Then the Egyptians, concerned at the growing menace, afflicted the Hebrews and "made their lives bitter with hard bondage in mortar and in brick and in all manner of service in the field."

Yet they grew and flourished. Pharaoh then ordered every male child that was born to be cast into the river. A woman of the house of Levi put her infant son in a basket of bulrushes, which she laid in the flags by the bank of the Nile. Pharaoh's daughter, coming down to bathe, took the child as her own and called him Moses.

## Moses and Aaron, Ex. 2-4

When Moses became a man he observed the burdens of his brethren; and one day he slew an Egyptian who was abusing one of them. Fearing that his deed would become known, he fled two or three hundred miles across the desert to Midian at the head of the Red Sea.

As he sat by a well there, the seven daughters of Jethro the priest came to draw water for their father's sheep. While they were filling the troughs, shepherds came and drove them away. Moses then stood up and defended them. Their father asked, when they returned home, "How is it that ye are come so soon today?" They replied: "An Egyptian delivered us out of the hand of the shepherds, and also drew water enough for us, and watered the flock." "Call him, that he may eat bread," said Jethro. So Moses was content to dwell in Midian and Jethro gave him his daughter Zipporah.

While he was with his father-in-law's flock on the far side of the wilderness near Mount Horeb, the Lord appeared to him in a flame of fire out of the midst of a bush which burned but was not consumed.

As Moses turned aside to observe the phenomenon, the Lord said to him: "Draw not nigh hither; put off thy shoes from off thy feet, for the place whereon thou standest is holy ground. . . I have surely seen the affliction of my people which are in Egypt. . . And I am come down to deliver them . . . and to bring them up out of that land unto a good land and a large, unto a land flowing with milk and honey; unto the place of the Canaanites."

Then the Lord appointed Moses to the leadership of the children of Israel; but Moses demurred, asking: "Who am I that I should go unto Pharaoh and that I should bring forth the children of Israel out of Egypt?" Whereupon the Lord gave him the assurance, "Certainly I will be with thee."

"Behold," continued Moses, "when I come unto the children of Israel, and shall say unto them, The God of your fathers hath sent me unto you; and they shall say to me, What is his name? what shall I say unto them?" The Lord answered: "I AM THAT I AM . . . Say unto the children of Israel, I AM hath sent me unto you."

## Rod Becomes Serpent, Ex. 4

Moses, still hesitating, declared, "They will not believe me nor hearken unto my voice." Then the Lord directed him to cast his rod on the ground. As Moses did so, the rod became a serpent and he fled. Whereupon the Lord said, "Put forth thine hand and take it by the tail." Moses obeyed, and the serpent became a rod in his hand.

The Lord said, "Put now thine hand into thy bosom." Moses complied, and when he took it out his hand was leprous as snow. "Put thine hand into thy bosom again," said the Lord. Moses did as directed, and when he drew it out "it was turned again as his other flesh."

"And it shall come to pass," continued the Lord, "if they will not believe thee, neither hearken to the voice of the first sign, that they will believe the voice of the latter sign."

Still wavering, Moses argued, "I am not eloquent" but "am slow of speech and of a slow tongue." At this the anger of the Lord kindled and he appointed Aaron spokesman. "Take this rod in thine hand," He said to Moses, "wherewith thou shalt do signs."

Moses, having gained the consent of his father-in-law, now departed with his family to Egypt, with the rod of God in his hand. Aaron, who was his brother and who had been instructed by the Lord, met him in the wilderness on the way. The two gathered together the elders of the children of Israel; and spoke the words the Lord had given Moses, and did the signs; and the people believed.

But when Moses and Aaron prayed Pharaoh that they might hold a feast and do sacrifice unto the God of Israel in the wilderness, as the Lord had instructed them, Pharaoh asked: "Who is the Lord, that I should obey his voice to let Israel go? I know not the Lord, neither will I let Israel go."

## Pharaoh's Heart Hardened, Ex. 5-11

And Pharaoh denounced the Hebrews as idlers and commanded them henceforth to find their own straw for brickmaking. So the people were scattered about the land to gather stubble instead of straw; while they were required to produce the usual tale or number of brick.

Moses complained to the Lord: "Wherefore hast thou so evil entreated this people? Why is it thou hast sent me? For since I came to Pharaoh to speak in thy name, he hath done evil to this people; neither hast thou delivered thy people at all."

The Lord, in reply, assured Moses that he had heard the groaning of the children of Israel, that he remembered his covenant with Abraham, and that he would bring them out from their bondage into the land of Canaan. He therefore commanded Moses and Aaron to ask Pharaoh to send the Israelites away; adding that He would harden Pharaoh's heart so that he would not hearken, and would multiply His signs and wonders, and would bring the children of Israel out of the land that "the Egyptians shall know that I am the Lord."

Pharaoh, when Moses and Aaron spoke to him, demanded a miracle. So Aaron cast down his rod, and it became a serpent. Then the magicians of Egypt "cast down every man his rod, and they became serpents; but Aaron's rod swallowed up their rods."

However the Lord had hardened Pharaoh's heart, that he hearkened not.

In the morning Moses lifted up his rod and smote the waters in the river, and they turned to blood. Then with his rod he brought forth successive plagues of frogs, lice, flies, diseases to the cattle, locusts, darkening of the sun, and storms of hail and fire. Still the Lord hardened Pharaoh's heart. He said to Moses: "Yet will I bring one plague more upon Pharaoh, and upon Egypt; afterward he will let you go hence."

## The Passover, Ex. 12

Then, speaking through Moses and Aaron, the Lord commanded the Israelites to take every man a lamb, the tenth day of the month, keep it until the fourteenth day, slay it in the evening, and strike the blood on the two sideposts and on the upper doorpost of the houses.

"And thus shall ye eat it: with your loins girded, your shoes on your feet, and your staff in your hand; and ye shall eat it in haste; it is the Lord's passover. For I will pass through the land of Egypt this night, and will smite all the firstborn in the land of Egypt, both man and beast . . . and when I see the blood, I will pass over you, and the plague shall not be upon you."

At midnight the Lord smote all the firstborn in Egypt, "from the firstborn of Pharaoh that sat on his throne unto the firstborn of the captive that was in the dungeon; and all the firstborn of cattle."

Pharaoh, calling for Moses and Aaron, cried: "Rise up and get you forth from among my people, both ye and the children of Israel; and go, serve the Lord, as ye have said. Also take your flocks and your herds, as ye have said, and be gone; and bless me also."

So urgent were the Egyptians that the Hebrews "took their dough before it was leavened, their kneading troughs being bound up in their clothes upon their shoulders." And they spoiled the Egyptians, borrowing of them jewels and raiment; for the Lord had said: "When ye go ye shall not go empty. But every woman shall borrow of her neighbor, and of her that sojourneth in her house, jewels of silver and jewels of gold, and raiment; and ye shall put them upon your sons and upon your daughters."

## Departure from Egypt, Ex. 12-14

So after sojourning in Egypt "four hundred and thirty years," the children of Israel journeyed eastward from "Rameses to Succoth, about six hundred thousand on foot that were men, beside children. And a mixed multitude went up also with them; and flocks and herds, even very much cattle."

The direct road to their destination would lead them through the land of the militant Philistines by the Mediterranean. Therefore the Lord, lest they turn about when confronted by war and go back to Egypt, led them southward through the way of the wilderness of the Red Sea. "And the Lord went before them by day in a pillar of a cloud, to lead them the way; and by night in a pillar of fire, to give them light."

The Egyptians, now concerned at the prospect of losing the Israelites' service, pursued and overtook them camping by the sea. There was instant consternation. They cried out to the Lord; and they said to Moses: "Because there were no graves in Egypt, hast thou taken us away to die in the wilderness? Wherefore hast thou dealt thus with us, to carry us forth out of Egypt? Is not this the word that we did tell thee in Egypt, saying, Let us alone that we may serve the Egyptians? For it had been better for us to serve the Egyptians than that we should die in the wilderness."

Moses answered: "Fear ye not, stand still and see the salvation of the Lord which he will show to you today; for the Egyptians whom ye have seen today, ye shall see them again no more forever. The Lord shall fight for you, and ye shall hold your peace."

Then said the Lord to Moses: "Lift thou up thy rod and stretch out thine hand over the sea." Moses did as directed and the Lord caused the water to go back by a strong east wind, so that the Israelites went into the sea upon the dry ground. The Egyptians followed. Moses again stretched forth his hand. The waters returned and overthrew all the

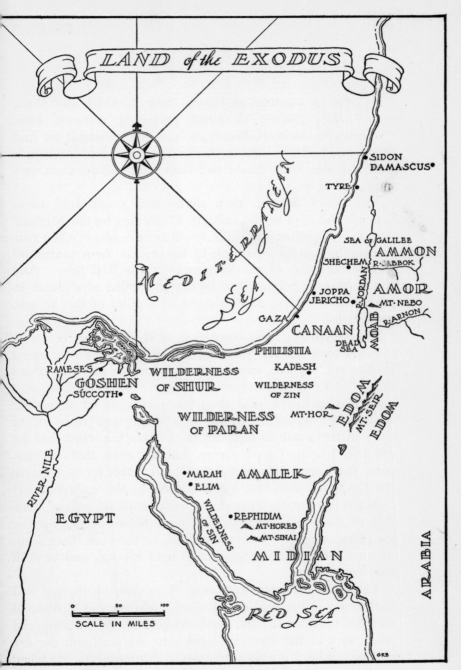

LAND of the EXODUS

SIDON
DAMASCUS

TYRE

SEA of GALILEE
AMMON
SHECHEM   R·JABBOK

MEDITERRANEAN SEA

JOPPA   AMOR
JERICHO   MT·NEBO
R·ARNON
GAZA
CANAAN   MOAB
PHILISTIA   DEAD
SEA
RAMESES   KADESH
WILDERNESS
GOSHEN   OF SHUR   WILDERNESS
SÚCCOTH   OF ZIN
EDOM
WILDERNESS   MT·HOR   MT·SEIR
OF PARAN   EDOM

RIVER NILE

MARAH   AMALEK
ELIM

EGYPT   REPHIDIM
MT·HOREB
MT·SINAI
WILDERNESS
OF SIN   MIDIAN

ARABIA

0    50    100
SCALE IN MILES   RED SEA

G·K·B

29

host of Pharaoh. "But the children of Israel walked upon
dry land in the midst of the sea, and the waters were a wall
unto them on their right hand and on their left."

Then sang Moses and the children of Israel a song of
triumph to the Lord. Miriam the prophetess, sister of Aaron,
took a timbrel in her hand; and all the women went out after
her with timbrels and with dances. And Miriam answered
them: "Sing ye to the Lord, for he hath triumphed glori-
ously; the horse and his rider hath he thrown into the sea."

## *Manna in Wilderness, Ex. 15-18*

The Red Sea passed, the Hebrews went three days into the
wilderness of Shur. At Marah the water was so bitter they
could not drink it. When the people murmured, Moses cast
a tree, which the Lord showed him, into the waters and they
were made fresh. At Elim were twelve wells of water and
threescore and ten palm trees. There they camped for a
time.

Moving southward to the wilderness of Sin, the people
again murmured: "Would to God we had died by the hand
of the Lord in the land of Egypt, when we sat by the flesh
pots, and when we did eat bread to the full." Then said the
Lord to Moses: "I have heard the murmurings of the children of Israel; speak unto them, saying, At even ye shall eat
flesh, and in the morning ye shall be filled with bread; and
ye shall know that I am the Lord your God."

In the evening quail came down and covered the camp.
And in the morning, when the dew was gone, there lay "a
small round thing, as small as the hoar frost on the ground
. . . It was like coriander seed, white; and the taste of it was
like wafers made with honey." When the people saw it
they said, "It is manna." Moses explained, "This is the
bread which the Lord hath given you to eat." They ate
·manna forty years, until they came to the borders of Canaan.

Moving farther south, they pitched in Rephidim. Find-

ing no water there, they blamed Moses. He cried to the
Lord: "What shall I do unto this people? they be almost
ready to stone me." The Lord replied: "Go on before the
people and take with thee of the elders of Israel; and thy
rod, wherewith thou smotest the river, take in thine hand
and go. Behold, I will stand before thee there upon the
rock in Horeb; and thou shalt smite the rock, and there shall
come water out of it, that the people may drink."

Moses did so in the sight of the elders. And he named
the place Massah, proof, and Meribah, complaint, because of
the "chiding of the children of Israel," and because they
tempted the Lord, saying, "Is the Lord among us or not?"

At Rephidim, Amalek appeared and fought with the children of Israel. And it came to pass that when Moses, on
the top of the hill with his rod, held up his hand, Israel prevailed; and when he let down his hand, Amalek prevailed.
"And Aaron and Hur stayed up his hands, the one on the
one side and the other on the other side; and his hands were
steady until the going down of the sun. And Joshua discomfited Amalek and his people."

## The First Judges, Ex. 18

The Israelites were now nearing Midian. Jethro therefore visited Moses, bringing along Zipporah and the two
children, whom Moses had sent back home. Jethro, much
pleased with his son-in-law's achievements, declared, "Now
I know that the Lord is greater than all gods." Accordingly
he brought a burnt offering; and Aaron and the elders joined
in the ceremony.

The next day Moses sat to judge the people. Jethro, observing the strain on Moses, asked, "Why sittest thou thyself alone and all the people stand by thee from morning
unto even?" Moses answered: "Because the people come
unto me to inquire of God. When they have a matter, they
come unto me; and I judge between one and another, and

I do make them know the statutes of God and his laws."

Jethro, pointing out that the system was archaic, recommended Moses to teach the people laws and ordinances, and show them the way wherein they must walk and the work they must do; and to provide able men, such as fear God, to be rulers of thousands, of hundreds, of fifties, and of tens, to judge the people at all seasons.

Moses hearkened to the voice of his father-in-law and appointed judges. Small matters were taken to them; the hard causes were brought to him. Then Jethro went his way into his own land.

## Mount Sinai and Commandments, Ex. 19-31

In the third month, after leaving Egypt, the children of Israel came to the wilderness of Sinai. There they camped before the mountain. The Lord called to Moses from the mountain to sanctify the people and get them ready, for on the third day He would come down in their sight.

There were thunders and lightnings the third morning, and a thick cloud upon the mountain, and the voice of a loud trumpet. As the people in fear and trembling gathered round, "Mount Sinai was altogether on a smoke, because the Lord descended upon it in fire." He called Moses up to the top; where Moses remained forty days and forty nights and received from the Lord the ten commandments, various laws and ordinances, and instructions for building the ark and tabernacle.

## Golden Calf, Ex. 32

The people, becoming impatient during Moses' long absence, appealed to Aaron: "Up, make us gods which shall go before us; for as for this Moses, the man that brought us

up out of the land of Egypt, we wot not what is become of
him." Aaron therefore directed them to break off their
golden earrings and bring them to him. Then he fashioned
them into a calf, built an altar before it, and proclaimed a
feast for the next day.

Moses, on coming down from the mountain with his "two
tables of testimony, tables of stone, written with the finger
of God," mistook the sound of merriment for the noise of
war in the camp. But when he saw the people eating and
dancing in idolatry, his anger waxed hot and he threw down
and broke the tables on which the commandments were in-
dited.

Turning to the Lord he said: "Oh, this people have sinned
a great sin and have made them gods of gold. Yet now, if
thou wilt forgive their sin—and if not, blot me, I pray thee,
out of thy book which thou hast written." The Lord replied: "Whosoever hath sinned against me, him will I blot
out of my book. Therefore now go, lead the people unto the
place of which I have spoken unto thee. Behold, mine angel
shall go before thee . . . for I will not go up in the midst
of thee, for thou art a stiffnecked people, lest I consume thee
in the way."

## *My Presence with Thee, Ex.* 33

Continuing, the Lord declared: "I will drive out the Canaanite, the Amorite, the Hittite, the Perizzite, the Hivite,
and the Jebusite . . . I will not drive them out from before
thee in one year; lest the land become desolate, and the
beast of the field multiply against thee. By little and little
I will drive them out from before thee until thou be increased and inherit the land."

Moses entered the tabernacle. As he did so, the pillar
of cloud descended and stood at the door. The people,
standing in their tent doors, looked on and worshipped. The
Lord spoke to Moses "face to face, as a man speaketh unto

his friend." "Show me now thy way," pleaded Moses, "that I may know thee, that I may find grace in thy sight; and consider that this nation is thy people." To which the Lord replied: "My presence shall go with thee, and I will give thee rest."

"If thy presence go not with me," continued Moses, "carry us not up hence. For wherein shall it be known here that I and thy people have found grace in thy sight? Is it not in that thou goest with us?" The Lord answered: "I will do this thing also that thou hast spoken; for thou hast found grace in my sight, and I know thee by name."

"I beseech thee," persisted Moses, "show me thy glory." The Lord agreed: "I will make all my goodness pass before thee, and I will proclaim the name of the Lord before thee; and will be gracious to whom I will be gracious, and will show mercy on whom I will show mercy.

"Thou canst not see my face; for there shall no man see me and live. Behold, there is a place by me, and thou shalt stand upon a rock; and it shall come to pass, while my glory passeth by, that I will put thee in a cleft of the rock, and will cover thee with my hand while I pass by. And I will take away mine hand, and thou shalt see my back parts, but my face shall not be seen."

## Second Tables of Stone, Ex. 34-39

"Hew thee two tables of stone like unto the first," the Lord resumed, "and I will write upon these tables the words that were in the first tables, which thou breakest." In the morning Moses ascended Sinai, taking the tables. The Lord descended in the cloud and stood with him there, saying, "Write thou these words, for after the tenor of these words I have made a covenant with thee and with Israel." And Moses wrote upon the tables the words of the covenant, the ten commandments.

After forty days Moses came down. When the people

saw him "the skin of his face shone" and they were afraid to
go nigh him.   But soon he gathered them all together and
said to them, "These are the words which the Lord hath
commanded, that ye should do them:"

## Ten Commandments, Ex. 20

*1* Thou shalt have no other gods before me.

*2* Thou shalt not make unto thee any graven image,
or any likeness of any thing that is in heaven above,
or that is in the earth beneath, or that is in the
water under the earth: thou shalt not bow down
thyself to them nor serve them; for I the Lord thy
God am a jealous God, visiting the iniquity of the
fathers upon the children unto the third and fourth
generation of them that hate me, and showing mercy
unto thousands of them that love me and keep my
commandments.

*3* Thou shalt not take the name of the Lord thy God
in vain; for the Lord will not hold him guiltless that
taketh His name in vain.

*4* Remember the sabbath day, to keep it holy.   Six
days shalt thou labor and do all thy work; but the
seventh day is the sabbath of the Lord thy God: in it
thou shalt not do any work, thou nor thy son nor thy
daughter, thy man servant nor thy maid servant nor
thy cattle nor thy stranger that is within thy gates;
for in six days the Lord made heaven and earth, the
sea, and all that in them is, and rested the seventh
day: wherefore the Lord blessed the sabbath day and
hallowed it.

Honor thy father and thy mother, that thy days may
be long upon the land which the Lord thy God giveth
thee.

Thou shalt not kill.

Thou shalt not commit adultery.

Thou shalt not steal.

Thou shalt not bear false witness against thy neighbor.

Thou shalt not covet thy neighbor's house, thou shalt not covet thy neighbor's wife nor his man servant nor his maid servant nor his ox nor his ass nor anything that is thy neighbor's.

## Ark and Tabernacle, Ex. 25, 26, 40

Moses now constructed the tabernacle and the ark of the covenant according to the Lord's instructions.   The ark was a chest of acacia wood about four feet long, two feet wide, and two feet deep, overlaid within and without with gold.   Inside were placed the commandments.   On the top or lid was the mercy seat of pure gold, with a golden cherub at each end.   The cherubim faced each other and their outstretched wings covered the seat.   "There," the Lord said "I will meet with thee and I will commune with thee from above the mercy seat, from between the two cherubim which are upon the ark of the testimony."   On the sides were rings through which were run poles for carrying.

The tabernacle was a structure about forty-five feet long, fifteen feet wide, and fifteen feet high.   The sides and the rear were boards; the front or entrance was a rich curtain linens and skins made up the roof.   It stood at the far end of a court made of canvas screens.

A veil separated the tabernacle into two compartments The first was called the "sanctuary"; the second the "holy of holies."   The ark rested in the holy of holies; while the sanctuary contained the golden candlestick, the table for shewbread, and the altar of incense.   In the court outside were the laver for the priests and the altar for burnt offerings.

It was the custom to set up the whole establishment in the middle of the camp. Surrounding it were the tents of the Levites, whom the Lord had assigned to Aaron to serve in the tabernacle and constitute the priestly class. Farther back were the tents of the other tribes.

On the first day of the first month, the tabernacle having been put in order, the Lord instructed Moses to bring Aaron and his sons to the door and anoint them that they might minister in the priest's office; for, said he, "Their anointing shall surely be an everlasting priesthood throughout their generations."

"Then a cloud covered the tent of the congregation, and the glory of the Lord filled the tabernacle. And Moses was not able to enter into the tent of the congregation, because the cloud abode thereon, and the glory of the Lord filled the tabernacle.

"And when the cloud was taken up from over the tabernacle, the children of Israel went onward in all their journeys; but if the cloud were not taken up, then they journeyed not till the day that it was taken up. For the cloud of the Lord was upon the tabernacle by day, and fire was on it by night, in the sight of all the house of Israel throughout all their journeys."

# Leviticus

## Priestly Codes, Lev. 1-18

The laws promulgated by Moses in Exodus, Numbers, and Deuteronomy were revised and codified by the priests in Leviticus. The book therefore contains little of incident or action. The penalty for departing from prescribed ceremonies appears in this tragedy told in the tenth chapter:

"Nadab and Abihu, the sons of Aaron, took either of them his censer and put fire therein and put incense thereon, and offered strange fire before the Lord, which he commanded them not. And there went out fire from the Lord and devoured them, and they died before the Lord." Then said Moses to Aaron: "This is it that the Lord spake, saying, I will be sanctified in them that come nigh me, and before all the people I will be glorified." Aaron accordingly held his peace.

## Ye Shall Be Holy, Lev. 19-26

The law reaches its highest expression in chapter nineteen, where it is written: "Ye shall be holy, for I the Lord your God am holy . . . Thou shalt not avenge, nor bear any grudge against the children of thy people, but thou shalt love thy neighbor as thyself."

38

The twenty-sixth chapter recites: "If ye walk in my statutes and keep my commandments and do them; then I will give you rain in due season, and the land shall yield her increase, and the trees of the field shall yield their fruit. And your threshing shall reach unto the vintage, and the vintage shall reach unto the sowing time; and ye shall eat your bread to the full and dwell in your land safely.

"And I will give peace in the land, and ye shall lie down, and none shall make you afraid; and I will rid evil beasts out of the land, neither shall the sword go through your land. And ye shall chase your enemies, and they shall fall before you by the sword. And five of you shall chase an hundred, and an hundred of you shall put ten thousand to flight.

"And I will walk among you and will be your God and ye shall be my people. I am the Lord your God, which brought you forth out of the land of Egypt, that ye should not be their bondmen; and I have broken the bands of your yoke and made you go upright."

# Numbers

## Departure from Sinai, Num. 1-12

Over a year has passed since the Israelites left Egypt. Ready now to leave the wilderness of Sinai, Moses ordered them to be numbered; and there were found to be 603,550 men over twenty years old, excluding the Levites.

The tabernacle was taken down and borne forward. The ark of the covenant, too, was carried forward to "search out a resting place for them." When the ark started, Moses would say: "Rise up, Lord, and let thine enemies be scattered; and let them that hate thee flee before thee." And when it halted, he would say: "Return, O Lord, unto the many thousands of Israel."

As they journeyed northward from Sinai, the people resumed their complaining, this time because they had only manna to eat. "Who shall give us flesh?" they asked. "We remember the fish which we did eat in Egypt freely; the cucumbers and the melons and the leeks and the onions and the garlic. But now our soul is dried away; there is nothing at all besides this manna before our eyes."

## The People Complain, Num. 11

When Moses acquainted the Lord with this complaint, he directed Moses to gather seventy of the elders and take them

40

to the tabernacle, saying: "I will come down and talk with thee there; and I will take of the spirit which is upon thee and will put it upon them; and they shall bear the burden of the people with thee that thou bear it not thyself alone."

The Lord then instructed the Israelites to sanctify themselves against the next day, and they would eat flesh for a whole month until it became loathsome to them; because, he said: "Ye have despised the Lord which is among you and have wept before him, saying, Why came we forth out of Egypt?"

When Moses marveled how six hundred thousand men could be so fed, the Lord exclaimed: "Is the Lord's hand waxed short? Thou shalt see now whether my word shall come to pass."

When the seventy elders set themselves round about the tabernacle, the spirit rested upon them and they prophesied. But two men, Eldad and Medad, went not out to the tabernacle but prophesied in the camp. "My lord Moses, forbid them!" exclaimed Joshua. But Moses replied: "Enviest thou for my sake? Would God that all the Lord's people were prophets, and that the Lord would put his spirit upon them!"

A wind now brought quail. They fell about the camp in great numbers. But as the people ate, the wrath of the Lord kindled against them and he visited them with a plague.

Aaron and Miriam here took it upon themselves to speak against Moses because of the Ethiopian woman whom he had married. Whereupon the Lord directed the three to come out to the tabernacle. There he commended Moses as a prophet to whom he did not speak in visions or dreams, but to whom he spoke "mouth to mouth, even apparently, and not in dark speeches."

And as the cloud departed from off the tabernacle, Miriam became leprous, white as snow. When Moses prayed the Lord to heal her, he answered: "Let her be shut out from the camp seven days, and after that let her be received in again." When she was brought in at the end of the time, the people resumed their northward journey.

*Stot*

## *Arrival at Canaan, Num. 13-15*

Having arrived at Kadesh in the wilderness of Paran, or Zin, not many miles from the southern boundary of Canaan, they sent forward twelve men to spy out the country. At the end of forty days they brought back a glowing account of a land flowing with milk and honey. But they also reported that they had seen great walled cities and "giants, the sons of Anak, which come of the giants; and we were in our own sight as grasshoppers, and so we were in their sight." Then the people lamented: "Would God that we had died in the land of Egypt! or would God we had died in this wilderness!" And they said to one another, "Let us make a captain and let us return into Egypt."

Joshua and Caleb, who were among those who had searched the land, rent their clothes, and insisted that the district was exceedingly inviting and that they were able to go up at once and possess it. Moses and Aaron fell upon their faces. And Moses prayed that the faithlessness of the people might be pardoned; but the Lord, provoked because, having witnessed his miracles in Egypt and on the journey, they continued to tempt him, decreed:

"Tomorrow turn you, and get you into the wilderness by the way of the Red Sea . . . Ye shall not come into the land concerning which I sware to make you dwell therein, save Caleb the son of Jephunneh, and Joshua the son of Nun. But your little ones, which ye said should be a prey, them will I bring in and they shall know the land which ye have despised. But as for you, your carcasses, they shall fall in this wilderness. And your children shall wander in the wilderness forty years . . . After the number of the days in which ye searched the land, even forty days, each day for a year, shall ye bear your iniquities, even forty years, and ye shall know my breach of promise."

Early in the morning the people, having changed their mind in view of the prospective punishment, resolved to go ahead. But Moses pointed out that their enterprise must fail, because they had turned away from the Lord and therefore He would not be with them. Nevertheless they presumed to go up and engage the Amalekites and Canaanites, and were chased precipitately back down the hill. "The ark of the covenant of the Lord, and Moses, departed not out of the camp."

## Rebellion Against Moses, Num. 16, 17

At this point certain of the congregation rebelled against Moses and Aaron and defied their authority. They declared: "Ye take too much upon you, seeing all the congregation are holy, every one of them, and the Lord is among them; wherefore then lift ye up yourselves above the congregation of the Lord?"

When Moses sent for the leaders of the insurgents, they rejoined: "We will not come up. Is it a small thing that thou hast brought us up out of a land that floweth with milk and honey, to kill us in the wilderness, except thou make thyself altogether a prince over us?"

Moses commanded the congregation to withdraw. The earth then opened and swallowed up the rebels. Others who were burning incense were consumed by fire. The next day the people murmured against Moses and Aaron, "Ye have killed the people of the Lord." Then came a plague upon them, which carried away nearly fifteen thousand. Aaron stayed its ravages by offering an atonement.

The Lord instructed Moses to take of each of the princes a rod, write every man's name upon his rod, and lay the twelve rods up in the tabernacle. On the morrow, when Moses went into the tabernacle, he found that Aaron's rod had blossomed and yielded almonds. The Lord said to him: "Bring Aaron's rod again before the testimony, to be kept for a token against the rebels; and thou shalt quite take away their murmurings from me, that they die not."

## Detour Around Edom, Num. 20, 21, 33; Deut. 2

Then followed thirty-eight years of roving in the wilderness, at the end of which the wanderers found themselves back in Kadesh. "All the generation of the men of war were wasted out from among the host." Finding no water, they arrayed themselves once more against Moses and Aaron. "Gather thou the assembly together," the Lord instructed Moses, "and speak ye unto the rock before their eyes, and it shall bring forth his water."

When the people assembled, Moses, magnifying himself rather than the Lord, cried: "Hear now, ye rebels; must we fetch you water out of this rock?" He then smote the rock twice with his rod; and the water came out abundantly and the people and their beasts drank.

Then said the Lord to Moses and Aaron: "Because ye believed me not, to sanctify me in the eyes of the children of Israel, therefore ye shall not bring this congregation into the land which I have given them." This was the water of Meribah, "because the children of Israel strove with the Lord and he was sanctified in them."

Moses now sent messengers from Kadesh to the king of Edom. "Thus saith thy brother Israel," they said, "thou knowest all the travail that hath befallen us . . . and behold, we are in Kadesh, a city in the uttermost of thy border. Let us pass, I pray thee, through thy country. We will go by the king's highway, we will not turn to the right hand nor to the left, until we have passed thy borders."

"Thou shalt not go through," replied Edom; and Edom came out against Israel with much people and with a strong hand. Therefore the Israelites turned away and journeyed from Kadesh till they came to Mount Hor on the frontier of Edom.

There Moses, at the Lord's command, took Aaron and his son Eleazar up to the top, where he put Aaron's garment on Eleazar. Then was Aaron gathered to his people "in the fortieth year after the children of Israel were come out of the land of Egypt, in the first day of the fifth month." He was not permitted to enter the promised land, nor was Moses, because they had rebelled against the word of the Lord at the water of Meribah. Miriam had passed away on the return to Kadesh.

The people, much discouraged because compelled to make the long detour around Edom by way of the Red Sea, spoke against God and against Moses when there was no bread or water. Thereupon the Lord sent fiery serpents among them. When Moses prayed for them, the Lord directed him to make a serpent of brass and put it upon a pole. "And it came to pass that if a serpent had bitten any man, when he beheld the serpent of brass, he lived."

Moving around the south end of Edom and up the east side, the Israelites traveled northward till they reached the top of the Pisgah, or Abarim, Mountains, opposite Jericho. The highest point of the range was known as Mount Nebo. There they negotiated with the Amorites, saying: "Let us pass through thy land; we will not turn into the fields or into the vineyards, we will not drink of the waters of the well, but we will go along by the king's highway until we be past thy borders."

But Sihon, king of the Amorites, gathered his people and went out against the Israelites in the wilderness. Israel overthrew him and took possession of his land from Arnon to Jabbok, "even unto the children of Ammon, for the border of the children of Ammon was strong."

The Israelites contended not with the Moabites, because the Lord had given Ar, one of their chief places, to the children of Lot for a possession.

Then turned the Israelites and went up by the way of Bashan. Og, king of Bashan, who "remained of the remnant of giants," met them in the battle of Edrei. They did to him as they had done to Sihon.

## Balak and Balaam, Num. 22, 24

They next pitched in the plains of Moab on the east side of Jordan. Balak, king of the Moabites, frightened by their numbers, sent messengers eastward to the prophet Balaam, asking him to curse the invaders; but God said to Balaam, "Thou shalt not curse the people, for they are blessed."

A second time Balak appealed to Balaam, this time sending princes. And Balaam answered: "If Balak would give me his house full of silver and gold, I cannot go beyond the word of the Lord my God to do less or more." Nevertheless Balaam went with the princes of Moab. Thereby was the Lord's anger kindled; and the angel of the Lord stood in his way for an adversary as Balaam rode along with his two servants.

The donkey he was riding saw the angel, with his sword drawn, and turned aside into the fields. Balaam smote the animal to turn her back into the road.

But the angel again stood in a path of the vineyards; and when the donkey saw the angel, she swerved to one side and struck Balaam's foot against the wall and Balaam smote her again.

The angel went farther and stood, this time in a narrow way. Thus confronted the donkey fell down under Balaam. This so enraged him that he hit her with his staff. "What have I done unto thee, that thou hast smitten me these three times?" she asked. The Lord then opened the eyes of Balaam, and he saw the angel; and he bowed down his head and fell flat on his face.

The angel said to Balaam: "Go with the men; but only the word that I shall speak unto thee, that thou shalt speak." So Balaam went with the princes of Balak.

But when he came to Balak he did not so much curse as bless. Therefore Balak, hoping for a more favorable outcome, took Balaam to Mount Pisgah, where he pointed out to him the Israelites and again asked him to curse them. At this point the Lord met and spoke to Balaam. Then Balak asked,

"What hath the Lord spoken?" Balaam replied: "God is not a man, that he should lie; neither the son of man, that he should repent: hath he said, and shall he not do it? or hath he spoken, and shall he not make it good? Behold, I have received commandment to bless: and he hath blessed; and I cannot reverse it."

Then Balak brought Balaam to the top of Peor. Here Balaam foretold the power and happiness of Israel. Balak, in his anger, smote his hands together and exclaimed: "I called thee to curse mine enemies, and behold, thou hast altogether blessed them these three times. Therefore now flee thou to thy place. I thought to promote thee unto great honor; but lo, the Lord hath kept thee back from honor."

## *Viewing the Promised Land, Num.* 27-33

The Israelites were now on the plains of Moab by Jordan near Jericho. Moses and Eleazar, at the Lord's command, took another census of the people, and found that there were 601,730, excluding the Levites, who held no property. "But among these there was not a man of them whom Moses and Aaron the priest numbered when they numbered the children of Israel in the wilderness of Sinai."

And the Lord said unto Moses: "Get thee up into this Mount Abarim and see the land which I have given unto the children of Israel. And when thou hast seen it, thou also shalt be gathered unto thy people as Aaron thy brother was gathered. For ye rebelled against my commandment in the desert of Zin, in the strife of the congregation, to sanctify me at the water before their eyes; that is the water of Meribah in Kadesh."

Moses asked the Lord to appoint a leader for the people, that they might not be as sheep which have no shepherd. The Lord answered: "Take thee Joshua the son of Nun, a man in whom is the spirit, and lay thine hand upon him."

Moses did as commanded, and took Joshua and set him before Eleazar the priest and before all the congregation.

## Apportionment of Land, Num. 32

The children of Reuben and Gad, observing that the region about them was suited to cattle, of which they had a great number, asked that they might settle there and not cross the Jordan. Moses protested, exclaiming, "Shall your brethren go to war and shall ye sit here?"

But when they promised to send their soldiers across Jordan to take part in the campaign against the Canaanites, and not to return to their homes until the war was over, Moses accepted their proposition. Accordingly they, with half the tribe of Manasseh, received their inheritance on the side of Jordan to the eastward.

The Lord instructed Moses to say to the children of Israel: "When ye are passed over Jordan into the land of Canaan, then ye shall drive out all the inhabitants of the land from before you and destroy all their pictures and destroy all their molten images and quite pluck down all their high places, and ye shall dispossess the inhabitants of the land and dwell therein, for I have given you the land to possess it.

"And ye shall divide the land by lot for an inheritance among your families. To the more ye shall give the more inheritance, and to the fewer ye shall give the less inheritance; every man's inheritance shall be in the place where his lot falleth, according to the tribes of your fathers ye shall inherit.

"But if ye will not drive out the inhabitants of the land from before you, then it shall come to pass that those which ye let remain of them shall be pricks in your eyes and thorns in your sides, and shall vex you in the land wherein ye dwell. Moreover, it shall come to pass that I shall do unto you as I thought to do unto them."

To the Levites, so the instructions ran, were to be given

cities to dwell in, with the suburbs for their goods and cattle.
Among them were to be six cities of refuge, three on the east
of Jordan and three on the west, to provide a haven for the
manslayer until he stood before the congregation in judgment.   Altogether the Levites were to have forty-eight cities
with their suburbs.

# Deuteronomy

## Farewell Address, Deut. 1-31

"In the fortieth year, in the eleventh month, on the first day of the month" of the memorable journey, Moses called the people together and delivered a farewell address.

He expressed his desire to proceed with them to their destination, and his regret that the Lord had said to him, "Thou shalt not go over this Jordan." He reviewed their adventures in the wilderness. He reminded them of the disasters that followed their disobedience during the journey. But he added: "If from thence thou shalt seek the Lord thy God, thou shalt find him if thou seek him with all thy heart and with all thy soul."

He called to mind, as well, the protection and guidance the Lord had accorded in bringing them out of Egypt and through the wilderness up to the promised land. "Thy raiment waxed not old upon thee, neither did thy foot swell, these forty years." And now "the Lord will take away from thee all sickness, and will put none of the evil diseases of Egypt which thou knowest upon thee."

Referring to the approaching conquest of Canaan, he emphasized that it was not because of their (the Israelites') righteousness that the Lord would drive out nations mightier than they, "for thou art," he said, "a stiffnecked people," but because of the wickedness of those nations.

In the course of his address he promulgated many ordinances and rules of conduct, and restated the ten commandments, all of which became known as "the law." He commanded the book of the law to be delivered to the priests to be put into the ark of the covenant; and directed that it be read "at the end of every seven years, in the solemnity of the year of release, in the feast of tabernacles."

Previously he had warned them against the abominations of other nations, saying: "There shall not be found among you any one that maketh his son or his daughter to pass through the fire, or that useth divination, or an observer of times or an enchanter or a witch or a charmer or a consulter with familiar spirits or a wizard or a necromancer. For all that do these things are an abomination unto the Lord; and because of these abominations the Lord thy God doth drive them out from before thee."

That his counsel and admonition should in no wise be thought remote or theoretical, he declared: "For this commandment which I command thee this day, it is not hidden from thee, neither is it far off. It is not in heaven that thou shouldest say, Who shall go up for us to heaven and bring it unto us that we may hear it and do it? Neither is it beyond the sea that thou shouldest say, Who shall go over the sea for us and bring it unto us that we may hear it and do it? But the word is very nigh unto thee, in thy mouth and in thy heart, that thou mayest do it."

"Hear, O Israel," he proclaimed, "the Lord our God is one Lord . . . And now Israel, what doth the Lord thy God require of thee, but to fear the Lord thy God, to walk in all his ways, and to love him, and to serve the Lord thy God with all thy heart and with all thy soul."

Finally, as though to vindicate his leadership, he concluded: "I call heaven and earth to record this day against you, that I have set before you life and death, blessing and cursing. Therefore choose life, that both thou and thy seed may live . . . For He is thy life and the length of thy days."

Moses was now one hundred and twenty years old, yet "his eye was not dim nor his natural force abated." He died

in sight of the land which the Lord had sworn unto Abraham
and Isaac and Jacob; and was buried "in a valley in the land
of Moab, over against Bethpeor; but no man knoweth of his
sepulcher unto this day."

> *O lonely tomb in Moab's land,*
> *O dark Bethpeor's hill,*
> *Speak to these curious hearts of ours*
> *And teach them to be still.*

## *Song of Moses, Deut. 32*

> *Give ear, O ye heavens, and I will speak;*
> *And hear, O earth, the words of my mouth.*
> *My doctrine shall drop as the rain,*
> *My speech shall distil as the dew,*
> *As the small rain upon the tender herb,*
> *And as the showers upon the grass;*
> *Because I will publish the name of the Lord:*
> *Ascribe ye greatness unto our God.*
>
> *He is the Rock, his work is perfect;*
> *For all his ways are judgment:*
> *A God of truth and without iniquity,*
> *Just and right is he.*
>
> *They have corrupted themselves,*
> *Their spot is not the spot of his children;*
> *They are a perverse and crooked generation.*
> *Do ye thus requite the Lord, O foolish people and*
> *    unwise?*
> *Is not he thy father that hath bought thee?*
> *Hath he not made thee and established thee?*
>
> *Remember the days of old,*
> *Consider the years of many generations:*

Ask thy father, and he will show thee;
Thy elders, and they will tell thee.
When the Most High divided to the nations their
    inheritance,
When he separated the sons of Adam,
He set the bounds of the people
According to the number of the children of Israel.
For the Lord's portion is his people;
Jacob is the lot of his inheritance.

He found him in a desert land,
And in the waste howling wilderness;
He led him about, he instructed him,
He kept him as the apple of his eye.
As an eagle stirreth up her nest,
Fluttereth over her young,
Spreadeth abroad her wings, taketh them,
Beareth them on her wings;
So the Lord alone did lead him,
And there was no strange god with him.

But Jeshurun waxed fat and kicked:
Thou art waxen fat, thou art grown thick,
Thou art covered with fatness;
Then he forsook God which made him,
And lightly esteemed the rock of his salvation.

# Joshua

## Fall of Jericho, Joshua 1-6

The dreary journey from Egypt was over. The former generation, too irresolute on leaving Goshen to face the Philistines, and lacking courage two years later to enter Canaan when at its doors in Kadesh, had faded out. A new generation, invigorated by the freedom and hardship of the desert, had sprung up. They were encamped on the east side of the Jordan, looking toward Jericho a few miles across the plain. The supreme adventure was at hand; for the Lord now commanded Joshua to take them across the river, saying by way of encouragement:

"As I was with Moses, so I will be with thee; I will not fail thee nor forsake thee." Accordingly Joshua (1400 to 1300 B.C.) instructed the people to make ready, because in three days they would cross Jordan to take possession of the land.

Spies sent ahead to Jericho, having been discovered, sought refuge with Rahab, who took them up on the roof of her house and hid them with stalks of flax. When pursuers arrived she sent them away with false directions. She then told the spies how the reputation of the Israelites for prowess had reached her country, declaring: "We have heard how the Lord dried up the water of the Red Sea for you when ye came

54

out of Egypt, and what ye did unto the two kings of the Amorites that were on the other side of Jordan, Sihon and Og."

The spies promised her and her family protection, instructing her to bind a scarlet cord on the window in order that the house, which stood upon the town wall, could be recognized. She then let them down by a rope through the window. Making their escape, they returned to Joshua with the joyful report that "all the inhabitants of the country do faint because of us."

The Israelites, thus heartened, prepared to cross the river. As the priests, going before and carrying the ark of the covenant, stepped into the stream, the waters "rose up upon an heap," and they "stood firm on dry ground in the midst of Jordan, and all the Israelites passed over on dry ground."

They encamped at Gilgal on the east border of Jericho. There they ate the passover. The day following they partook of the fruit of the land of Canaan, whereupon the manna ceased.

Joshua, while by Jericho, observed a man with his sword drawn. Approaching him he asked, "Art thou for us or for our adversaries?" And he said: "Nay, but as captain of the host of the Lord am I now come . . . Loose thy shoe from off thy foot, for the place whereon thou standest is holy."

The inhabitants of Jericho now shut its gates against the Israelites; none went out and none came in. Joshua, in obedience to the Lord's command, had armed men, followed by priests with the ark, march around Jericho every day for six days, the priests blowing trumpets of rams' horns. On the seventh day they compassed the city seven times. This done, Joshua commanded, "Shout; for the Lord hath given you the city."

When the people shouted and the priests blew the trumpets, the wall fell down flat. Entering the city, they destroyed "both man and woman, young and old, and ox and sheep and donkey, with the edge of the sword." Only Rahab and her family were spared. "And they burned the city with fire, and all that was therein; only the silver and the gold and the vessels of brass and of iron, they put into the treasury of the house of the Lord."

## Overthrow of Other Cities, Joshua 7-10

Jericho taken, the Israelites next fought against the men of Ai and were defeated. Joshua was troubled at this change in his fortunes, until the Lord told him that one of his men, contrary to instructions, had taken to himself some of the spoils of Jericho—a rare Babylonian garment, shekels of silver, and a wedge of gold. The offender discovered and punished, the anger of the Lord was appeased, and the Israelites won their next battle with Ai.

Alarmed at the growing power of Joshua, the kings of the Hittites, Amorites, Canaanites, Perizzites, Hivites, and Jebusites gathered themselves together to fight him. But the Hivites, inhabitants of Gibeon, forgetting the compact, made overtures to Joshua. They donned old clothes and took moldy bread, when they went to meet him, representing that they had come from a far country and wished to make a league with the Israelites.

Joshua therefore made peace with them and allowed them to live. But a few days later, on reaching the cities of Gibeon and discovering the duplicity of the inhabitants, he condemned them to become hewers of wood and drawers of water.

And when the other five kings learned of the truce effected by the Hivites, they planned an attack on them. Joshua, coming to the rescue of the Hivites, put the five kings and their armies to flight. During one of the battles the sun, at Joshua's command, stood still and the moon stayed, until the people had avenged themselves upon their enemies.

The war continued until Joshua smote his foes from Kadesh to Gaza and all the country of Goshen, even unto Gibeon. Then he, and all Israel with him, returned to the camp at Gilgal.

## Division of Territory, Joshua 11-22

Other kings banded together and went out as the sand that is upon the sea shore in multitude, with horses and chariots. When they pitched together at the waters of Merom to fight the Israelites, Joshua and his men of war fell upon them, and the Lord delivered them into the hand of Israel.

So that with the exception of the Hivites, Joshua overthrew all the tribes, sacking their cities and taking over their land; and he gave the country "for an inheritance unto Israel according to their divisions by their tribes."

Caleb, who with Joshua survived the wanderings in the wilderness, asked for Mount Hebron, reminding Joshua: "I am this day fourscore and five years old. As yet I am as strong this day as I was in the day that Moses sent me." Joshua blessed him and granted his petition.

The conquest completed, Reuben and Gad, and the half tribe of Manasseh, returned to their own land in Gilead east of the Jordan in accordance with their previous agreement with Moses.

## End of Career, Joshua 23, 24

Joshua, now stricken in age, gathered Israel around him and warned them against idolatry. Reviewing their experience from the time of Terah to the present, he declared: "I have given you a land for which ye did not labor, and cities which ye built not, and ye dwell in them; of the vineyards and oliveyards which ye planted not do ye eat. Now therefore fear the Lord and serve him in sincerity and in truth; and put away the gods which your fathers served on the other side of the flood and in Egypt; and serve ye the Lord."

The people answered, "God forbid that we should forsake the Lord to serve other gods." Joshua continued, "Ye are witnesses against yourselves that ye have chosen you the Lord, to serve him." They replied, "We are witnesses."

That day Joshua made a covenant with the people, and, formulating rules for them at Shechem, wrote them in the book of the law.   He took a great boulder and set it up under an oak, saying to the people: "Behold, this stone shall be a witness unto us; for it hath heard all the words of the Lord which he spake unto us."   Every man then departed to his inheritance.

Joshua died at the age of one hundred and ten years.   He was buried in the border of his inheritance in Timnath-serah. Israel served the Lord all the days of Joshua, and all the days of the elders who outlived him and who had known of the works of the Lord.

The remains of Joseph, which the Israelites brought up out of Egypt, were buried in Shechem in a parcel of ground which Jacob had bought of the sons of Hamor.   Today the district is marked by the town of Nablus, with Jacob's well nearby.

## Covenant Fulfilled, Psalm 105

O give thanks unto the Lord, call upon his name;
Make known his deeds among the people.

He hath remembered his covenant for ever,
The word which he commanded to a thousand gen-
    erations.
Which covenant he made with Abraham,
And his oath unto Isaac;
And confirmed the same unto Jacob for a law,
And to Israel for an everlasting covenant,
Saying: Unto thee will I give the land of Canaan,
The lot of your inheritance.

When they were but a few men in number,
Yea, very few, and strangers in it,
When they went from one nation to another,
From one kingdom to another people,
He suffered no man to do them wrong;

Yea, he reproved kings for their sakes,
Saying, Touch not mine anointed
And do my prophets no harm.

Moreover he called for a famine upon the land;
He brake the whole staff of bread.
He sent a man before them,
Even Joseph, who was sold for a servant,
Whose feet they hurt with fetters,
He was laid in iron;
Until the time that his word came
The word of the Lord tried him.
The king sent and loosed him,
Even the ruler of the people, and let him go free.
He made him lord of his house
And ruler of all his substance
To bind his princes at his pleasure
And teach his senators wisdom.

Israel also came into Egypt
And Jacob sojourned in the land of Ham.
And he increased his people greatly
And made them stronger than their enemies.
He turned their heart to hate his people,
To deal subtilly with his servants.
He sent Moses his servant,
And Aaron whom he had chosen.
They showed his signs among them
And wonders in the land of Ham.
He sent darkness and made it dark,
And they rebelled not against his word.
He turned their waters into blood
And slew their fish.
Their land brought forth frogs in abundance
In the chambers of their kings.

He spake and there came divers sorts of flies
And lice in all their coasts.

He gave them hail for rain,
And flaming fire in their land.
He smote their vines also and their fig trees,
And brake the trees of their coasts.
He spake and the locusts came,
And caterpillars, and that without number,
And did eat up all the herbs in their land
And devoured the fruit of their ground.
He smote also all the firstborn in their land,
The chief of all their strength.

He brought them forth also with silver and gold;
And there was not one feeble person among their
tribes.
Egypt was glad when they departed,
For the fear of them fell upon them.
He spread a cloud for a covering,
And fire to give light in the night.
The people asked and he brought quails,
And satisfied them with the bread of heaven.
He opened the rock and the waters gushed out;
They ran in the dry places like a river.
For he remembered his holy promise
And Abraham his servant.
And he brought forth his people with joy
And his chosen with gladness,
And gave them the lands of the heathen,
And they inherited the labor of the people
That they might observe his statutes
And keep his laws.
Praise ye the Lord.

# Judges

*A New Regime, Judges 1-3*

Still was the land far from complete subjugation. Taking possession of the territories allotted to the different tribes, and afterward defending them against invasion, involved war after war. Victory and defeat alternated according as the people were obedient to the Lord or turned toward strange gods.

Thus when Israel made a league with the people at Bethel, and did not throw down their altars, the Lord declared: "I will not drive them out from before you; but they shall be as thorns in your sides, and their gods shall be a snare unto you."

But while the anger of the Lord was, on occasion, stirred against Israel because of their evil and disobedience, nevertheless he raised up judges, who from time to time delivered them out of the hand of those who spoiled them. Othniel was the first judge, Samuel the last.

Yet the people did not always hearken to their judge; and when there was none, they returned and corrupted themselves more than their fathers in following other gods to serve them. "They ceased not from their own doings nor from their stubborn way."

Therefore the Lord said: "I also will not henceforth drive out any from before them of the nations which Joshua left when he died; that through them I may prove Israel, whether they will keep the way of the Lord to walk therein, as their fathers did keep it, or not."

Among the nations thus surviving were the five lords of the Philistines. The Philistines had been a long time in this region. Abraham found them in his day and for a while lived with them. They were invading Canaan from the west; the Hebrews from the east. Unavoidable collisions between the two wore on intermittently for generations.

The Hebrews dwelt among the Canaanites, Hittites, and other peoples, intermarrying with them and serving their gods. Therefore was the anger of the Lord hot against Israel; and at one time he sold them into the hand of the king of Mesopotamia, whom they served eight years. Hearing their cry, the Lord raised up Othniel, son of Caleb's brother, who judged Israel and in war was victorious. The land then had rest for forty years.

After the death of Othniel, however, the Israelites again did evil in the sight of the Lord. Whereupon he strengthened Eglon, king of Moab, who brought them under subjection for eighteen years, until Ehud, a left-handed man, led them to victory over the Moabites, and there was peace fourscore years.

Having given themselves up to idolatry once more after the death of Ehud, the Lord sold them into the hand of Jabin, king of Canaan, who for twenty years mightily oppressed them. The captain of his hosts was Sisera.

## Deborah and Sisera, Judges 4-5

At that time Deborah the prophetess judged Israel. She assured Barak of Kedesh, a Galilean city of refuge, that if he would draw near Mount Tabor with his army, she would deliver Sisera with his chariots and multitude into his hand. To which Barak answered, "If thou wilt go with me, then I will go." She consented, reminding him, however, that the journey should not be for his honor, because the Lord would sell Sisera into the hand of a woman.

When the armies met, the Lord discomfited Sisera and his host. Alighting from his chariot he fled on foot to the tent of Jael, wife of Heber, for there was peace between Jabin and Heber. Inviting Sisera in she gave him a drink, covered him with a mantle, and as he slept dispatched him. When Barak arrived he found Sisera was no more.

Jabin having therefore been subdued, Deborah and Barak celebrated the victory with the song:

> *They fought from heaven;*
> *The stars in their courses fought against Sisera.*
> *At her feet he bowed, he fell, he lay down:*
> *At her feet he bowed, he fell:*
> *Where he bowed, there he fell down dead.*
>
> *The mother of Sisera looked out at a window*
> *And cried through the lattice,*
> *Why is his chariot so long in coming?*
> *Why tarry the wheels of his chariots?*

After forty years of peace the Lord delivered Israel into the hand of Midian for seven years, because again had they done evil in his sight. The Midianites, coming up as grasshoppers for multitude, greatly impoverished Israel.

## Gideon and the Midianites, Judges 6-12

To Gideon, as he threshed wheat by the wine press to hide it from the Midianites, an angel of the Lord came, saying, "Thou shalt save Israel from the hand of the Midianites." Gideon, doubtful of his ability for such an undertaking, asked a sign. The angel told him to bring forth a present.

In response Gideon prepared a kid and unleavened cakes, and took them to the angel as he sat under an oak. Thereupon the angel instructed him to place his gift on a rock and pour broth upon it. The angel then touched the offering with his staff; and there rose up fire out of the rock and consumed the flesh and the unleavened cakes.

That night Gideon threw down the altar of Baal which his father Joash had erected, cut down the nearby grove, and offered a sacrifice. In the morning the men of the city, having learned what Gideon had done, demanded of Joash that he bring forth his son that they might kill him. But Joash answered: "Will ye plead for Baal? will ye save him? He that will plead for him, let him be put to death whilst it is yet morning; if he be a god, let him plead for himself, because one hath cast down his altar."

Gideon still demanded a sign, saying: "Behold, I will put a fleece of wool in the floor; and if the dew be on the fleece only, and it be dry upon all the earth beside, then shall I know that thou wilt save Israel by mine hand as thou hast said." The next morning he wrung a bowl full of water out of the fleece. Gideon, yet hesitating, said: "Let it now be dry only upon the fleece, and upon all the ground let there be dew." In the morning it was so.

When Gideon and his army pitched beside the wall of Harod, the host of the Midianites being to the north of them, the Lord told him that his army was too large. Therefore Gideon allowed those who were fearful to return home. Ten thousand men remained.

The army yet too large, Gideon brought them down to the water to try them. Then said the Lord: "Every one that lappeth of the water with his tongue, as a dog lappeth, him shalt thou set by himself; likewise every one that boweth down upon his knees to drink." The number of them that lapped, putting their hand to their mouth, were three hundred; all the rest bowed down upon their knees to drink. With these three hundred, Gideon went out to engage the Midianites.

## Subjugation of Midian, Judges 7-12

One of the men dreamed that "a cake of barley bread tumbled into the host of Midian, and came unto a tent and smote it that it fell." His companion, when told the dream, answered, "This is nothing else save the sword of Gideon, the son of Joash, a man of Israel, for into his hand hath God delivered Midian."

When Gideon was told the dream, and the interpretation thereof, he worshipped, and, returning to the host of Israel, said, "Arise, for the Lord hath delivered into your hand the host of Midian."

Gideon now divided the three hundred men into three companies, giving each man a trumpet and an empty pitcher with a lamp in it. When they came to the outside of the enemy's camp at the beginning of the middle watch of the night, "the three companies blew the trumpets and brake the pitchers, and held the lamps in their left hands, and the trumpets in their right hands to blow withal; and they cried, The sword of the Lord and of Gideon! And they stood every man in his place round about the camp; and all the host ran and cried and fled."

Thus were the Midianites subdued so that they lifted up their heads no more; and the country was in quietness forty years. The men of Israel asked Gideon to become their ruler, but he answered: "I will not rule over you, neither shall my son rule over you; the Lord shall rule over you."

Gideon left seventy sons. One of them, Abimelech, wickedly disposed of all but the youngest, and then was made king. In a revolt led by Gaal, Abimelech himself was killed by a piece of millstone hurled by a woman.

After him arose Tola, who judged for a quarter of a century; following Tola, Jair judged for a like period. After him, the children of Israel again having done evil in the sight of the Lord, he sold them into the hands of the Philistines and the children of Ammon.

When they called to the Lord in their distress, he replied: "Go and cry unto the gods which ye have chosen; let them deliver you in the time of your tribulation." At this they put away the strange gods from among them and served the Lord; and his soul was grieved for their misery. In later years, under the leadership of Jephthah, they overthrew the Ammonites.

## *Samson and the Philistines, Judges 13-16*

Now there was a man of Zorah, of the family of the Danites, whose name was Manoah and whose wife had no children. An angel appeared to tell her that she should bear a son; "and no razor shall come on his head, for the child shall be a Nazarite unto God, and he shall begin to deliver Israel out of the hand of the Philistines."

Manoah prayed that he might see the angel to be instructed by him regarding the care of the boy. So when the angel again appeared to the woman, she ran and called her husband. The instructions repeated, Manoah offered to make ready a kid for the visitor, not knowing that he was an angel. But the angel directed a burnt offering to be made to the Lord. Manoah obeying, "it came to pass, when the flame went up toward heaven from off the altar, that the angel of the Lord ascended in the flame."

They named the son Samson. "The child grew and the Lord blessed him. And the Spirit of the Lord began to move him at times."

Coming back one day from Timnath, he told his parents he had seen a Philistine woman there who pleased him. But they protested his taking a wife of another race. "Get her for me, for she pleaseth me well," he insisted. His parents "knew not that it was of the Lord, that He sought an occasion against the Philistines."

Afterward, when they were on their way to Timnath, a young lion roared at Samson. With no weapon in his hand, he rent the animal as though it were a kid; but he told not his parents of the adventure.

He talked with the woman, on arriving at Timnath, and was satisfied. Later on when he went back to take her, he turned aside to see the carcass of the lion and found a swarm of bees and honey in it. He took thereof and ate, and, coming to his father and mother, gave them to eat, but did not tell where he had obtained the honey.

At the wedding feast he propounded to his thirty companions this riddle:

> From the eater came something to eat,
> From the strong came something sweet.

'If ye can certainly declare it me within the seven days of the feast," he said, "then I will give you thirty sheets and thirty change of garments; but if ye cannot declare it me, then shall ye give me thirty sheets and thirty change of garments."

Unable to guess the riddle, the men threatened Samson's wife that they would burn her and her father's house if she did not obtain the answer. She pleaded and wept until he told her. The men of the city, on the seventh day before the sun went down, asked him, "What is sweeter than honey? and what is stronger than a lion?" He answered, "If ye had not plowed with my heifer, ye had not found out my riddle."

"And the Spirit of the Lord came upon him, and he went down to Ashkelon and slew thirty men of them, and took their spoil and gave change of garments unto them which expounded the riddle." Still furious he went up to his father's house.

A while afterward, in the time of wheat harvest, he took his wife a present of a kid, but her father would not allow him to see her, saying: "I verily thought that thou hadst utterly hated her; therefore I gave her to thy companion; is not her younger sister fairer than she? take her, I pray thee, instead of her."

Samson, now bent on mischief toward the Philistines, "caught three hundred foxes and took firebrands and turned tail to tail and put a firebrand in the midst between two tails. And when he had set the brands on fire, he let them go into the standing corn of the Philistines and burnt up both the shocks and also the standing corn, with the vineyards and olives."

When the Philistines discovered what Samson had done, they burned out his wife and her father as previously threat-

ened. In revenge Samson "smote them hip and thigh with
a great slaughter; and he went down and dwelt in the top of
the rock Etam."

Then the Philistines camped in Judah, giving as a reason
that they had come to bind Samson. The people of Judah
said to him: "Knowest thou not that the Philistines are rulers
over us? What is this that thou hast done unto us?" He
replied, "As they did unto me, so have I done unto them."

Samson permitted them to seize him, upon their assurance
that they themselves would do him no harm but only deliver
him to the Philistines. Accordingly "they bound him with
two new cords and brought him up from the rock. And
when he came unto Lehi, the Philistines shouted against him;
and the Spirit of the Lord came mightily upon him, and the
cords that were upon his arms became as flax that was burnt
with fire, and his bands loosed from off his hands. And he
found a new jawbone of a donkey, and put forth his hand
and took it and slew a thousand men therewith."

Samson then judged Israel twenty years in the days of the
Philistines.

One night when he was in Gaza, the Gazites waited for
him at the gate of the city that they might kill him. He
"arose at midnight and took the doors of the gate and the two
posts and went away with them, bar and all, and put them
upon his shoulders and carried them up to the top of an
hill that is before Hebron."

## Delilah and Samson, Judges 16

After that he fancied a woman in the valley of Sorek,
named Delilah. The Philistine lords bribed her to learn the
secret of his strength. Samson evaded her a number of
times, but finally yielding to her importunities, confessed that
if his hair were cut off his strength would leave him. Thereupon Delilah sent for the Philistines; and while Samson was
asleep, she called a man who shaved his head.

Then she cried, "The Philistines be upon thee, Samson." As he awoke he boasted, "I will go out as at other times before and shake myself;" for he knew not that the Lord had departed from him. "But the Philistines took him and put out his eyes, and brought him down to Gaza and bound him with fetters of brass; and he did grind in the prison house."

But his hair began to grow again; and when the Philistines gathered together to offer sacrifice to their god Dagon and to rejoice because he had delivered Samson into their hand, they called for him out of the prison house and he made them sport.

While seated between the pillars, he said to the lad that held him by the hand, "Suffer me that I may feel the pillars whereupon the house standeth, that I may lean upon them." Now the house was full of men and women, three thousand being on the roof, and all of the lords of the Philistines were there.

Then Samson pleaded: "O Lord God, remember me, I pray thee, and strengthen me, I pray thee, only this once, O God, that I may be at once avenged." Taking hold of the two middle pillars, he bowed himself with all his might and the house fell, so that they whom he slew at his death were more than they whom he slew in his life.

After Samson "there was no king in Israel; every man did that which was right in his own eyes."

# Ruth

## Gleaning after Reapers, Ruth, 1, 2

In the days of the judges there was a famine. Therefore Elimelech of Bethlehem, with his wife Naomi and their two sons, went into the country of Moab to sojourn. Soon after Elimelech died. The two sons married women of Moab, Orpah and Ruth; and afterward died.

Naomi, now hearing that the Lord had visited his people in giving them bread, resolved to return home. She directed her daughters-in-law to go each to her mother's house. Orpah obeyed but Ruth clung to Naomi. They came to Bethlehem in the beginning of the barley harvest.

Ruth went to glean after the reapers. She chose a part of the field belonging to Boaz, who was of the kindred of Elimelech. When he learned who she was he said to her, "Go not to glean in another field, neither go from hence, but abide here fast by my maidens."

Then she said: "Let me find favor in thy sight, my lord; for that thou hast comforted me, and for that thou hast spoken friendly unto thine handmaid, though I be not like unto one of thine handmaidens."

## Visiting Boaz, Ruth 3, 4

Boaz replied, "At mealtime come thou hither and eat of the bread and dip thy morsel in the vinegar." As she sat beside

70

the reapers he reached her parched corn. She ate, was sufficed, and left.

When she was risen up to glean, Boaz commanded his young men: "Let her glean even among the sheaves, and reproach her not; and let fall also some of the handfuls of purpose for her, and leave them that she may glean them." So she gleaned with the maidens of Boaz to the end of barley harvest and of wheat harvest, dwelling with her mother-in-law.

One night she visited Boaz as he winnowed grain on the threshing floor. He said to her: "There is a kinsman nearer than I. . . But if he will not do the part of a kinsman to thee, then will I." Ruth's kinsman, unable or unwilling to redeem her inheritance and marry her, according to the custom of the times, Boaz, as he promised, took her as his wife. They had a son called Obed. He became "the father of Jesse, the father of David."

# I Samuel

### Eli and His Sons, I Sam. 1-3

There was a man of the highlands of Ephraim named
Elkanah. His two wives were Hannah and Penninah. Hannah had no children, which greatly grieved her. Penninah
had sons and daughters and provoked Hannah.

Each year they went to Shiloh, where Eli and his two sons
were priests, to worship and offer sacrifice. After they had
eaten, on one of their visits, Hannah rose up and vowed: "O
Lord of hosts, if thou wilt indeed look on the affliction of
thine handmaid" and give her "a man child, then I will give
him unto the Lord all the days of his life, and there shall no
razor come upon his head."

As Eli watched her he exclaimed, "How long wilt thou be
drunken? put away thy wine from thee." But Hannah assured him she had not been drinking but had poured out her
soul before the Lord. "Go in peace," answered Eli, "and
the God of Israel grant thee thy petition."

Elkanah and Hannah returned to their home, where she
bore a son and called him Samuel. While the lad was still
young she took him to Eli, saying: "I am the woman that
stood by thee here praying unto the Lord. For this child I
prayed; and the Lord hath given me my petition which I
asked of him. Therefore also I have lent him to the Lord;
as long as he liveth he shall be lent to the Lord."

Samuel therefore remained with Eli and ministered unto the Lord. The sons of Eli, Hophni and Phinehas, were worshippers of Belial, depraved and unfit for the priestly office.

## Samuel Called, I Sam. 2, 3

"The word of the Lord was precious in those days; there was no open vision." One evening after Eli and Samuel had lain down, the Lord called Samuel. He ran to Eli, supposing the call had come from him; but Eli said, "I called not, lie down again."

Again the Lord spoke, and again Samuel went to Eli; only to be told to lie down once more as he had not spoken. A third time the Lord called Samuel; and when he went to Eli, Eli perceived that the Lord had called the child. So Eli said: "Go, lie down; and it shall be, if He call thee, that thou shalt say, Speak, Lord, for thy servant heareth." Samuel went to his place and lay down. And the Lord came and stood and called as at other times, "Samuel, Samuel." Samuel replied, "Speak, for thy servant heareth."

The Lord then told Samuel that he intended to punish Eli's household, because Eli knew his sons blasphemed the Lord and did not stop them. In the morning Samuel was afraid to tell Eli of the vision, but Eli insisted upon knowing. Therefore Samuel withheld nothing; and Eli said, "It is the Lord; let him do what seemeth him good."

"Samuel grew . . . and all Israel from Dan even to Beersheba knew that Samuel was established to be a prophet of the Lord. And the Lord appeared again in Shiloh; for the Lord revealed himself to Samuel."

## Ark of Covenant, I Sam. 5-7

Now the Israelites went out against the Philistines. Meeting with defeat, they came back to camp, where the elders said: "Wherefore hath the Lord smitten us today before the Philistines? Let us fetch the ark of the covenant of the Lord out of Shiloh unto us, that, when it cometh among us, it may save us out of the hand of our enemies."

Accordingly they sent for the ark, and Hophni and Phinehas came with it. On its arrival the Israelites shouted with a great shout. The Philistines, when they heard it, were afraid, crying: "God is come into the camp. Woe unto us! . . . These are the gods that smote the Egyptians with all the plagues in the wilderness. Be strong and quit yourselves like men."

The Israelites were routed; the ark of God was taken; and the two sons of Eli were slain. A man of Benjamin ran to Shiloh to tell Eli of the disaster. When Eli heard that his sons were killed and the ark taken, he fell off his seat backward and expired, for he was ninety-eight years old and very heavy. He had judged Israel forty years.

The Philistines set the ark up by their god Dagon in Ashdod. On two successive mornings Dagon was found fallen to the earth in front of the ark. And the hand of the Lord was heavy upon the people of Ashdod, visiting them with severe afflictions. They therefore insisted that the Philistines take away the ark.

It was carried to Gath. The Lord smote the men of that city until they protested and sent the ark to Ekron. As the ark approached the city the Ekronites cried, "They have brought about the ark of the God of Israel to us to slay us and our people."

The Philistines then put the ark on a cart drawn by two cows. The animals, given free rein to go wherever they would, took the highway to Beth-shemesh, turning neither to right nor left till they came to a standstill in the field of Joshua, a Beth-shemite. The Levites joyfully received the ark, while the five lords of the Philistines who had followed the cart turned back to Ekron.

The Lord smote the men of Beth-shemesh because they looked into the ark. Accordingly they sent word to the inhabitants of Kirjath-jearim, "The Philistines have brought

again the ark of the Lord; come ye down and fetch it to you."
They did so and took it to the home of Abinadab on the hill,
where it abode twenty years until David had it brought to
Jerusalem.

The people now put away strange gods and served the
Lord only. Samuel called them together at Mizpah to worship. When the Philistines learned of the gathering they
went up against the Israelites. The people being much
frightened, Samuel offered a burnt sacrifice. As he did so the
enemy drew near. "But the Lord thundered with a great
thunder on that day upon the Philistines and discomfited
them; and they were smitten before Israel."

The Philistines, thus subdued, came no more within the
borders of Israel. And there was peace between Israel and
the Amorites.

Samuel judged Israel all the days of his life. He went
from year to year in circuit to Bethel, Gilgal, and Mizpah,
deciding affairs in all these places; and he returned to Ramah,
where his house was. There he judged Israel and built an
altar unto the Lord.

## Demand for a King, I Sam. 8, 9

As years came upon him, Samuel made his sons judges.
They "walked not in his ways, but turned aside after lucre,
and took bribes and perverted judgment." The elders protested to Samuel and asked for a king. But Samuel pointed
out the disadvantages of such a course, telling them that a
king would take their sons and daughters, their vineyards and
oliveyards, their sheep and cattle.

Nevertheless the people insisted, saying: "Nay, but we will
have a king over us, that we also may be like all the nations,
and that our king may judge us and go out before us and fight
our battles." Samuel, displeased with the idea, repeated
their words to the Lord, who said, "Hearken unto their voice
and make them a king."

Now there was a man of Benjamin whose name was Kish. He had a son named Saul, a fine stalwart young man. Kish sent Saul out with a servant to find some donkeys which had been lost. After several days' unsuccessful search they arrived in Zuph. Here Saul proposed that they should return, lest his "father leave caring for the donkeys and take thought for us."

But the servant suggested that they consult a seer who was in the city, to learn which way to go. They went on into town and soon met Samuel, who was expecting them because the Lord had told him the night before that he would meet Saul and appoint him captain over the Israelites.

Samuel invited Saul to accompany him to the high place where he was to bless the sacrifice. "As for thine donkeys that were lost three days ago," said he, "set not thy mind on them, for they are found. And on whom is all the desire of Israel? Is it not on thee and on all thy father's house?"

Greatly astonished, Saul protested that he was of the tribe of Benjamin, the smallest of the tribes of Israel, and that his family was least among the Benjaminites. But Samuel took him along and made him sit in the chief place among the guests, serving him the portion that had been put aside for him.

The next morning Samuel went with Saul to the outskirts of the city. Having sent the servant ahead, Samuel took a vial of oil and poured it upon Saul's head, and said, "Is it not because the Lord hath anointed thee to be captain over his inheritance?"

Then as Saul departed homeward, Samuel told him that two men would meet him at Rachel's sepulcher and tell him that the donkeys had been found; that three other men would meet him at Tabor and give him two loaves of bread; and finally that he would meet a company of prophets coming down from the high place with a psaltery, a tabret, a pipe, and a harp. He instructed Saul to prophesy with them, because the Spirit of the Lord would come upon him and he would be turned into another man.

Speaking further to Saul, Samuel said: "Go down before me to Gilgal; and behold, I will come down unto thee to offer burnt offerings and to sacrifice sacrifices of peace offerings. Seven days shalt thou tarry, till I come to thee and show thee what thou shalt do." As Saul proceeded the signs were all fulfilled and the people were amazed to see him prophesying.

## Saul Anointed, I Sam. 10-15

Samuel called the people together at Mizpah. When they fetched Saul he stood shoulders above all the others. And Samuel said to the people, "See ye him whom the Lord hath chosen, that there is none like him among all the people?" They shouted, "God save the king!"

"Samuel told the people the manner of the kingdom, and wrote it in a book and laid it up before the Lord." Then the people dispersed, every man going to his own house. Saul "also went home to Gibeah; and there went with him a band of men whose hearts God had touched."

The Ammonites now encamped against Jabesh-gilead. Saul called the people to follow him and Samuel. When they assembled he put them in three companies; "and they came into the midst of the host in the morning watch, and slew the Ammonites until the heat of the day."

Then Samuel called them to Gilgal to renew the kingdom there. And they all went and made Saul king. While the people were still assembled, Samuel made an oration, reminding them of his integrity, upbraiding them for adding to their sins in asking for a king, and exhorting them to obey the voice of the Lord. He called on the Lord to send thunder and rain that they might perceive their wickedness in desiring a king.

Then they greatly feared the Lord and Samuel; and he assured them that the Lord would not "forsake his people for his great name's sake." "As for me," he continued, "God forbid that I should sin against the Lord in ceasing to pray for you; but I will teach you the good and the right way."

Saul, thirty years old, began his reign a thousand years or so before Christ. Soon he sounded an alarm against the

Philistines and the people rallied about him at Gilgal.  But
they became frightened as the Philistines gathered, and hid in
caves and thickets, some even crossing the Jordan to the land
of Gad and Gilead.

## Saul Offends Samuel, I Sam. *13, 14*

Saul, at Gilgal, offered a sacrifice.  As soon as the ceremony was finished, Samuel arrived and demanded an expla-
nation.  Saul replied that he had waited the appointed number of days for Samuel and that the Philistines had camped
at Michmash and the people were deserting.  He continued:
"Therefore said I, the Philistines will come down now upon me
to Gilgal, and I have not made supplication unto the Lord.
I forced myself therefore and offered a burnt offering."

Then Samuel told him that if he had not thus acted foolishly, the Lord would have established his kingdom upon
Israel forever.  "But now," he proceeded, "the Lord hath
sought him a man after his own heart, and the Lord hath
commanded him to be captain over his people, because thou
hast not kept that which the Lord commanded thee."

The Philistines had abolished smiths lest the Hebrews
make swords and spears.  Saul's son Jonathan nevertheless
led them, unarmed, to victory, and the Philistines returned
to their own land.  "So Saul took the kingdom over Israel
and fought against all his enemies on every side."  Whithersoever he turned he vexed them.  There was war against the
Philistines all the days of Saul; and when he saw any strong
or valiant man he added him to his army.

Because the Amalekites had opposed Israel in coming out
of Egypt, Samuel now sent Saul out against them, directing
him to spare no one and even to destroy their sheep and oxen.
The Amalekites were scattered.  But after the battle Samuel,
coming out to meet Saul, heard the bleating of sheep and the
lowing of kine.  Saul explained that the people had spared
the best of the animals to sacrifice unto the Lord.

But said Samuel: "Hath the Lord as great delight in burnt offerings and sacrifices as in obeying the voice of the Lord? Behold, to obey is better than sacrifice, and to hearken than the fat of rams. For rebellion is as the sin of witchcraft, and stubbornness is as iniquity and idolatry. Because thou hast rejected the word of the Lord, he hath also rejected thee from being king."

Then Saul confessed: "I have sinned, for I have transgressed the commandment of the Lord and thy words; because I feared the people and obeyed their voice. Now therefore, I pray thee, pardon my sin and turn again with me that I may worship the Lord."

But Samuel refused; and as he turned to go, Saul caught hold of the skirt of his mantle and tore it. Samuel exclaimed, "The Lord hath rent the kingdom of Israel from thee this day." They parted and Samuel visited Saul no more.

"How long wilt thou mourn for Saul," said the Lord to Samuel, "seeing I have rejected him from reigning over Israel? Fill thine horn with oil and go, I will send thee to Jesse the Bethlehemite, for I have provided me a king among his sons."

"How can I go?" asked Samuel, "if Saul hear it he will kill me." "Take an heifer with thee," instructed the Lord, "and say, I am come to sacrifice." At Bethlehem Samuel called Jesse and his sons to the sacrifice which he had prepared. When he saw Eliab he said, "Surely the Lord's anointed is before him." But the Lord declared: "Look not on his countenance, or on the height of his stature, because I have refused him; for the Lord seeth not as man seeth; for man looketh on the outward appearance, but the Lord looketh on the heart."

## David and Goliath, I Sam. *16-27*

Jesse then made seven of his sons pass before Samuel, but Samuel, rejecting them, asked if he had seen all the children.

When Jesse told him that David, the youngest, was keeping the sheep, Samuel insisted upon seeing him.

Jesse sent and fetched David in. "Now he was ruddy and withal of a beautiful countenance and goodly to look to." "Arise, anoint him," said the Lord, "for this is he." Samuel then took the horn of oil and anointed David in the midst of his brethren; and the Spirit of the Lord came upon David from that day forward.

But the Spirit of the Lord departed from Saul and an evil spirit troubled him. He therefore asked his servants to provide him a man who could play well. They brought David. As David stood before Saul, Saul loved him greatly, and David became his armor-bearer. And when the evil spirit was upon Saul, David took his harp and played so that Saul was refreshed and was well and the spirit departed.

War again broke out. The Philistines stood on a mountain on one side, and Israel stood on a mountain on the other side. Between them was a valley. A champion named Goliath, six cubits and a span in height, stepped from the ranks of the Philistines. The staff of his spear was like a weaver's beam. "I defy the armies of Israel this day," he shouted, "give me a man that we may fight together." Then were Saul and his men dismayed.

For forty days Goliath repeated his challenge. David, meanwhile, went to and fro, attending Saul and feeding his father's sheep. Visiting his brothers in the army to learn how they fared, he overheard the giant's challenge. And when Saul next sent for him he said: "Let no man's heart fail because of him; thy servant will go and fight with this Philistine." But Saul replied: "Thou art not able to go against this Philistine to fight with him; for thou art but a youth, and he a man of war from his youth."

David then related how he had slain a lion and a bear, and argued that the Lord who had delivered him from these wild beasts would deliver him from the Philistine. Saul answered, "Go, and the Lord be with thee."

Saul put his own armor on David and gave him his sword; but said David, "I cannot go with these, for I have not proved them." Putting them off, therefore, he took his staff, chose five smooth stones out of the brook, and started out with his sling in his hand.

As the two drew near each other Goliath disdained David because of his youth and ruddy complexion, and boasted that he would give him to the fowls of the air and the beasts of the field. David replied: "Thou comest to me with a sword and with a spear and with a shield; but I come to thee in the name of the Lord of hosts, the God of the armies of Israel, whom thou hast defied. This day will the Lord deliver thee into mine hand . . . And all this assembly shall know that the Lord saveth not with sword and spear; for the battle is the Lord's, and he will give you into our hands."

As he ran forward David took a stone from his bag, slung it, and smote Goliath in the forehead; and he fell upon his face to the earth. When the Philistines saw their champion fall, they fled and the Israelites pursued them to the gates of Ekron.

Saul, watching the encounter, did not recognize David; and when David was afterward brought before him he asked, "Whose son art thou, thou young man?" David answered, "I am the son of thy servant Jesse."

A close friendship now arose between Saul's son Jonathan and David. They made a covenant and Jonathan put his own robe and garments and weapons on David.

## Saul Envious of David, I Sam. 18

Saul set David over the men of war; and it came to pass that when they returned from battle, the women, coming out to meet Saul with singing and dancing, said one to another, "Saul hath slain his thousands and David his ten thousands."

Saul was wroth with this. "What can he have more but the kingdom?" he asked. And from that day he eyed David. On two occasions, while David was playing for him, he cast his javelin at him. But David evaded it each time. Then

Saul realized that the Lord had departed from him and was
with David.

Jonathan's friendship with David continued. He interceded with Saul but without success. Indeed Saul's enmity
increased rather than diminished, until David became a fugitive.

Once, when he and his men were hungry, he entered the
house of God and inveigled hallowed bread from the priest.
Jesus afterward cited this incident to justify his disciples in
plucking ears of corn in the field and eating them on the sabbath.

One night Saul, while searching for David, slept in the
same cave where David had taken refuge. During the night
David cut off a piece of Saul's robe; and his men would have
slain Saul, but David stayed their hands. In the morning,
on the outside, Saul confessed to David: "Thou art more
righteous than I . . . I know well that thou shalt surely be
king . . . Swear now therefore unto me by the Lord that
thou wilt not cut off my seed after me."

At another time, when Saul was in pursuit, David crept
into Saul's camp and found him asleep. His armor-bearer
was ready to smite Saul, but David would not permit it because Saul was the Lord's anointed. But he carried away
Saul's spear and cruse of water.

Then, at safe distance, the men conversed with each other,
Saul ending the dialogue by saying, "Behold, I have played
the fool and have erred exceedingly." So each man went his
own way. David, still fearful, now fled to the land of the
Philistines, taking up his abode at Ziklag.

### Witch of Endor, I Sam. 28-31; I Chr. 10

Again hostilities broke out with the Philistines. David
would have joined them but they distrusted him. Saul trembled greatly as he saw their host. And when he sought the
Lord, for Samuel was no more, he received no answer. Then

he asked for a woman with a familiar spirit. But his men reminded him that he had put the witches and soothsayers out of the country. Yet they told him of one left at Endor. Saul, disguising himself, went with two men to her at night and said, "Bring me him up whom I shall name unto thee."

The woman, fearing a trap was being set for her, hesitated until Saul promised that she should not be harmed. Then he asked her to bring up Samuel. When she saw the prophet she was greatly alarmed and asked, "Why hast thou deceived me? for thou art Saul." Reassuring her, he asked what she saw. "I saw gods ascending out of the earth," she answered.

"What form is he of?" he inquired. "An old man cometh up," she replied, "and he is covered with a mantle." Whereupon "Saul perceived that it was Samuel, and he stooped with his face to the ground and bowed himself."

"Why hast thou disquieted me, to bring me up?" asked Samuel. "I am sore distressed," replied Saul, "for the Philistines make war against me, and God is departed from me and answereth me no more, neither by prophets nor by dreams." Samuel answered: "The Lord will also deliver Israel with thee into the hand of the Philistines; and tomorrow shalt thou and thy sons be with me."

Saul fell to the ground. There was no strength left in him, for he had eaten no bread all day. The woman and his men, with much persuasion, induced him to remain while she prepared dinner. After eating he rose up and went away.

When the Philistines made their attack the Hebrews fled. Three of Saul's sons, including Jonathan, were slain. Saul, hard pressed, took his own life.

# II Samuel

## David Made King, II Sam. *1-12*, I Chr. *11*

When news of the disaster reached David at Ziklag in Philistia, he and his men rent their clothes and fasted and
mourned until evening.   In their grief they sang:

> Tell it not in Gath,
> Publish it not in the streets of Askelon;
> Lest the daughters of the Philistines rejoice,
> Lest the daughters of the uncircumcised triumph.

> Saul and Jonathan were lovely and pleasant in their
>     lives,
> And in their death they were not divided;
> They were swifter than eagles,
> They were stronger than lions.

> O Jonathan, thou wast slain in thine high places.
> I am distressed for thee, my brother Jonathan;
> Very pleasant hast thou been unto me;
> Thy love to me was wonderful,
> Passing the love of women.
> How are the mighty fallen,
> And the weapons of war perished!

84

David now went up from Ziklag to Hebron, where he was anointed king over the house of Judah. Abner, captain of Saul's army, made Ish-bosheth, Saul's surviving son, king over Israel. Then was there long war between the house of Saul and the house of David, in which David waxed stronger and stronger until Abner came over to him.

Afterward both Abner and Ish-bosheth were slain. Then the elders of Israel went to Hebron and anointed David king over all Israel (about 960 B.C.). He now proceeded against the Jebusites in Jerusalem. Taking over the city, he established his abode in the castle of Zion. "Therefore they called it the city of David."

## *Ark Taken to Jerusalem, II Sam. 2-12, I Chr. 11-17*

The ark of the covenant had been neglected during the days of Saul. Now the people went with David to Kerjath-jearim to bring it up to Jerusalem. They put the ark in a new cart driven by Uzza and Ahio. When they came to the threshing floor of Chidon, Uzza put forth his hand to steady the ark because the oxen stumbled. This so kindled the anger of the Lord that he smote Uzza.

David, filled with apprehension, abandoned the journey and put the ark in the house of Obed-edom, where it remained three months, and the blessing of the Lord was upon the house.

Now Hiram, king of Tyre, sent David timber of cedars, with masons and carpenters; and David built himself a house in Jerusalem. He also prepared a place for the ark of God and pitched for it a tent. The Levites, having sanctified themselves to take charge of the ark, carried it from Obed-edom to Jerusalem on their shoulders. As they started the journey they sang Psalm 30:

*I will extol thee, O Lord; for thou hast lifted me up*
*And hast not made my foes to rejoice over me.*

O Lord my God,
I cried unto thee, and thou hast healed me.
O Lord, thou hast brought up my soul from the
grave;
Thou hast kept me alive, that I should not go down
to the pit.

Sing unto the Lord, O ye saints of his,
And give thanks at the remembrance of his holiness.
For his anger endureth but a moment;
In his favor is life:
Weeping may endure for a night,
But joy cometh in the morning.

As the procession entered the city, the 24th Psalm was
sung:

Lift up your heads, O ye gates;
And be ye lift up, ye everlasting doors;
And the King of glory shall come in.
Who is this King of glory?
The Lord strong and mighty,
The Lord mighty in battle.

Lift up your heads, O ye gates;
Even lift them up, ye everlasting doors;
And the King of glory shall come in.
Who is this King of glory?
The Lord of hosts,
He is the King of glory.

The ark brought in and placed in the tent, David sang
Psalm 132:

Lord, remember David
And all his afflictions,
How he sware unto the Lord,
And vowed unto the mighty God of Jacob:
Surely I will not come into the tabernacle of my
house,

Nor go up into my bed;
I will not give sleep to mine eyes,
Or slumber to mine eyelids,
Until I find out a place for the Lord,
An habitation for the mighty God of Jacob.
Lo, we heard of it at Ephratah;
We found it in the fields of the wood.
We will go into his tabernacles;
We will worship at his footstool.

Now David returned to bless his household, singing Psalm 101:

I will sing of mercy and judgment;
Unto thee, O Lord, will I sing.
I will behave myself wisely in a perfect way.
O when wilt thou come unto me?
I will walk within my house with a perfect heart.
I will set no wicked thing before mine eyes;
I hate the work of them that turn aside;
It shall not cleave to me.

One day as David sat in his house, after the Lord had given him rest from his enemies, he said to Nathan the prophet, "Lo, I dwell in an house of cedars but the ark of the covenant of the Lord remaineth under curtains." That night, however, word came from the Lord through Nathan that not David but David's son should build a house to the Lord, because David had been a man of war.

After this David subdued the Philistines, Moabites, Ammonites, Edomites, and Syrians.

## *Affair with Bathsheba, II Sam. 11, 12*

One evening in Jerusalem, as he walked on the roof, he observed a woman who pleased him. She was Bathsheba, wife of Uriah, who was away with the army in a campaign against

the Ammonites.   David wrote Joab, who was in command of
the troops: "Set ye Uriah in the forefront of the hottest
battle, and retire ye from him, that he may be smitten."
Joab followed instructions and Uriah was slain.   When the
time for mourning was past, Bathsheba became David's wife;
but the thing that David had done displeased the Lord.

Then Nathan told him a parable of the rich man who had
many flocks, and the poor man who had only one little lamb;
and when a traveler came to the rich man, he spared to take
of his own herd and took the poor man's lamb for the way-
farer's entertainment.   David's anger was greatly kindled and
he roundly denounced the wrong.   Then said Nathan, "Thou
art the man."

The Lord struck Bathsheba's first child and he was very
sick.   David fasted and besought the Lord but on the seventh
day the boy died.

In his mourning David reflected: "While the child was yet
alive, I fasted and wept; for I said, Who can tell whether
God will be gracious to me, that the child may live?   But
now he is dead, wherefore should I fast?   Can I bring him
back again?   I shall go to him, but he shall not return to
me."

The second son by Bathsheba David called Solomon; and
the Lord loved him.

## Revolt of Absalom, II Sam. *13-24*

Among David's sons was one named Absalom.   In all
Israel there was none so much praised for his beauty; from
the sole of his feet to the crown of his head there was no
blemish on him.   When he cut his hair at the end of each
year, it weighed four pounds.

Absalom slew his brother Ammon, on account of a family
grievance, and fled to Geshur.   After three years there he returned to Jerusalem and became reconciled with his father.

He made it a practice to rise early in the morning and stand

Absalom stirred up a rebellion

by the gate of the capital and accost those coming with their grievances to the king, exclaiming: "O that I were made judge in the land, that every man which hath any suit or cause might come unto me, and I would do him justice!" In this way he ingratiated himself with people from all parts of the kingdom.

In the course of a few years he gained permission of David, under pretense that he had a vow to pay unto the Lord, to go to Hebron. As he went he sent spies throughout Israel saying: "As soon as ye hear the sound of the trumpet, then ye shall say, Absalom reigneth in Hebron."

In the rebellion thus stirred up, David fled from Jerusalem across Jordan. Absalom entered Jerusalem and enjoyed the palace for a time and might have succeeded in his revolt but for the intrigues of David's friend Hushai.

The decisive battle was fought in Ephraim wood. There, as Absalom rode under an oak, his hair became entangled in an overhanging branch, and he was lifted from his mule and left swinging in the air.

A man who found Absalom in this predicament refrained from slaying him, because David had given orders that no harm should be done his rebellious son. But when the man told Joab, Joab promptly took advantage of the situation and dispatched him.

When runners brought the news to David, he retired to his chamber over the gate and lamented: "O my son Absalom, my son, my son Absalom! would God I had died for thee, O Absalom, my son, my son!"

When Joab heard that David was turning victory into mourning, he went to him and told him that unless he presented himself to the people and spoke "comfortably" to them, there would not tarry one with him that night. Then David arose and sat in the gate, and all the people came before him.

The rebellion suppressed, David permitted the people of Judah, alone, to escort him back to Jerusalem. Jealousy of the other tribes against Judah was the result, and another rebellion, headed by Sheba, a Benjaminite, broke out. When Sheba was delivered up to Joab by a woman in Abel, hostilities ceased.

Then there was a famine for three years, because of Saul's offense in slaying Gibeonites. Another war with the Philistines followed. David in these days waxing faint, his men said to him: "Thou shalt go no more out with us to battle, that thou quench not the light of Israel."

David, at last rescued from the power of his enemies, sang a song of thanksgiving:

> The Lord is my rock and my fortress and my deliverer;
> The God of my rock; in him will I trust:
> He is my shield, and the horn of my salvation,
> My high tower and my refuge, my savior;
> Thou savest me from violence.
> As for God his way is perfect;
> The word of the Lord is tried;
> He is a buckler to all them that trust in him.
> For who is God, save the Lord?
> And who is a rock, save our God?
> God is my strength and power;
> And he maketh my way perfect.

# I Kings

## Reign of Solomon, I Kings 1-11, I Chr. 28, II Chr. 1

David being now old and stricken in years, Adonijah, Absalom's brother, proclaimed himself king. Bathsheba, the mother of Solomon, reminded David of his promise to make Solomon king. Nathan strengthened Bathsheba's plea. Then David ordered that Solomon should be anointed. When the ceremony took place "the people piped with pipes and rejoiced with great joy, so that the earth rent with the sound of them."

As his end drew nigh, David charged Solomon: "I go the way of all the earth: be thou strong therefore and show thyself a man; and keep the charge of the Lord thy God to walk in his ways, to keep his statutes and his commandments and his judgments."

So David slept with his fathers, and was buried in the city of Jerusalem. He was thirty years old when called to the throne. He reigned over Israel forty years, seven years in Hebron and thirty-three years in Jerusalem.

Solomon took Pharaoh's daughter as his wife. Going to Gibeon, where there was a great high place, he offered a thousand burnt offerings. The Lord appeared to him and said, "Ask what I shall give thee." Solomon answered: "Give therefore thy servant an understanding heart to judge thy people that I may discern between good and bad; for who is able to judge this thy so great a people?"

Much pleased with Solomon's speech, the Lord promised him not only a wise and understanding heart but riches and honor as well. He promised also to lengthen Solomon's days if he would walk in His ways and keep His statutes and commandments.

A strange controversy between two women was brought before Solomon for decision. One accused the other of taking away her living child and putting in its place her own dead child. The other denied the accusation and insisted that the living child was hers. Solomon called for a sword and ordered, "Divide the living child in two and give half to the one and half to the other."

Immediately one of the women exclaimed, "Give her the living child and in no wise slay it!" But the other said, "Let it be neither mine nor thine but divide it!" The king answered: "Give her (the first speaker) the living child and in no wise slay it; she is the mother thereof." And all Israel heard of the decision, and saw that the wisdom of God was in their king to do judgment.

## Erection of Temple, I Kings 6, II Chr. 2-8

Solomon now set about to build the temple. He arranged with King Hiram to have timbers hewed in the forests of Lebanon. He had stone made ready in the quarries. So that when the materials were brought together "there was neither hammer nor ax nor any tool of iron heard in the house while it was in building."

Solomon was seven years building the house. When the work was ended he brought in the things which David had dedicated, the silver and gold and vessels. With the elders of Israel and the heads of the tribes assembled, "the priests brought in the ark of the covenant of the Lord unto his place, into the oracle of the house, to the most holy place, even under the wings of the cherubim."

There was nothing in the ark save the two tables of stone

Israel prosper
under Solomon

which Moses had put there at Horeb. When the priests came out of the holy place a cloud filled the house so that they could not stand to minister. "The glory of the Lord had filled the house of the Lord."

Solomon having constructed the temple and his own house, and rebuilt various cities, next built a navy on the shore of the Red Sea in the land of Edom. Hiram sent his seamen to man the ships along with Solomon's servants. They went to Ophir and fetched gold and jewels and sandalwood.

Solomon also had a fleet which sailed from Tharshish with Hiram's navy to distant places. Every third year it brought home gold and silver, ivory, apes, and peacocks. Besides he traded with spice merchants. He imported horses and chariots. Both in wisdom and in riches he surpassed all other kings of his time. All the earth sought him to hear his wisdom.

## Queen of Sheba, I Kings 10, 11, II Chr. 9

When the Queen of Sheba heard of the fame of Solomon, she came and communed with him of all that was in her heart. Solomon was able to answer her hard questions, for there was nothing hid from him. When she saw his wisdom and the house he had built and the splendor of his court "there was no more spirit in her." She exclaimed: "The half was not told me; thy wisdom and prosperity exceedeth the fame which I heard!" She made him many and costly presents. He gave her whatsoever she desired, and she returned to her own country.

"But King Solomon loved many strange women, together with the daughter of Pharaoh, women . . . of the nations concerning which the Lord said . . . Ye shall not go in to them, neither shall they come in unto you." These foreign wives, as years crept upon Solomon, turned away his heart after other gods.

Angered with him, the Lord declared: "I will surely rend the kingdom from thee and will give it to thy servant. Notwithstanding in thy days I will not do it, for David thy father's sake, but I will rend it out of the hand of thy son." So the Lord stirred up adversaries against Solomon.

One of them was Jeroboam, a mighty man of valor, son of Nebat. The prophet Ahijah, rending his garment in twelve pieces one day when he met Jeroboam in the field, cried: "Take thee ten pieces; for thus saith the Lord, I will rend the kingdom out of the hand of Solomon and will give ten tribes to thee."

## Division of Kingdom, I Kings 12, II Chr. 10

After a reign of forty years Solomon slept with his fathers and was interred in the city of David. His son Rehoboam went to Shechem, for all Israel gathered there to make him king. Jeroboam, who had fled to Egypt for safety, now appeared, having been called back by his friends after Solomon's demise. He and the congregation of Israel asked Rehoboam to make their yoke lighter. But Rehoboam, listening to his young advisers rather than to the old men who had been with Solomon, exclaimed: "Now whereas my father did lade you with a heavy yoke, I will add to your yoke. My father hath chastised you with whips but I will chastise you with scorpions."

To which the people replied: "What portion have we in David? Neither have we inheritance in the son of Jesse. To your tents, O Israel; now see to thine own house, David." So Israel, the ten tribes of the North, rebelled against the house of David, the two tribes of Judah and Benjamin in the South. Israel now made Jeroboam king and later established their capital at Samaria; while the tribes of the South gathered to Rehoboam in Jerusalem. Thus after a brief existence of less than a century did the kingdom fall apart (931 B. C.).

*Dirge for the Fall, Psalm 80*

> O Lord God of hosts,
> How long wilt thou be angry against the prayer of
>    thy people?
> Thou feedest them with the bread of tears;
> And givest them tears to drink in great measure.
>
> Thou makest us a strife unto our neighbors;
> And our enemies laugh among themselves.
> Turn us again, O God of hosts,
> And cause thy face to shine, and we shall be saved.
>
> Thou hast brought a vine out of Egypt;
> Thou hast cast out the heathen, and planted it.
> Thou preparedst room before it,
> And didst cause it to take deep root, and it filled the
>    land.
> The hills were covered with the shadow of it,
> And the boughs thereof were like the goodly cedars.
> She sent out her boughs unto the sea,
> And her branches unto the river.
> Why hast thou then broken down her hedges,
> So that all they which pass by the way do pluck her?

War followed war between the kingdom of Israel in the North and the kingdom of Judah in the South. Cruel civil strife also raged. In their weakened condition the Hebrews became easy victims to their powerful neighbors. The Egyptians were the first to assert dominion over them. One after another the Arameans, Assyrians, Babylonians swooped down upon them. Yet despite internal dissension and foreign aggression the Northern Kingdom endured for two centuries, when it was absorbed by Sargon, king of Assyria (722 B. C.). The Southern Kingdom struggled on a century and a half longer, eventually to fall a prey to Nebuchadnezzar, king of Babylon (587 B. C.). Now for a more detailed history of the two kingdoms.

## The Northern Kingdom, I Kings 12, 13

Jeroboam was a distinct disappointment as king of Israel. The bad precedents he established proved stumbling blocks to his successors. It at once occurred to him, when he came to the throne, that his followers might return to the house of David if they continued to go to the temple in Jerusalem to sacrifice. He therefore made two calves of gold and set one up at Bethel and the other at Dan, saying to the people: "It is too much for you to go up to Jerusalem; behold thy gods, O Israel, which brought thee up out of the land of Egypt." Accordingly they worshipped and offered sacrifices before the idols.

He built an house of high places and made priests out of the lowest of the people who were not sons of Levi. These things became "sin unto the house of Jeroboam even to cut it off and to destroy it from off the face of the earth."

He continued his questionable practices throughout a reign of twenty-two years. As a penalty the Lord demanded the life of his son Abijah. The prophet Ahijah, when the mother appealed to him, foretold the demise.

Jeroboam was followed on the throne by his son Nadab. Nadab walked in the footsteps of his father. In two years he was slain by Baasha, who reigned after him. Baasha exterminated the house of Jeroboam, leaving "not any that breathed."

There was war between Baasha and Asa, king of Judah, all their days. Baasha built Ramah, that no one might go out or come in to Asa. Like Nadab he walked in the footsteps of Jeroboam. He was followed by his son Elah.

After a reign of two years Elah was assassinated by Zimri, who ascended the throne. When word of the assassination reached the army, the men in camp made Omri king over Israel. Besieged by Omri at Tirzah, Zimri, after a reign of seven days, burned the king's house over himself and died. Omri now built the city of Samaria. In his days also was Jericho rebuilt.

Like his predecessors Omri wrought evil in the eyes of the Lord. At his death his son Ahab became king. He did worse than all that were before him. He even married Jezebel the daughter of Ethbaal, king of the Zidonians, and went and served Baal.

## Elijah, I Kings 17-22

Therefore the prophet Elijah of Gilead warned Ahab that there would not be dew or rain for years except according to his word. The Lord commanded Elijah to hide by the brook Cherith toward Jordan and promised that the ravens would feed him. Elijah did so and the ravens fed him bread and flesh in the morning and in the evening; and he drank from the stream.

But after a time the brook dried up because there was no rain. Then the Lord directed Elijah to go to Zarephath in Zidon and dwell with a widow who would sustain him. When he came to the gates of the city he found her gathering sticks. He asked for food and water. She answered: "As the Lord thy God liveth, I have not a cake, but an handful of meal in a barrel, and a little oil in a cruse; and behold, I am gathering two sticks that I may go in and dress it for me and my son that we may eat it and die."

Elijah told her to first make him a cake and then prepare for her son and herself. "For thus saith the Lord God of Israel," he assured her, "the barrel of meal shall not waste, neither shall the cruse of oil fail, until the day that the Lord sendeth rain upon the earth." The woman obeyed and the three ate for many days.

One day the son became so sick that there was no breath left in him. Elijah took the boy to his loft and cried: "O Lord my God, hast thou also brought evil upon the widow with whom I sojourn, by slaying her son? . . . I pray thee, let this child's soul come into him again." The child revived; and when Elijah presented him to his mother she said:

"Now by this I know that thou art a man of God, and that the word of the Lord in thy mouth is truth."

After three years of famine the Lord ordered Elijah to show himself to Ahab, and promised to send rain. Ahab asked Elijah, "Art thou he that troubleth Israel?" Elijah rejoined that it was Ahab who was troubling Israel by forsaking the Lord and following Baal.

## Prophets of Baal, I Kings 18

Now Elijah directed Ahab to gather all Israel to Mount Carmel, also the four hundred and fifty prophets of Baal and the four hundred prophets of the grove who ate at Jezebel's table. When the people had assembled, Elijah asked: "How long halt ye between two opinions? If the Lord be God, follow Him; but if Baal, then follow him." The people answered not a word.

Elijah proceeded: "I, even I only, remain a prophet of the Lord; but Baal's prophets are four hundred and fifty men. Let them therefore give us two bullocks; and let them choose one bullock for themselves, and cut it in pieces and lay it on wood and put no fire under; and I will dress the other bullock and lay it on wood and put no fire under. And call ye on the name of your gods, and I will call on the name of the Lord; and the God that answereth by fire, let him be God." The people all agreed.

The prophets of Baal dressed their bullock first. They called on Baal from morning until noon, "O Baal, hear us." But there was no voice or answer. And they leaped upon the altar.

Then Elijah mocked them: "Cry aloud, for he is a god; either he is talking or he is pursuing or he is in a journey or peradventure he sleepeth and must be awaked." They cried and prophesied until the time of the evening sacrifice. Still there was neither voice nor any to answer nor any that regarded.

Elijah now took twelve stones and built an altar. He also made a trench around it. He put the wood and the offering in place and ordered four barrels of water to be poured on them. Three times was this done. The trench filled with water.

When the hour came to offer the evening sacrifice, Elijah approached the altar and prayed: "Lord God of Abraham, Isaac, and of Israel, let it be known this day that thou art God in Israel and that I am thy servant and that I have done all these things at thy word. Hear me, O Lord, hear me, that this people may know that thou art the Lord God and that thou hast turned their heart back again."

Then the "fire of the Lord fell and consumed the burnt sacrifice and the wood and the stones and the dust, and licked up the water that was in the trench." When the people saw it they fell on their faces and cried: "The Lord, he is the God; the Lord, he is the God."

Elijah now told Ahab to eat and drink for there was a sound of abundance of rain. He next went up to the top of Carmel. As he prayed there he told his servant to look toward the sea. The servant reported that there was nothing in sight. Elijah bade him to go again seven times. At the seventh time he said, "Behold, there ariseth a little cloud out of the sea like a man's hand." Elijah instructed him to warn Ahab. "And it came to pass in the meanwhile that the heaven was black with clouds and wind and there was a great rain. And Ahab rode and went to Jezreel."

## Still Small Voice, I Kings 19

When he told Jezebel how Elijah had triumphed over the prophets, she sent Elijah a messenger threatening him with vengeance. Whereupon Elijah fled into the wilderness near Beersheba. Sitting down under a juniper tree, he prayed that he might die. Presently he fell asleep. Then an angel touched him and said, "Arise and eat."

As Elijah looked he beheld "a cake baken on the coals and a cruse of water at his head. And he did eat and drink and laid him down again." A second time the angel touched him and said, "Arise and eat, because the journey is too great for thee." He did so and went in the strength of that food forty days and forty nights to Mount Horeb.

There he took shelter in a cave, where the Lord came to him and inquired, "What doest thou here?" He answered: "I have been very jealous for the Lord God of hosts. For the children of Israel have forsaken thy covenant, thrown down thine altars, and slain thy prophets with the sword; and I, even I only, am left; and they seek my life to take it away."

The Lord said, "Go forth and stand upon the mount." And "behold, the Lord passed by and a great and strong wind rent the mountains and brake in pieces the rocks before the Lord; but the Lord was not in the wind: and after the wind an earthquake; but the Lord was not in the earthquake: and after the earthquake a fire; but the Lord was not in the fire; and after the fire a still, small voice."

The Lord commanded Elijah to take the wilderness road to Damascus and there anoint Hazael king over Syria. He also directed him to anoint Jehu king over Israel; and Elisha prophet in his own place. "It shall come to pass," the Lord continued, "that him that escapeth the sword of Hazael shall Jehu slay; and him that escapeth from the sword of Jehu shall Elisha slay. Yet I have left me seven thousand in Israel, all the knees which have not bowed unto Baal, and every mouth which hath not kissed him."

Elijah departed and found Elisha plowing with twelve yoke of oxen. As he passed by Elisha, he threw his mantle upon him. Elisha then followed and ministered to Elijah.

# II Kings

## Departure of Elijah, II Kings 1

After Ahab, his son Ahaziah reigned in Israel. Injured by a fall through the lattice in his upper chamber, he sent messengers to Baalzebub to inquire if he would recover. Elijah, meeting them on their way, gave them this message to the king: "Is it not because there is not a God in Israel that thou sendest to inquire of Baalzebub, the god of Ekron? Therefore thou shalt not come down from that bed on which thou art gone up, but shalt surely die."

Then the king sent a captain and fifty men to fetch Elijah. Elijah said to the captain, "If I be a man of God, then let fire come down from heaven and consume thee and thy fifty." Accordingly they were consumed. The king sent another captain with fifty men. They met the same fate. The third captain fell on his knees before Elijah and prayed that he and his men might be spared. An angel said to Elijah, "Go down with him; be not afraid of him." Elijah went and repeated his prophecy to the king, who died according to the word of the Lord.

"And it came to pass, when the Lord would take up Elijah into heaven by a whirlwind, that Elijah went with Elisha from Gilgal." They passed through Bethel and Jericho. The sons of the prophets there asked Elisha if he did not know that the Lord would take away his master that day. He an-

101

swered, "Yea, I know it; hold ye your peace."   At both places
Elijah told Elisha to tarry, but Elisha replied, "As the Lord
liveth and as thy soul liveth, I will not leave thee."   When
they came to the Jordan "Elijah took his mantle and wrapped
it together and smote the waters, and they were divided hither
and thither, so that they two went over on dry ground."

Then Elijah said to Elisha, "Ask what I shall do for thee
before I be taken away."   Elisha answered, "I pray thee, let
a double portion of thy spirit be upon me."   Elijah responded: "Thou hast asked a hard thing.   Nevertheless if
thou see me when I am taken from thee, it shall be so unto
thee; but if not, it shall not be so."   As they went on, talking,
"there appeared a chariot of fire and horses of fire, and parted
them both asunder; and Elijah went up by a whirlwind into
heaven."   Elisha saw it and cried, "My father, my father, the
chariot of Israel and the horsemen thereof."   And he saw
Elijah no more.

### Elisha Succeeds Elijah, II Kings 2

Elisha took up the mantle that had fallen from Elijah and
went back to the bank of Jordan.   He smote the waters and
cried, "Where is the Lord God of Elijah?"   The waters parted
and he went over.   Fifty men of the sons of the prophets who
had viewed both incidents from afar, exclaimed, "The spirit
of Elijah doth rest on Elisha!"   And they went out, against
the injunction of Elisha, and searched three days for Elijah
but found him not.

While Elisha tarried at Jericho the people pointed out to
him: "The situation of this city is pleasant, as my lord seeth;
but the water is naught and the ground barren."   He replied,
"Bring me a new cruse and put salt therein."   When they
brought it he went to the spring and cast the salt in the water.
"Thus saith the Lord," he exclaimed, "I have healed these

waters; there shall not be from thence any more death or barren land." And the waters were purified.

On his way up to Bethel little children came out and mocked him, "Go up, thou bald head; go up, thou bald head." He looked back and cursed them in the name of the Lord. And there came forth two she bears out of the wood and tore forty and two of them.

After Ahaziah, his brother Jehoram reigned in Israel. The king of Moab, who had been paying tribute to Israel, rebelled against Jehoram. Enlisting the aid of Jehoshaphat, king of Judah, and of the king of Edom, Jehoram proceeded against the Moabites. After seven days' journey they found themselves without water. Jehoshaphat demanded, "Is there not here a prophet of the Lord that we may inquire of the Lord by him?"

One of Jehoram's servants reminded them of Elisha. Elisha, when approached, exclaimed to Jehoram, who still carried on sinful practices although he had put away the image of Baal: "What have I to do with thee . . . Were it not that I regard the presence of Jehoshaphat, the king of Judah, I would not look toward thee nor see thee. But now bring me a minstrel."

"Thus saith the Lord," declared Elisha as the minstrel played, "make this valley full of ditches. Ye shall not see wind, neither shall ye see rain; yet that valley shall be filled with water that ye may drink, both ye and your cattle and your beasts." In the morning water came by way of Edom and filled the country.

The sun shining on the water made it look red. The Moabites, up early and ready for action, exclaimed: "This is blood; the kings are surely slain and they have smitten one another! Now therefore, Moab, to the spoil." When they came to the camp of Israel, the Israelites smote them and pursued them into their own country. So fierce were the battles which followed, and so hard pressed were the Moabites, that their king offered his eldest son as a sacrifice upon the wall.

## The Pot of Oil, II Kings 4

A widow called on Elisha one day to tell him that a creditor had come to take away her two sons as bondmen. "What hast thou in the house?" he asked. "Not anything," she replied, "save a pot of oil."

"Go, borrow thee vessels abroad of all thy neighbors," he directed, "borrow not a few. And when thou art come in, thou shalt shut the door upon thee and upon thy sons, and shalt pour out into all those vessels." When they were full, she asked her son to bring another. "There is not a vessel more," he replied; and the oil stayed. "Go, sell the oil and pay thy debt," said Elisha, "and live thou and thy children of the rest."

## The Shunammite Woman, II Kings 4

In Shunam was a great woman with whom Elisha ate bread whenever he passed by. Perceiving that the prophet was a man of God, she had her husband provide a room for him. He, learning that she had no children and wishing to do something for her, promised a son. She was incredulous. Nevertheless the promise was fulfilled.

One day when the boy was out with the reapers he exclaimed to his father, "My head! My head!" Carried to his mother, he sat on her knees until noon and then died. She laid him on Elisha's bed and started post haste on a donkey to Carmel to find Elisha. When he saw her coming he sent his servant to inquire if it were well with her and her husband and the child. She answered, "It is well."

Throwing herself at Elisha's feet she asked, "Did I desire a son of my lord? Did I not say, Do not deceive me?" "As the Lord liveth," she continued, "and as thy soul liveth, I will not leave thee." He therefore arose and followed her, first dispatching his servant before them to lay the prophet's staff upon the boy's face. But the child was not revived.

Elisha, when he arrived, at once repaired to the room. He "shut the door upon them twain and prayed unto the Lord." The child sneezed seven times and opened his eyes. "Take up thy son," said he to the mother.

## Feeding the People, II Kings 4

On his next visit to Gilgal Elisha found a famine in the land. He said to his servant, "Set on the great pot and seethe pottage for the sons of the prophets." One man brought in from the field a lapful of wild gourds, which he shred into the pot not knowing what they were. As the men were eating they cried out, "O thou man of God, there is death in the pot." But Elisha cast meal into the mess and said, "Pour out for the people that they may eat." Then there was no harm in the food.

A man from Baal-shalisha brought Elisha "bread of the firstfruits, twenty loaves of barley and full ears of corn in the husk." Elisha directed, "Give unto the people that they may eat." But his servitor cried, "What, should I set this before an hundred men?" Elisha repeated the command, adding, "For thus saith the Lord, They shall eat and shall leave thereof." Accordingly they ate and there was some left over.

## Naaman of Syria, II Kings 5

Naaman, captain of the host of the king of Syria, was a mighty man in valor but he was a leper. His wife had a maid who had been brought captive from Israel. She said to her mistress, "Would God my lord were with the prophet

that is in Samaria! for he would recover him of his leprosy."
Whereupon the king of Syria sent Naaman to the king of
Israel with this letter, "Behold, I have therewith sent Naaman
my servant to thee that thou mayest recover him of his
leprosy."

The king of Israel, when he read the letter, rent his clothes
and exclaimed: "Am I God, to kill and to make alive . . .
see how he seeketh a quarrel against me." But Elisha interposed, "Let him come now to me." As Naaman stood at the
door of Elisha, he received this message from the prophet,
"Go and wash in Jordan seven times and thy flesh shall come
again to thee and thou shalt be clean."

Naaman was wroth and went away, saying: "I thought he
will surely come out to me and stand and call on the name of
the Lord his God and strike his hand over the place and recover the leper. Are not Abana and Pharpar, rivers of Damascus, better than all the waters of Israel? May I not wash
in them and be clean?"

His servant reasoned with him, "My father, if the prophet
had bid thee do some great thing, wouldest thou not have
done it?" Then Naaman went down and dipped himself in
Jordan seven times; and his flesh became like that of a little
child. Returning to Elisha he said, "Now I know that there
is no God in all the earth but in Israel." He offered Elisha
a gift but the prophet declined it.

### Further Miracles, II Kings 6-8

The sons of the prophets, finding their house too small,
went down to the Jordan to cut timber for a larger building.
As one of them was felling a beam, his ax head dropped into
the water. "Alas, master," he cried, "for it was borrowed."
When Elisha was shown the place, he thrust in a stick and
made the iron swim. The man put out his hand and took it.

The king of Syria warred against Israel. In taking counsel
with his servants he said, "In such and such a place shall be

my camp." Then sent Elisha word to the king of Israel,
"Beware that thou pass not such a place, for thither the Syrians are come down." Therefore was the heart of the king
of Syria troubled; and he demanded of his servants, "Will ye
not show me which of us is for the king of Israel?"

"None, my lord, O king; but Elisha the prophet that is in
Israel telleth the king of Israel the words that thou speakest
in thy bedchamber." Therefore the king of Syria sent a great
host, which by night compassed the city of Dothan where
Elisha was. Early in the morning Elisha's servant exclaimed,
"Alas, my master! how shall we do?"

"Fear not," answered Elisha, "for they that be with us are
more than they that be with them." And Elisha prayed the
Lord to quicken the vision of the young man. Then he beheld that the mountain was full of horses and chariots of fire
round about them.

When the enemy came down to him, Elisha asked the
Lord to smite them with blindness. He then said, "Follow
me and I will bring you to the man whom ye seek." But he
led them to Samaria. When they entered the town the Lord,
at Elisha's request, opened their eyes and they realized where
they were. The king of Israel wanted to slay them but Elisha
forbade. Instead he set bread and water before them; and
when they had eaten he sent them back to their master.

## *Rulers in the North*, II *Kings* 9-16

Elisha commissioned one of the children of the prophets
to go to Ramoth-gilead and find Jehu, the son of Jehoshaphat,
the son of Nimshi, and anoint him king. The young man
obeyed without delay. "Thus saith the Lord God of Israel,"
he declared as he poured oil on Jehu's head, "I have anointed
thee king over the people of the Lord, even over Israel. And
thou shalt smite the house of Ahab thy master, that I may
avenge the blood of my servants the prophets, and the blood
of all the servants of the Lord, at the hand of Jezebel."

Now Jehoram, son of Ahab and king of Israel, lay convalescing from wounds in Jezreel; and Ahaziah, king of Judah, was visiting him. Jehu started thither at once. As he approached the city the watchman remarked, "The driving is like the driving of Jehu, the son of Nimshi, for he driveth furiously."

Jehoram and Ahaziah went out to meet him, each in his own chariot. Detecting treachery they turned to flee. Jehu followed and overcame them both. Entering the city, and finding Jezebel looking out of a window, he commanded her to be thrown to the street.

Writing to Samaria, he had the seventy sons of Ahab in the city executed. Then on his way to Samaria, meeting the brethren of Ahaziah at the shearing house, he did away with them to the number of forty-two.

Pretending friendliness with the prophets of Baal, after his arrival in Samaria, he invited them to gather for a great sacrifice. While they were assembled in their temple, he commanded the guard and the captains to go in and dispatch them.

After this unprecedented ferocity Jehu lived twenty-eight years. He was followed on the throne by his son Jehoahaz, who reigned seventeen years. During that period Hazael, king of Syria, oppressed Israel.

Jehoahaz was succeeded by his son Jehoash. He recovered the cities which Hazael had taken. He went up against Jerusalem, broke down the wall, and took the gold and vessels from the house of the Lord and the treasury of the king. Elisha's last days were passed during the reign of Jehoash, who was succeeded by his son Jeroboam II. They all did that which was evil in the sight of the Lord.

During the reign of Jeroboam II in Israel, and of Amaziah in Judah, arose the prophet Amos from the shepherds of Tekoa, a small town near Jerusalem. He denounced the injustice and wickedness of the time. He predicted that Jeroboam should die of the sword and that Israel should be led captive out of their own land. Amaziah, the priest of Bethel, reminded Amos that he had better do his preaching in his own country.

Jeroboam II was followed by Zechariah, who reigned six
months, when he was assassinated by Shallum. Shallum
reigned only a month, before he was assassinated by Menahem.

Menahem turned back the king of Assyria by payment of a
thousand talents of silver exacted from the mighty men of
wealth in Israel.  He was followed by Pekahiah, who reigned
two years.  Like the kings before him he departed not from
the sins of Jeroboam the son of Nebat.  Pekah conspired
against and slew him.  In Pekah's days the king of Assyria
made encroachments on the territory of Israel.  After a reign
of twenty years Pekah was slain by Hoshea.


## Fall of Northern Kingdom, II Kings 17

Hoshea yielded to the king of Assyria and paid him tribute
year by year.  After a time, however, the king of Assyria shut
him up in prison, because he defaulted in his annual present
and besides made an alliance with the king of Egypt.

Finally the Assyrians invaded Israel in earnest, took Samaria
after a siege of three years, carried away the better class of the
inhabitants to Assyria, and in their place in Samaria planted
aliens.  Thus the Northern Kingdom came to an end (722
B.C.) and its people became known to history as the Ten Lost
Tribes.  "For so it was that the children of Israel had sinned
against the Lord their God, which had brought them up out
of the land of Egypt . . . And walked in the statutes of the
heathen, whom the Lord cast out from before the children of
Israel."

They built high places, they set up images and groves, they
burned incense, they served idols, they caused their sons and
daughters to pass through the fire, they used divination and
enchantments, they sold themselves to do evil in the sight of
the Lord to provoke him to anger.  Hence the Lord was
wroth with Israel and removed them out of his sight.

The newcomers to Samaria feared not the Lord.  There-

fore he sent lions among them.   The king of Assyria, when
told of the predicament, returned one of the deported priests
to teach them the way of the God of Israel.   However they
did not hearken but worshipped the gods of their own country
as well as the God of Israel.

## Southern Kingdom, I Kings 14, II Chr. 11-16

In the South, where were the tribes of Judah and Benjamin,
Rehoboam, who followed Solomon, reigned seventeen years.
There was war between him and Jeroboam all their days.   He
built cities for defense, fortified strongholds, stored supplies
and weapons.

The Levites of Israel resorted to him because Jeroboam and
his sons had excluded them from executing their priestly office.   Therefore devout people from the Northern Kingdom
came to Jerusalem to sacrifice to the God of their fathers.

So for three years Rehoboam strengthened his kingdom,
walking in the way of David and Solomon.   Thereafter he
forsook the law of the Lord, and the people went with him.
Then, in the fifth year of his reign, the Egyptians came up
against Jerusalem and took away the treasures of the house
of the Lord and the treasures of the king's house and the
shields of gold which Solomon had made.

Rehoboam was followed by his son Abijam.   For three
years he reigned in Jerusalem, walking in all the sins of his
father.   He too fought with Jeroboam.   Asa, who succeeded
him, did that which was right in the sight of the Lord.   He
repelled an attack by the Ethiopians.   He continued the con-
test with Israel.   In the thirty-ninth year of his reign he became diseased in his feet; yet in his affliction he sought not the
Lord but the physicians, and slept with his fathers.

## *Jehoshaphat,* I *Kings 2 2 ,* II *Chr. 1 7 - 2 0*

His son Jehoshaphat, following him on the throne, walked
in the commandments of the Lord. He sent out teachers
and priests to instruct the people in the law. He pulled
down the shrines of the idolaters. He built up the nation's
defenses. Therefore the Lord established the kingdom in his
hand, and he had riches and honor in abundance.

While he was on a visit to Ahab, king of Israel, Ahab invited him to join forces and attack Ramoth-gilead. Four
hundred prophets whom Ahab gathered gave assurance that
the campaign would succeed. One lone prophet, Micaiah,
warned against the venture, saying, "The Lord hath put a lying spirit in the mouth of all these thy prophets." Ahab was
slain and the battle lost.

On Jehoshaphat's return to Jerusalem he set up judges in the
fenced cities, instructing them: "Take heed what ye do; for
ye judge not for man but for the Lord, who is with you in the
judgment. Wherefore now let the fear of the Lord be upon
you; take heed and do it: for there is no iniquity with the
Lord our God nor respect of persons nor taking of gifts."

After this the inhabitants of Moab, Ammon, and Mount
Seir came against Jehoshaphat. Alarmed at the huge host, he
sought the Lord's protection. He proclaimed a fast throughout Judah. All the people came to the house of the Lord,
where he uttered a long prayer depicting their helplessness.

Then the Spirit of the Lord came upon Jahaziel, a Levite.
"Thus saith the Lord unto you," he declared, "be not afraid
nor dismayed by reason of this great multitude; for the battle
is not yours but God's. Tomorrow go ye down against them:
behold, they come up by the cliff of Ziz . . . Ye shall not
need to fight in this battle: set yourselves, stand ye still, and
see the salvation of the Lord."

The following day the Ammonites and Moabites attacked
the people of Mount Seir. Annihilating them, they next
fell upon each other. So that when the people of Judah

looked out from the watch tower in the wilderness, they saw the earth strewn with their enemies.

The spoil was so tremendous that they were three days in gathering it. The fourth day they assembled in the valley of Berachah and blessed the Lord. So the realm of Jehoshaphat was quiet, for his God gave him rest round about.

## *Jehoram to Amaziah,* II *Kings* 8, *11,* II *Chr.* 21-25

After Jehoshaphat came his son Jehoram. During his reign Edom and Libnah revolted; also the Arabians made a vicious attack on Jerusalem, carrying away all his sons but the youngest.

Jehoram's wife was the daughter of Ahab. He therefore walked in the way of the kings of Israel, which was an offense to his own people. After ruling eight years, he "departed without being desired."

He was succeeded by Ahaziah, the son who had eluded the Arabians. Ahaziah, after a reign of twelve months, came to an end at the hand of Jehu, as previously related. His mother Athaliah promptly usurped the kingdom and dispatched the seed royal. His sister, wife of Jehoiada the priest, rescued his youngest son, Jehoash, from the grandmother's villainy and kept him safe in seclusion.

After six years Jehoiada brought the boy forth and anointed him. "God save the king!" shouted the people. When Athaliah cried, "Treason!" she was driven out at Jehoiada's command.

"Jehoash did that which was right in the sight of the Lord all his days wherein Jehoiada the priest instructed him." He was minded to repair the house of the Lord. King Hazael made a hostile gesture toward Jerusalem, but desisted when Jehoash gave him the gold and hallowed things out of the temple and the palace. After Jehoash had reigned forty years his officers conspired and assassinated him.

As soon as the kingdom was confirmed in the hand of his

son Amaziah, Amaziah dispatched his father's assassins. But their children he spared, according to the law of Moses: "The fathers shall not be put to death for the children, nor the children be put to death for the fathers; but every man shall be put to death for his own sin."

He defeated the Edomites. Afterward he challenged the king of Israel, who responded: "Thou hast indeed smitten Edom, and thine heart hath lifted thee up. Glory of this and tarry at home, for why shouldest thou meddle to thy hurt that thou shouldest fall." But Amaziah would not listen. Judah got the worst of the clash which followed and fled to their tents. Israel broke down the wall of Jerusalem, sacked the city, and took away hostages to Samaria. Soon after, Amaziah came to his end in a conspiracy.

## *Uzziah to Ahaz,* II *Kings 15,* II *Chr. 26-28*

He was followed by his son Azariah, also called Uzziah, who reigned fifty-two years. He did that which was right in the sight of the Lord, save that he did not remove the high places. The Lord helped him in his struggles against the Philistines, the Arabians, the Ammonites.

In strengthening his army and military equipment he placed engines, invented by cunning men, on the towers and bulwarks in Jerusalem to shoot arrows and hurl great stones. So powerful did he become that his fame extended as far as Egypt. But he was much more than a man of war. He loved husbandry. He planted vines in the mountains. He had cattle both in the low country and on the plains. He built towers at the gates in Jerusalem and dug wells in the desert.

But in his strength his heart was lifted up to his destruction. He went into the temple to burn incense, which was not for him but for the priests to do. As they looked upon him "he was leprous in his forehead, and they thrust him out from thence; yea, himself hasted also to go out, because the Lord had smitten him."

In the face of this tragedy Jotham ruled for him, and eventually ascended the throne. He built cities in the mountains and castles and towers in the forests. "He did that which was right in the sight of the Lord, according to all that his father Uzziah did: howbeit he entered not into the temple of the Lord." He reigned sixteen years. Then came Ahaz his son. Ahaz made molten images for Baalim, he burned incense in the valley of the son of Hinnom, he followed the abominations of the heathen whom the Lord had cast out before the children of Israel.

His reign was a turbulent one. He encountered the Syrians, the Philistines, the Edomites, the Israelites. The Lord brought him low because of his transgressions. In his distress he gave from the treasures of the palace and temple to the king of Assyria, but the Assyrians helped him not. He sacrificed to the gods of Damascus, saying, "Because the gods of the kings of Syria help them therefore will I sacrifice to them that they may help me." He broke up the vessels of the house of God, he shut its doors, he made altars in every corner of Jerusalem and burned incense to other gods.


## *Hezekiah*, II *Kings* 18, II *Chr.* 29-33, *Isa.* 36

Ahaz was succeeded by his son Hezekiah. In the first month of his reign Hezekiah set about to open and repair the doors of the temple. He "trusted in the Lord God of Israel; so that after him was none like him among all the kings of Judah, nor any that were before him." He gathered together the priests and Levites and instructed them to sanctify themselves, cleanse the house of the Lord, repair the altars and utensils. The work finished, Hezekiah offered sacrifices and all the congregation worshipped. So the service of the house of the Lord was set in order.

Hezekiah now sent word throughout all Israel and Judah, and to Ephraim and Manasseh, bidding them come to Jerusalem to keep the passover. "Be ye not stiffnecked as your fathers were," he said. "For if ye turn again unto the Lord your brethren and your children shall find compassion before them that lead them captive, so that they shall come again into this land, for the Lord your God is gracious and merciful and will not turn away his face from you if you return unto him."

Outside the kingdom of Judah many of the people scorned the couriers and messengers. Others, however, humbled themselves and responded to the call. In Judah the Lord gave them one heart to do the commandment of the king. The feast lasted seven days. There was great joy, for since the time of Solomon there was not the like in Jerusalem. "Then the priests the Levites arose and blessed the people; and their voice was heard and their prayer came up to his holy dwelling place even unto heaven."

In the fourteenth year of Hezekiah's reign Sennacherib, king of Assyria, came up against Judah and took the fenced cities. Hezekiah offered to pay any sum Sennacherib might demand. He gave him all the silver to be found in the temple and in the palace. He even stripped the gold from the doors of the temple.

Sennacherib's officers said: "Hearken not unto Hezekiah when he persuadeth you, saying, The Lord will deliver us. Hath any of the gods of the nations delivered at all his land out of the hand of the king of Assyria . . . have they delivered Samaria out of mine hand?" The people answered not a word. When the boast was carried to Hezekiah, he rent his clothes and sent messengers to Isaiah the prophet.

"Thus saith the Lord," answered Isaiah, "be not afraid of the words which thou hast heard, with which the servants of the king of Assyria have blasphemed me. Behold, I will send a blast upon him, and he shall hear a rumor and shall return to his own land; and I will cause him to fall by the sword in his own land."

Sennacherib continuing to send threatening messages, Hezekiah prayed, "Now therefore, O Lord our God, I beseech thee, save thou us out of his hand that all the kingdoms of the earth may know that thou art the Lord God, even thou only." Isaiah assured him that the Lord would defend and save the

city. "And it came to pass that night that the angel of the
Lord went out and smote in the camp of the Assyrians an
hundred fourscore and five thousand." So Sennacherib departed and dwelt at Nineveh. As he was worshipping in the
house of his god, two of his sons smote him with the sword.

In those days Hezekiah was at the point of death. Said
Isaiah to him, "Set thine house in order, for thou shalt die."
Then Hezekiah asked the Lord to remember how he had
walked in goodness and truth. Whereupon the Lord spoke
again to Isaiah and promised to add fifteen years to Hezekiah's
life and to defend Jerusalem against the Assyrians.

Berodach-baladan, king of Babylon, hearing that Hezekiah
had been sick, sent him letters and a present. Hezekiah
showed the messengers his gold and silver and precious things.
There was nothing in his house nor in all his dominion that
Hezekiah showed them not. Isaiah inquired about the men
and what they had seen. When Hezekiah told him that the
men were from Babylon and that they had seen all his possessions, Isaiah replied: "Behold, the days come that all that
is in thine house, and that which thy fathers have laid up in
store unto this day, shall be carried into Babylon . . . thy
sons . . . shall they take away." Hezekiah answered, "Is it
not good, if peace and truth be in my days?"

Hezekiah died after a reign of twenty-nine years. His son
Manasseh restored the altars of Baal, used enchantments, dealt
with familiar spirits and wizards, and wrought much wickedness in the sight of the Lord. Therefore the Lord declared
through his prophets: "Behold, I am bringing such evil upon
Jerusalem and Judah, that whosoever heareth of it, both his
ears shall tingle . . . I will wipe Jerusalem as a man wipeth
a dish, wiping it and turning it upside down."

The Lord brought the Assyrians against Manasseh. They
bound him in fetters and carried him away to Babylon. In
his affliction he humbled himself and prayed. The Lord
heard his prayers and allowed him to return to Jerusalem.
Manasseh then overthrew the altars and cast out the idols
which he had raised to strange gods and offered sacrifices to

the Lord. After a reign of fifty-five years he was succeeded by his son Amon.⓪

## Josiah and Hilkiah, II Kings 22, II Chr. 34, 35

Scarcely two years elapsed when Amon was assassinated by his officers. His son Josiah, only eight years old, followed him. Josiah turned to the Lord and destroyed the images, groves, and high places throughout the land.

More than this, he repaired the house of the Lord. During the work of reconstruction, Hilkiah the priest found a book of the law of the Lord given by Moses. When the book was read to Josiah, he rent his clothes and commanded Hilkiah: "Go ye, inquire of the Lord for me and for the people and for all Judah, concerning the words of this book that is found; for great is the wrath of the Lord that is kindled against us, because our fathers have not hearkened unto the words of this book."

Hilkiah consulted Huldah the prophetess. She predicted that the Lord would bring evil upon Judah, but not during the days of Josiah because he had humbled himself before the Lord.

Josiah gathered the priests and prophets and people around him, and read in their ears all the words of the book. He made a covenant before the Lord to keep his statutes and commandments. He directed the people to keep the passover, and never was such a passover held from the days of the judges. Neither before nor after him was there a king who turned so wholeheartedly to the Lord. But because of the provocations of Manasseh, the Lord declared, "I will remove Judah also out of my sight as I have removed Israel."

After all this Josiah joined the Assyrians in their war against the king of Egypt and lost his life. Jeremiah the prophet lamented for Josiah, as did the singing men and the singing women and all the people.

His son Jehoahaz reverted to the abominations of his predecessors and ruled only three months. For then the king of Egypt seized Jerusalem, levied heavy tribute, and carried Jehoahaz to Egypt, where he died. His brother Eliakim, whom Pharaoh made king of Judah and renamed Jehoiakim, taxed land and people throughout the realm to pay the tribute. He carried on the evil practices of the kings before him.

## *Fall of Jerusalem,* II *Kings* 24; II *Chr.* 36; *Jer.* 27

Now came upon the scene Nebuchadnezzar, king of Babylon. Jehoiakim became his subject for three years; then rebelled. The Lord sent against Jehoiakim Chaldees, Syrians, Moabites, and Ammonites. The wars which followed continued during the days of Jehoiakim. He was succeeded by his son Jehoiachin.

The Egyptians came not again out of their land, for Nebuchadnezzar "had taken from the river of Egypt unto the River Euphrates all that pertained to the king of Egypt." Nebuchadnezzar next took over Jerusalem (597 B. C.). He carried to Babylon its treasures and its people—"all the princes, and all the mighty men of valor, even ten thousand captives, and all the craftsmen and smiths. None remained, save the poorest sort of the people of the land."

He even took Jehoiachin captive and made Jehoiachin's uncle, Mattaniah, whom he renamed Zedekiah, king over Judah. Zedekiah did "evil in the sight of the Lord his God, and humbled not himself before Jeremiah the prophet speaking from the mouth of the Lord." He also rebelled against Nebuchadnezzar.

Nebuchadnezzar then pitched against Jerusalem and after a two years' siege broke up the city. The men of war fled by night. The Chaldees overtook and scattered them in the plains of Jericho, capturing Zedekiah and taking him to Babylon.

Shortly afterward an officer of King Nebuchadnezzar entered Jerusalem, burned the temple, the palace, and every great house. He confiscated the gold and silver and brass work. He broke down the walls of the city. He made further deportations, leaving "the poor of the land to be vine-dressers and husbandmen." So it was that "Judah was carried away out of their land."

Nebuchadnezzar made Gedaliah ruler over the people who remained in Judah. Gedaliah assured them: "Fear not to be the servants of the Chaldees: dwell in the land, and serve the king of Babylon; and it shall be well with you." But he soon faced rebellion and was slain. The people, afraid of the Chaldees, fled to Egypt (587 B. C.).

A century and a half before, the ten tribes of the North had been deported by the Assyrians, to lose their identity among the people with whom they were planted. The two tribes of the Southern Kingdom were now broken into three groups. The first remained in Judah, the second was carried by Nebuchadnezzar captive to Babylon, while the third fled to Egypt. In the course of half a century Babylon fell to Cyrus, king of Persia.

# I *and* II *Chronicles*

## *Scope of Books*

The books of Chronicles are largely a repetition of the books of Kings, because for the most part they cover the same period. Therefore they have been incorporated in previous chapters. Little remains here to be said of them.

First Chronicles starts off with nine chapters of genealogy, stretching from Adam to David. Then follows a history of the kingdom, with emphasis on the events of spiritual rather than political significance.

## *Building of Temple*

In the twenty-second and twenty-eighth chapters David addresses Solomon: "My son, as for me, it was in my mind to build an house unto the name of the Lord my God. But the word of the Lord came to me, saying, Thou hast shed blood abundantly and hast made great wars; thou shalt not build an house unto my name, because thou hast shed much blood upon the earth in my sight. Behold, a son shall be born to thee who shall be a man of rest; and I will give him rest from all his enemies round about, for his name shall be Solomon, and I will give peace and quietness unto Israel in his days. He shall build an house for my name; and he shall be my son and I will be his father; and I will establish the throne of his kingdom over Israel forever. Now, my son, the Lord be with thee; and prosper thou and build the house of the Lord thy God as he hath said of thee."

When the people and princes contributed generously to the building of the temple, David rejoiced and declared: "Thine, O Lord, is the greatness and the power and the glory and the victory and the majesty. For all that is in the heaven and in the earth is thine; thine is the kingdom, O Lord, and thou art exalted as head above all. Both riches and honor come of thee, and thou reignest over all; and in thine hand is power and might, and in thine hand it is to make great and to give strength unto all. Now therefore, our God, we thank thee and praise thy glorious name."

The second book takes up the history of Solomon and of the Southern Kingdom. It closes with a reference to the plan of Cyrus, king of Persia, to encourage the rebuilding of the temple in Jerusalem.

# Daniel

## Captivity in Babylon, Dan. 1

The vivid experiences of Daniel, one of the Hebrews taken to Babylon, run through the reign of Nebuchadnezzar into the reign of Cyrus. He first came into prominence when Nebuchadnezzar commanded that some of the most favored Hebrew captives be brought to the palace and taught the culture of the Chaldeans. When the day came Hananiah, Mishael, and Azariah accompanied him. The name Belteshazzar was given to Daniel, Shadrach to Hananiah, Meshach to Mishael, and Abednego to Azariah.

The king appointed them a daily provision of his meat and wine that they might stand before him at the end of three years. But Daniel and his companions persuaded their guard to give them, instead, vegetables and water for ten days. At the end of that time their countenances were found "fairer and fatter" than those who had eaten "the portion of the king's meat." Thereafter the keeper permitted them to follow their restricted diet.

When the time came for presenting the Hebrews to the king, he found none like Daniel and his three countrymen. "Therefore stood they before the king. And in all matters of wisdom and understanding that the king inquired of them, he found them ten times better than all the magicians and astrologers."

## King's Troubled Dreams, Dan. 2

In the second year of his reign Nebuchadnezzar had such troubled dreams that "his sleep brake from him." He appealed to his wisemen. They said, "Tell thy servants the dream and we will show the interpretation." He answered, "The thing is gone from me . . . Therefore show me the dream and the interpretation thereof."

They protested that no ruler ever made such a demand of a magician, astrologer, or Chaldean; adding, "There is none other that can show it before the king except the gods, whose dwelling is not with flesh." This so stirred the king that he ordered the wisemen of Babylon to be executed.

When the king's officer came to take Daniel and his friends, Daniel counseled: "Destroy not the wisemen of Babylon . . . I will show unto the king the interpretation." Brought before the king, Daniel declared: "There is a God in heaven that revealeth secrets, and maketh known to the king Nebuchadnezzar what shall be in the latter days. Thy dream, and the visions of thy head upon thy bed, are these." Then Daniel recalled the forgotten dream and interpreted it.

Nebuchadnezzar fell upon his face and worshipped Daniel. "Of a truth," he declared, "your God is a God of gods and a Lord of kings and a revealer of secrets, seeing thou couldest reveal this secret." Then the king made Daniel a great man, appointing him ruler over the whole province of Babylon and making him chief of the governors over the wisemen. "Then Daniel requested of the king, and he set Shadrach, Meshach, and Abednego over the affairs of the province of Babylon; but Daniel sat in the gate of the king."

## Story of Fiery Furnace, Dan. 3

After this Nebuchadnezzar set up an image of gold on the plain of Dura in the province of Babylon. At the dedication

a herald announced that whenever the people heard the sound
of the cornet and other musical instruments, they should fall
down and worship the image. Those who failed to obey the
decree would be cast into a burning furnace. Therefore when
the music started, people of all nations and languages fell
down and worshipped the golden image.

But certain Chaldeans, gaining an audience with the king,
said: "Shadrach, Meshach, and Abednego, these men, O king,
have not regarded thee; they serve not thy gods nor worship
the golden image which thou hast set up." Whereupon Nebuchadnezzar, in his rage, commanded the three to be brought
before him. "Is it true?" he asked.

"If it be so," they answered, "our God whom we serve is
able to deliver us from the burning fiery furnace, and he will
deliver us out of thine hand, O king. But if not, be it known
unto thee, O king, that we will not serve thy gods nor worship
the golden image."

Full of fury Nebuchadnezzar ordered the men to be thrown
into the furnace. The order was carried out. Presently he
arose in haste and asked his counselors, "Did not we cast
three men bound into the midst of the fire?" They replied,
"True, O king." He answered: "Lo, I see four men loose,
walking in the midst of the fire, and they have no hurt; and
the form of the fourth is like the Son of God."

Approaching the mouth of the furnace, Nebuchadnezzar
cried to the men to come forth. When they did so the on-
lookers saw that the fire had no power on their bodies, "nor
was an hair of their head singed, neither were their coats
changed, nor the smell of fire had passed on them."

### King Driven from Men, Dan. 4

Now Nebuchadnezzar saw, in a dream, "a tree in the midst
of the earth, and the height thereof was great. The tree grew

and was strong, and the height thereof reached unto heaven, and the sight thereof to the end of all the earth: the leaves thereof were fair and the fruit thereof much, and in it was meat for all: the beasts of the field had shadow under it, and the fowls of the heaven dwelt in the boughs thereof, and all flesh was fed of it . . . And behold, a watcher and an holy one came down from heaven; he cried aloud: Hew down the tree and cut off his branches, shake off his leaves and scatter his fruit; let the beasts get away from under it and the fowls from his branches; nevertheless leave the stump of his roots in the earth."

Daniel, called upon to explain the vision, declared: "My lord, the dream be to them that hate thee, and the interpretation thereof to thine enemies. The tree that thou sawest . . . it is thou, O king, that art grown and become strong; for thy greatness is grown and reacheth unto heaven, and thy dominion to the end of the earth.

"This is the interpretation, O king, and this is the decree of the Most High, which is come upon my lord the king: That they shall drive thee from men, and thy dwelling shall be with the beasts of the field, and they shall make thee to eat grass as oxen, and they shall wet thee with the dew of heaven, and seven times shall pass over thee, till thou know that the Most High ruleth in the kingdom of men and giveth it to whomsoever he will. And whereas they commanded to leave the stump of the tree roots; thy kingdom shall be sure unto thee, after that thou shalt have known that the heavens do rule."

Twelve months afterward, as Nebuchadnezzar walked in his palace and meditated upon his greatness, there fell a voice from heaven, saying, "The kingdom is departed from thee." The same hour he was driven from men and ate grass and was wet with the dew "till his hairs were grown like eagles' feathers and his nails like birds' claws." At the end of the days he lifted up his eyes to heaven and blessed the Most High. His reason returned and his glory and kingdom were restored.

## *Fall of Belshazzar, Dan. 5*

Belshazzar the king made a great feast.  As the guests drank from golden vessels which his father Nebuchadnezzar had taken from the temple in Jerusalem, and praised the gods of gold and silver and brass and wood and stone, there came forth the fingers of a man's hand, which Belshazzar saw, and wrote over against the candlestick upon the wall.  Then the king's countenance changed and his thoughts troubled him so that "his knees smote one against another."

Daniel, called in to read the writing, exclaimed: "O thou king, the most high God gave Nebuchadnezzar thy father a kingdom and majesty and glory and honor . . . But when his heart was lifted up and his mind hardened in pride, he was deposed from his kingly throne and they took his glory from him. . . And thou his son, O Belshazzar, hast not humbled thine heart, though thou knewest all this."

The writing was this: "Mene, Mene, Tekel, Upharsin." And here is the interpretation: "Mene; God hath numbered thy kingdom and finished it.  Tekel; Thou art weighed in the balances and art found wanting.  Peres; Thy kingdom is divided and given to the Medes and Persians."

That night was Belshazzar slain; and Darius the Median took the kingdom.

## *The Den of Lions, Dan. 6*

Darius preferred Daniel above his presidents and princes, because of his excellent spirit, and thought to set him over the whole realm.  Whereupon the presidents and princes prevailed on the king to establish a decree that whosoever should petition any God or man for thirty days, save the king, should be thrown to the lions.

Daniel nevertheless continued to kneel down three times a day and give thanks to God as was his custom.  When the king was informed, he labored to the going down of the sun to deliver Daniel. But the statute had been signed and could not be changed "according to the law of the Medes and Persians, which altereth not."

Then Daniel was cast into the den of lions. The king passed the night fasting. Early in the morning he hastened to the place and cried with a lamentable voice: "O Daniel, servant of the living God, is thy God, whom thou servest continually, able to deliver thee from the lions?"

Daniel answered: "My God hath sent his angel and hath shut the lions' mouths, that they have not hurt me, for as much as before him innocency was found in me, and also before thee, O king, have I done no hurt." The king, exceedingly glad, had Daniel taken up out of the den. Then he made a decree that throughout his kingdom men tremble and fear before the God of Daniel. "He delivereth and rescueth, and he worketh signs and wonders in heaven and in earth, who hath delivered Daniel from the power of the lions."

From time to time there came to Daniel strange dreams and visions which, like the foregoing incidents, when put in writing, comforted and encouraged his hard pressed countrymen of the homeland. So Daniel prospered in the reign of Darius and in the reign of Cyrus the Persian.

## *Lament of the Captives, Psalm 137*

By the rivers of Babylon,
There we sat down, yea, we wept,
When we remembered Zion.
We hanged our harps
Upon the willows in the midst thereof.
For there they that carried us away captive
Required of us a song,
And they that wasted us
Required of us mirth, saying,

Sing us one of the songs of Zion.
How shall we sing the Lord's song
In a strange land?
If I forget thee, O Jerusalem,
Let my right hand forget her cunning.
If I do not remember thee,
Let my tongue cleave to the roof of my mouth,
If I prefer not Jerusalem above my chief joy.

# Ezra

## Return to Jerusalem, Ezra 1, II Chr. 36, Hag. 1

In his first year (536 B. C.) Cyrus, king of Persia, made a proclamation in writing: "All the kingdoms of the earth hath the Lord God of heaven given me; and he hath charged me to build him an house in Jerusalem, which is in Judah. Who is there among you of all his people? The Lord his God be with him and let him go up." For this generosity is Cyrus referred to in Isaiah as the "Lord's anointed."

Thus encouraged, certain of the Hebrews resolved to return and restore their temple. Cyrus ordered those who remained behind to contribute money, goods, and beasts of burden to the enterprise. He brought forth, that they might be returned, the gold and silver vessels of the house of the Lord which Nebuchadnezzar had taken from Jerusalem and put into the house of his gods.

Reaching Judah, after a long journey across the desert, the people scattered to their various towns. But at the end of seven months they came together in Jerusalem. Fearful of the inhabitants round about, they built an altar and burned offerings according to their ancient custom. They also observed the set feasts of the Lord.

## Rebuilding the Temple, Ezra 3-6

During the next two years they made preparations for building the temple. Masons and carpenters were hired. Men of Sidon and Tyre were given meat and drink and oil to bring cedars from Lebanon. This accomplished, Zerubbabel and Jeshua appointed the Levites, over twenty years of age, to start the work. When the foundation was laid, some shouted with joy, while others, old men who had seen the first house, wept with a loud voice, so that the shouting could not be distinguished from the lamenting.

When the adversaries of Judah and Benjamin heard that the children of the captivity were building the temple, they went to Zerubbabel and offered to assist. But he would have nothing to do with them. They then tried to frustrate his purpose. They wrote letters to the Persian court, representing that these people had been rebellious in the past and would be so again when re-established. Accordingly Artaxerxes, a successor of Cyrus, commanded the work to cease; and building operations were stayed until the second year of the reign of the Persian king Darius.

Then the prophets Haggai and Zechariah urged resumption of the work; Haggai exclaiming: "This people say, The time is not come, the time that the Lord's house should be built. Is it time for you, O ye, to dwell in your cieled houses, and this house lie waste? . . . Go up to the mountain and bring wood and build the house; and I will take pleasure in it and I will be glorified, saith the Lord."

Thereupon Zerubbabel and Jeshua went to work. Again opposition arose. The matter was placed before Darius. Searching his records and finding the decree of Cyrus, he ordered the opponents to desist and to furnish the builders with funds, animals for sacrifice, and daily supplies of food.

From then on the work prospered, and the temple was finished in the sixth year of the reign of Darius. The priests and Levites and all the children of the captivity celebrated the dedication with great joy.

## Second Expedition, Ezra 7-10

In the seventh year of Artaxerxes II another band of exiles
left Babylon for Jerusalem. They were led by Ezra, a descendant of Aaron. "He was a ready scribe in the law of
Moses"; and "had prepared his heart to seek the law of the
Lord, and to do it, and to teach in Israel statutes and judgments." The king's decree in the matter authorized Ezra to
gather those who were willing to go, and provided funds and
equipment for the undertaking. En route the Lord delivered them from the hand of the enemy and from those who
lay in wait. In four months they reached their destination.

Ezra was astonished and grieved, on arrival, to find that the
Hebrews had intermarried with the Canaanites and other inhabitants of the land. He tore his garments and cast himself
down before the house of God. The people who had assembled wept with him. One of the men said, "Now therefore
let us make a covenant with our God to put away all the
wives and such as are born of them."

Three days after, when they all congregated in Jerusalem,
Ezra stood up and said: "Ye have transgressed, and have
taken strange wives, to increase the trespass of Israel. Now
therefore make confession unto the Lord God of your fathers
and do his pleasure; and separate yourselves from the people
of the land and from the strange wives." The congregation
answered with a loud voice, "As thou hast said, so must we
do."

# Nehemiah

## Rebuilding the Wall, Neh. 1-3

Thirteen years later Nehemiah, cup-bearer to Artaxerxes, having obtained royal permission, headed an expedition to rebuild the wall of Jerusalem. Three days after his arrival he rode out at night to inspect the premises. Looking at the ruined walls, he said to his men: "Ye see the distress that we are in, how Jerusalem lieth waste and the gates thereof are burned with fire; come and let us build up the wall of Jerusalem that we be no more a reproach." They responded, "Let us rise up and build."

But when Sanballat the Horonite and Tobiah the Ammonite and Geshem the Arabian heard of the project they inquired, "What is this thing that ye do? will ye rebel against the king?" Nehemiah replied: "The God of heaven, he will prosper us; therefore we his servants will arise and build; but ye have no portion nor right nor memorial in Jerusalem."

Each tribe was assigned to repair a certain gate or portion of the wall. Sanballat was wroth and mocked the workers. Speaking before his brethren and the army of Samaria, he exclaimed: "What do these feeble Jews? will they fortify themselves? will they sacrifice? will they make an end in a day? will they revive the stones out of the heaps of the rubbish which are burned?" Tobiah, standing by, answered, "Even that which they build, if a fox go up, he shall even break down their stone wall."

## Mind to Work, Neb. 4-13

But "the people had a mind to work." Then Sanballat
and Tobiah, with their followers, conspired to fight against
Jerusalem. Whereupon Nehemiah posted armed guards
about. From that time forth half the men worked while the
other half bore arms. The laborers wrought with one hand
and with the other held a weapon. The builders each had
his sword girded by his side. The trumpeter stood by Nehemiah, who said: "The work is great and large, and we are
separated upon the wall, one far from another. In what place
therefore ye hear the sound of the trumpet, resort ye thither
unto us: our God shall fight for us."

There came a great cry from the inhabitants of the land,
that they had mortgaged their property to buy corn and pay
taxes, and that their sons and daughters were in bondage to
their brethren for the indebtedness. Nehemiah, very angry
when he heard of the situation, rebuked the rulers and nobles
for exacting usury from their brother Jews. He ordered them
to restore the vineyards and oliveyards and houses. They
did so.

As the work on the wall proceeded Sanballat, Tobiah, and
Geshem proposed a meeting with Nehemiah in one of the
villages on the plain of Ono. But he, discerning that they
planned mischief, answered: "I am doing a great work, so that
I cannot come down; why should the work cease whilst I leave
it and come down to you?" Other devices were equally un-
availing. So the wall was finished at the end of fifty-two
days.

The people now gathered in the street which was before the
water gate, where Ezra read to them from the book of the
law of Moses from morning until midday. Certain of the
Levites "caused the people to understand the law." When
they heard the words of the law they wept. But Nehemiah
and Ezra said to them: "This day is holy unto the Lord your
God; mourn not nor weep . . . Go your way, eat the fat
and drink the sweet and send portions unto them for whom

nothing is prepared . . . The joy of the Lord is your strength."

## Singing and Rejoicing, Psalm 126

> When the Lord turned again the captivity of Zion,
> We were like them that dream.
> Then was our mouth filled with laughter,
> And our tongue with singing:
> Then said they among the heathen,
> The Lord hath done great things for them.
> The Lord hath done great things for us;
> Whereof we are glad.
> Turn again our captivity, O Lord,
> As the streams in the south.
> They that sow in tears shall reap in joy.
> He that goeth forth and weepeth, bearing precious
>     seed,
> Shall doubtless come again with rejoicing,
>     bringing his sheaves with him.

The rulers dwelt in Jerusalem. The rest of the people cast lots to bring one out of ten to dwell in Jerusalem and the other nine to dwell in other cities.

The wall finished and dedicated (445 B. C.) Nehemiah returned to Babylon for a time. Revisiting Jerusalem he saw the people treading wine presses and marketing produce on the sabbath. He also found that some had married foreign wives. Correcting these practices he cried: "Remember me, O my God, concerning this also, and spare me according to the greatness of thy mercy."

# Esther

## Queen of Persia, Esther 1, 2

Xerxes (Ahasuerus) king of Persia, his wife Vashti having offended him by refusing to appear at a feast, caused young women to be brought before him that he might select a new queen. Among them was Esther, a beautiful young Jewess; for many of the Hebrews chose to remain in Babylon and Persia rather than return to their native land when Cyrus gave them permission.

Esther was an orphan reared by her cousin Mordecai of the tribe of Benjamin. Taking Mordecai's advice, she did not divulge to the king her kindred or nationality. Preferring her to all the others, the king set the royal crown upon her head and made her queen instead of Vashti.

## Haman's Conspiracy, Esther 3

Now Mordecai, learning of a plot to assassinate the king, told Esther. She in turn warned the king; whereupon the guilty men were brought to justice. Mordecai, however, neglected to reverence Haman, who had been promoted above all the princes. Scorning to have Mordecai alone punished for this lack of respect, Haman persuaded the king to destroy all the Jews in the kingdom. Mordecai sent a copy of the king's decree to this effect to Esther, and asked her to plead before the king for her people.

She reminded him that the law, under penalty of death, forbade any person to come to the king in the inner court without being summoned, except those to whom he should hold out the golden scepter. Mordecai then said to her, "Think not with thyself that thou shalt escape in the king's house, more than all the Jews."

Then answered Esther: "Go, gather together all the Jews that are present in Shushan and fast ye for me, and neither eat nor drink three days, night or day: I also and my maidens will fast likewise; and so will I go in unto the king, which is not according to the law: and if I perish, I perish." Mordecai went his way and did accordingly.

The third day, when the king saw Esther standing in the court, he held out to her the golden scepter which was in his hand. As she drew near and touched its top he asked: "What wilt thou, Queen Esther? And what is thy request? It shall be even given thee to the half of the kingdom."

She responded, "If it seem good unto the king, let the king and Haman come this day unto the banquet that I have prepared for him." They came, yet she would not make her request. Instead she invited them to another banquet the day following.

Haman went forth with a glad heart; but when Mordecai, sitting at the king's gate, did not stand up or move for him, he was full of indignation. However he refrained himself. On reaching home he boasted to his wife and friends of his glory and riches. "Yet all this availeth me nothing so long as I see Mordecai the Jew sitting at the king's gate," he added. They advised him to have made a gallows fifty cubits high and to ask the king to have Mordecai hanged thereon. The plan pleased him and he caused the gallows to be erected.

## Mordecai Exonerated, Esther 6

That night the king could not sleep. He therefore commanded the book of records, which told how Mordecai had protected him, to be read. He then asked, "What honor and dignity hath been done to Mordecai for this?" "There is nothing done for him," his servants answered.

At this point Haman came to speak with the king about the gallows. The king inquired, "What shall be done unto the man whom the king delighteth to honor?" Haman, supposing the king had him in mind, recommended that the man be clothed in royal apparel, taken on the king's horse through the streets of the city, and a proclamation made before him: "Thus shall it be done to the man whom the king delighteth to honor."

The king answered: "Make haste and take the apparel and the horse, as thou hast said, and do even so to Mordecai the Jew." Haman, astonished and mortified, set about to pay public tribute to the man he had purposed to hang. Mordecai came again to the king's gate. And Haman hurried to his house, mourning and having his head covered. Then said his wife and his wisemen: "If Mordecai be of the seed of the Jews, before whom thou hast begun to fall, thou shalt not prevail against him but shalt surely fall before him."

The next day at the banquet the king asked Esther to make known her petition. She answered: "If I have found favor in thy sight, O king, and if it please the king, let my life be given me at my petition, and my people at my request; for we are sold, I and my people, to be destroyed, to be slain and to perish."

"Who is he, and where is he, that durst presume in his heart to do so?" cried the king. "The adversary and enemy is this wicked Haman," answered the queen. As the king rose up full of wrath, one of his chamberlains pointed out the gallows Haman had erected for Mordecai. "Hang him thereon!" thundered the king. So Haman came to an end.

The king gave Haman's house to Esther. His ring, which

he had taken from Haman, he gave to Mordecai.   And Esther set Mordecai over the house of Haman.   She then besought the king to reverse his decree against the Jews.   He granted her petition and directed Mordecai to send letters throughout the realm, according the Jews the right to gather themselves together and to stand for their lives against those who might assault them.

Mordecai went out from the presence of the king in royal apparel.   In every province and city the Jews had joy and gladness, a feast and a good day.   Many of the people of the land became Jews, for the fear of the Jews fell upon them.

*          *          *

Here is a convenient point to digress from our narrative to a brief consideration of the books of prophecy, wisdom, and poetry contained in the Old Testament.

# Early Minor Prophets

*Amos*

Rather continuously throughout Hebrew history the voice of prophecy was raised against the folly and oppression of the rulers, and the wickedness and backsliding of the people. The first of the prophets, that is, the speakers for God, to write as well as declaim, was Amos. He was a shepherd of Tekoa, a small town south of Jerusalem, although he did much of his preaching in the Northern Kingdom. He was active for twenty years or so during the first half of the eighth century B. C.

"Hear this word that the Lord hath spoken against you, O children of Israel," he cried. "I hate, I despise your feast days, and I will not smell in your solemn assemblies. Though ye offer me burnt offerings and your meat offerings, I will not accept them; neither will I regard the peace offerings of your fat beasts. Take thou away from me the noise of thy songs; for I will not hear the melody of thy viols. But let judgment run down as waters, and righteousness as a mighty stream.

"Have ye offered unto me sacrifices and offerings in the wilderness forty years, O house of Israel? But ye have borne the tabernacle of your Moloch and Chium your images, the star of your god, which ye made to yourselves. Therefore will I cause you to go into captivity beyond Damascus . . .

"I will not utterly destroy the house of Jacob . . . In that day will I raise up the tabernacle of David that is fallen and close up the breaches thereof . . . The plowman shall overtake the reaper, and the treader of grapes him that soweth seed; and the mountains shall drop sweet wine, and all the hills shall melt. And I will bring again the captivity of my people of Israel, and they shall build the waste cities and inhabit them; and they shall plant vineyards and drink the wine thereof; they shall also make gardens and eat the fruit of them. And I will plant them upon their land, and they shall no more be pulled up out of their land which I have given them."

## Hosea

Closely following Amos, in the reigns of Uzziah, Hezekiah, and Jeroboam, came Hosea in the Northern Kingdom, emphasizing God's love and forbearance. "Hear the word of the Lord, ye children of Israel," he admonished, "for the Lord hath a controversy with the inhabitants of the land, because there is no truth nor mercy nor knowledge of God in the land . . . When Israel was a child, then I loved him and called my son out of Egypt . . . O Israel, thou hast destroyed thyself; but in me is thine help.

"I will ransom them from the power of the grave; I will redeem them from death. O death, I will be thy plagues; O grave, I will be thy destruction . . . I will heal their backsliding, I will love them freely; for mine anger is turned away from him. I will be as the dew unto Israel. He shall grow as the lily and cast forth his roots as Lebanon. His branches shall spread and his beauty shall be as the olive tree and his smell as Lebanon."

## *Micah*

After Hosea had run his career in the North, Micah arose in the South. Unlike his great contemporary Isaiah, he sprang from the common people. "Wherewith," he proclaimed, "shall I come before the Lord and bow myself before the high God? Shall I come before him with burnt offerings, with calves of a year old? Will the Lord be pleased with thousands of rams or with ten thousands of rivers of oil? Shall I give my firstborn for my transgression, the fruit of my body for the sin of my soul? He hath showed thee, O man, what is good; and what doth the Lord require of thee but to do justly and to love mercy and to walk humbly with thy God?"

## *Joel*

Droughts and pests had swept the land, and a strong nation had been laid waste, when the word of the Lord came to Joel: "Sanctify ye a fast, call a solemn assembly, gather the elders and all the inhabitants of the land into the house of the Lord your God, and cry unto the Lord . . . Rend your heart and not your garments . . . Be glad . . .

"He will cause to come down for you the rain, the former rain and the latter rain in the first month. And the floors shall be full of wheat, and the vats shall overflow with wine and oil. And I will restore to you the years that the locust hath eaten, the cankerworm and the caterpillar and the palmerworm, my great army which I sent among you."

# Isaiah

## The Lord Hath Spoken, Isa. 1

The book of Isaiah contains the flower of Hebrew prophecy. Statesman as well as prophet, Isaiah was active during the half century from 740 to 700 B. C. Internal evidence is persuasive that chapters 40 to 66 were written at a much later period and hence should not be ascribed to him. Chapter one proclaims, "Hear, O heavens, and give ear, O earth, for the Lord hath spoken:

"I have nourished and brought up children and they have rebelled against me. The ox knoweth his owner, and the ass his master's crib; but Israel doth not know, my people doth not consider . . . Why should ye be stricken any more? Ye will revolt more and more. The whole head is sick and the whole heart faint . . . Your country is desolate, your cities are burned with fire, your land, strangers devour it in your presence . . .

"To what purpose is the multitude of your sacrifices unto me? . . . Bring no more vain oblations . . . Your new moons and your appointed feasts my soul hateth . . . And when ye spread forth your hands, I will hide mine eyes from you . . . Wash you, make you clean; put away the evil of your doings from before mine eyes; cease to do evil; learn to do well; seek judgment, relieve the oppressed, judge the fatherless, plead for the widow.

"Come now and let us reason together.   Though your sins be as scarlet they shall be as white as snow; though they be red like crimson they shall be as wool."

## End of Strife, Isa. 2-8

"And it shall come to pass in the last days," the prophet foresees, "that the mountain of the Lord's house shall be established in the top of the mountains and shall be exalted above the hills; and all nations shall flow unto it . . .   And He shall judge among the nations and shall rebuke many people; and they shall beat their swords into plowshares and their spears into pruninghooks.   Nation shall not lift up sword against nation, neither shall they learn war any more.

"And the loftiness of man shall be bowed down, and the haughtiness of men shall be made low; and the Lord alone shall be exalted in that day . . .   Cease ye from man whose breath is in his nostrils; for wherein is he to be accounted of? . . .

"And when they shall say unto you, Seek unto them that have familiar spirits and unto wizards that peep and that mutter, should not a people seek unto their God?"

## Prince of Peace, Isa. 9, 11

"The people that walked in darkness have seen a great light," the prophet continues, "they that dwell in the land of the shadow of death, upon them hath the light shined . . . For unto us a child is born, unto us a son is given; and the government shall be upon his shoulder; and his name shall be called Wonderful, Counselor, The mighty God, The everlasting Father, The Prince of Peace.

"Of the increase of his government and peace there shall be no end upon the throne of David and upon his kingdom to order it and to establish it with judgment and with justice from henceforth even forever. The zeal of the Lord of hosts will perform this . . .

"And there shall come forth a rod out of the stem of Jesse and a branch shall grow out of his roots. And the Spirit of the Lord shall rest upon him, the spirit of wisdom and understanding, the spirit of counsel and might, the spirit of knowledge and of the fear of the Lord; and shall make him of quick understanding in the fear of the Lord.

"And he shall not judge after the sight of his eyes, neither reprove after the hearing of his ears. But with righteousness shall he judge the poor, and reprove with equity for the meek of the earth; and he shall smite the earth with the rod of his mouth, and with the breath of his lips shall he slay the wicked. And righteousness shall be the girdle of his loins and faithfulness the girdle of his reins.

"The wolf also shall dwell with the lamb, and the leopard shall lie down with the kid; and the calf and the young lion and the fatling together; and a little child shall lead them. And the cow and the bear shall feed; their young ones shall lie down together; and the lion shall eat straw like the ox. And the sucking child shall play on the hole of the asp, and the weaned child shall put his hand on the cockatrice' den. They shall not hurt nor destroy in all my holy mountain; for the earth shall be full of the knowledge of the Lord, as the waters cover the sea.

"And in that day there shall be a root of Jesse, which shall stand for an ensign of the people; to it shall the Gentiles seek: and his rest shall be glorious.

"And it shall come to pass in that day that the Lord shall set his hand again the second time to recover the remnant of his people, which shall be left, from Assyria and from Egypt and from Pathros and from Cush and from Elam and from Shinar and from Hamath and from the islands of the sea."

## Rending of the Veil, Isa. 25, 26

"And in this mountain shall the Lord of hosts make unto all people a feast of fat things: a feast of wines on the lees, of fat things full of marrow, of wines on the lees well refined. And he will destroy in this mountain the face of the covering cast over all people, and the veil that is spread over all nations. He will swallow up death in victory; and the Lord God will wipe away tears from off all faces; and the rebuke of his people shall he take away from off all the earth: for the Lord hath spoken it.

"And it shall be said in that day: Lo, this is our God; we have waited for him, and he will save us: this is the Lord; we have waited for him, we will be glad and rejoice in his salvation . . . In that day shall this song be sung in the land of Judah: We have a strong city; salvation will God appoint for walls and bulwarks. Open ye the gates, that the righteous nation which keepeth the truth may enter in. Thou wilt keep him in perfect peace whose mind is stayed on thee, because he trusteth in thee."

## The Lord Instructs the Prophet, Isa. 35. 40-45

"Strengthen ye the weak hands and confirm the feeble knees. Say to them that are of a fearful heart: Be strong, fear not; behold your God will come with vengeance, even God with a recompense; he will come and save you. Then the eyes of the blind shall be opened and the ears of the deaf shall be unstopped. Then shall the lame man leap as an hart and the tongue of the dumb sing.

"For in the wilderness shall waters break out, and streams in the desert. And the parched ground shall become a pool, and the thirsty land springs of water. In the habitation of dragons, where each lay, shall be grass with reeds and rushes. And an highway shall be there, and a way, and it shall be called The Way of Holiness. The unclean shall not pass over it; but it shall be for those. The wayfaring men, though fools, shall not err therein. . .

"O Zion that bringest good tidings, get thee up into the high mountain; O Jerusalem that bringest good tidings, lift up thy voice with strength; lift it up, be not afraid; say unto the cities of Judah, Behold your God!

"Behold, the Lord God will come with strong hand, and his arm shall rule for him; behold, his reward is with him and his work before him. He shall feed his flock like a shepherd; he shall gather the lambs with his arm and carry them in his bosom, and shall gently lead those that are with young . . .

"Hast thou not known? hast thou not heard that the everlasting God, the Lord, the Creator of the ends of the earth, fainteth not, neither is weary? There is no searching of his understanding. He giveth power to the faint; and to them that have no might he increaseth strength. Even the youths shall faint and be weary, and the young men shall utterly fall. But they that wait upon the Lord shall renew their strength; they shall mount up with wings as eagles; they shall run and not be weary; and they shall walk and not faint."

"Fear not," saith the Lord, "for I have redeemed thee, I have called thee by thy name, thou art mine. When thou passest through the waters, I will be with thee; and through the rivers, they shall not overflow thee. When thou walkest through the fire, thou shalt not be burned; neither shall the flame kindle upon thee."

### Bearer of Good Tidings, Isa. 52, 53

"How beautiful upon the mountains," resumes the prophet, "are the feet of him that bringeth good tidings, that publisheth peace; that bringeth good tidings of good, that publisheth salvation; that saith unto Zion, Thy God reigneth! Thy watchmen shall lift up the voice; with the voice together shall they sing: for they shall see eye to eye when the Lord shall bring again Zion.

"Break forth into joy, sing together ye waste places of Jerusalem; for the Lord hath comforted his people. He hath redeemed Jerusalem. The Lord hath made bare his holy arm in the eyes of all the nations; and all the ends of the earth shall see the salvation of our God . . .

"Who hath believed our report? and to whom is the arm of the Lord revealed? For he shall grow up before Him as a tender plant, and as a root out of a dry ground. He hath no form nor comeliness; and when we shall see him, there is no beauty that we should desire him. He is despised and rejected of men; a man of sorrows and acquainted with grief. And we hid as it were our faces from him; he was despised and we esteemed him not.

"Surely he hath borne our griefs and carried our sorrows; yet we did esteem him stricken, smitten of God, and afflicted. But he was wounded for our transgressions, he was bruised for our iniquities. The chastisement of our peace was upon him; and with his stripes we are healed. All we like sheep have gone astray; we have turned everyone to his own way; and the Lord hath laid on him the iniquity of us all.

"He was oppressed, and he was afflicted, yet he opened not his mouth; he is brought as a lamb to the slaughter, and as a sheep before her shearers is dumb, so he openeth not his mouth. He was taken from prison and from judgment: and who shall declare his generation? for he was cut off out of the land of the living: for the transgression of my people was he stricken. And he made his grave with the wicked, and with the rich in his death; because he had done no violence, neither was any deceit in his mouth. . . Therefore will I divide him a portion with the great, and he shall divide the spoil with the strong; because he hath poured out his soul unto death. And he was numbered with the transgressors; and he bare the sin of many and made intercession for the transgressors."

"The Spirit of the Lord God is upon me; because the Lord hath anointed me to preach good tidings unto the meek; he hath sent me to bind up the brokenhearted, to proclaim liberty to the captives, and the opening of the prison to them that are bound; to proclaim the acceptable year of the Lord, and the day of vengeance of our God; to comfort all that mourn; to appoint unto them that mourn in Zion, to give unto them beauty for ashes, the oil of joy for mourning, the garment of praise for the spirit of heaviness; that they might be called trees of righteousness, the planting of the Lord, that he might be glorified."

## Come to the Waters, Isa. 55

"Ho, everyone that thirsteth, come ye to the waters, and he that hath no money; come ye, buy and eat; yea, come, buy wine and milk without money and without price. Wherefore do ye spend money for that which is not bread? and your labor for that which satisfieth not? Hearken diligently unto me, and eat ye that which is good, and let your soul delight itself in fatness.

"Incline your ear and come unto me: hear, and your soul shall live; and I will make an everlasting covenant with you, even the sure mercies of David. Behold, I have given him for a witness to the people, a leader and commander to the people. Behold, thou shalt call a nation that thou knowest not, and nations that knew not thee shall run unto thee, because of the Lord thy God and for the Holy One of Israel; for he hath glorified thee.

"Seek ye the Lord while he may be found, call ye upon him while he is near. Let the wicked forsake his way, and the unrighteous man his thoughts; and let him return unto the Lord and he will have mercy upon him, and to our God for he will abundantly pardon."

His Way and Word, Isa. 55, 65, 66

"For my thoughts are not your thoughts, neither are your ways my ways," saith the Lord. "For as the heavens are higher than the earth, so are my ways higher than your ways, and my thoughts than your thoughts.

"For as the rain cometh down and the snow from heaven, and returneth not thither but watereth the earth and maketh it bring forth and bud, that it may give seed to the sower and bread to the eater, so shall my word be that goeth forth out of my mouth.   It shall not return unto me void, but it shall accomplish that which I please and it shall prosper in the thing whereto I sent it.

"For ye shall go out with joy and be led forth with peace. The mountains and the hills shall break forth before you into singing, and all the trees of the field shall clap their hands. Instead of the thorn shall come up the fir tree, and instead of the brier shall come up the myrtle tree.   And it shall be to the Lord for a name, for an everlasting sign that shall not be cut off. . .

"They shall not labor in vain nor bring forth for trouble; for they are the seed of the blessed of the Lord, and their offspring with them.   And it shall come to pass that before they call, I will answer; and while they are yet speaking, I will hear . . .   As one whom his mother comforteth, so will I comfort you."

# Jeremiah

## Call to Prophecy, Jer. 1, 8

Jeremiah lived in those troublous days which permitted him to witness both the first and the second fall of Jerusalem to Nebuchadnezzar. Disfavor with the later Judean kings of his period, because he prophesied the overthrow of the Holy City, brought him, on occasion, to the stocks and even to the dungeon.

Nebuchadnezzar gave orders that Jeremiah should be well treated. Therefore the victorious Babylonians, finding him in the "court of the prison," gave him the choice to be taken to Babylon or to remain in Jerusalem or to go whithersoever he would. He chose to stay in Jerusalem, until, following the assassination of Gedaliah the governor, he fled with others to Egypt.

He was the first of the prophets to make use of the "scroll." King Jehoiakim burned the first copy when it was read to him. But the document was reproduced, under Jeremiah's direction, by his secretary Baruch. In it were the beginnings, undoubtedly, of the present book of Jeremiah.

The word of the Lord came to him, saying, "Before I formed thee . . . I ordained thee a prophet unto the nations." Jeremiah replied, "Ah, Lord God! behold, I cannot speak, for I am a child." But the Lord insisted: "Say not, I am a child; for thou shalt go to all that I shall send thee, and

vhatsoever I command thee thou shalt speak. Be not afraid
of their faces, for I am with thee to deliver thee . . . Be-
nold, I have put my words in thy mouth. See, I have this
lay set thee over the nations and over the kingdoms to root
out and to pull down, and to destroy and to throw down, to
build and to plant . . .

"Why then is this people of Jerusalem slidden back by a
perpetual backsliding? They hold fast deceit, they refuse to
eturn. I hearkened and heard but they spake not aright; no
man repented him of his wickedness, saying, What have I
done? Everyone turned to his course, as the horse rusheth
nto the battle. Yea, the stork in the heaven knoweth her appointed times; and the turtle and the crane and the swallow
observe the time of their coming; but my people know not
the judgment of the Lord . . .

"The wisemen are ashamed, they are dismayed and taken.
Lo, they have rejected the word of the Lord; and what wisdom is in them? Therefore will I give their wives unto
others and their fields to them that shall inherit them; for
everyone from the least even unto the greatest is given to
covetousness, from the prophet even unto the priest everyone
dealeth falsely. For they have healed the hurt of the daughter of my people slightly, saying, Peace, peace, when there is
no peace . . .

"Why have they provoked me to anger with their graven
images and with strange vanities? The harvest is past, the
summer is ended, and we are not saved. For the hurt of the
daughter of my people am I hurt; I am black; astonishment
hath taken hold on me. Is there no balm in Gilead? is there
no physician there? Why then is not the health of the
daughter of my people recovered?"

## The Potter's Clay, Jer. 18

At the word of the Lord, Jeremiah went down to the potter's house as he wrought a work on the wheels. The vessel

that he made of clay was marred. So he made it again another vessel. "O house of Israel, cannot I do with you as this potter?" saith the Lord. "Behold, as the clay is in the potter's hand, so are ye in mine hand, O house of Israel.

"At what instant I shall speak concerning a nation, and concerning a kingdom, to pluck up and to pull down and to destroy it; if that nation against whom I have pronounced turn from their evil, I will repent of the evil that I thought to do unto them. And at what instant I shall speak concerning a nation, and concerning a kingdom, to build and to plant it; if it do evil in my sight that it obey not my voice, then I will repent of the good wherewith I said I would benefit them. Now therefore go to, speak to the men of Judah and to the inhabitants of Jerusalem, Behold, I frame evil against you and devise a device against you; return ye now every one from his evil way and make your ways and your doings good."

They answered: "There is no hope; but we will walk after our own devices, and we will every one do the imagination of his evil heart . . . Come and let us devise devices against Jeremiah; for the law shall not perish from the priest nor counsel from the wise nor the word from the prophet. Come and let us smite him with the tongue, and let us not give heed to any of his words."

Then cried Jeremiah: "Give heed to me, O Lord, and hearken to the voice of them that contend with me . . . Thou knowest all their counsel against me to slay me. Forgive not their iniquity, neither blot out their sin from thy sight, but let them be overthrown before thee; deal thus with them in the time of thine anger."


## Submission to Babylon, Jer. 27

Came this word to Jeremiah from the Lord: "Make thee bonds and yokes and put them upon thy neck, and send them to the king of Edom and to the king of Moab and to the king of the Ammonites and to the king of Tyrus and to the king of Zidon, by the hand of the messengers which come to Jerusalem unto Zedekiah, king of Judah, and command them to say unto their masters: Now have I given all these lands into the hand of Nebuchadnezzar . . . And all nations shall serve him . . . And it shall come to pass that the nation and kingdom which will not serve the same Nebuchadnezzar, the king of Babylon, and that will not put their neck under the yoke of the king of Babylon, that nation will I punish with the sword and with the famine and with the pestilence until I have consumed them by his hand."

Accordingly Jeremiah spoke also to Zedekiah: "Bring your necks under the yoke of the king of Babylon and serve him and his people and live. Why will ye die, thou and thy people, by the sword, by the famine, and by the pestilence, as the Lord hath spoken against the nation that will not serve the king of Babylon? Therefore hearken not unto the words of the prophets that speak unto you, saying, Ye shall not serve the king of Babylon; for they prophesy a lie unto you."

### Return from Exile, Jer. 29

For thus saith the Lord: "After seventy years be accomplished at Babylon I will visit you and perform my good word toward you in causing you to return to this place. For I know the thoughts that I think toward you, thoughts of peace and not of evil, to give you an expected end. Then shall ye call upon me, and ye shall go and pray unto me, and I will hearken unto you. And ye shall seek me and find me, when ye shall search for me with all your heart.

"And I will be found of you, and I will turn away your captivity, and I will gather you from all the nations and from all the places whither I have driven you, and I will bring you again into the place whence I caused you to be carried away captive . . .

"And it shall come to pass that like as I have watched over them to pluck up and to break down and to throw down and

to destroy and to afflict, so will I watch over them to build
and to plant.   In those days they shall say no more, The
fathers have eaten a sour grape and the children's teeth are
set on edge.   But every one shall die for his own iniquity.
Every man that eateth the sour grape his teeth shall be set
on edge."

# Ezekiel

## The Roll of Prophecy, Ezek. 1-3

Ezekiel was a priest in Jerusalem at the time of its fall (597 B. C.). He was taken in exile to Babylon, where he appears to have put in the remainder of his life as pastor and prophet. In the fifth year of king Jehoiachin's captivity the word of the Lord came to Ezekiel in a vision of the four cherubim and the four wheels:

"Son of man, I send thee to the children of Israel, to a rebellious nation that hath rebelled against me. They and their fathers have transgressed against me even unto this very day. For they are impudent children and stiffhearted . . . Be not afraid of them, neither be afraid of their words, though briers and thorns be with thee and thou dost dwell among scorpions . . .

"Be not thou rebellious like that rebellious house. Open thy mouth and eat that I give thee." As Ezekiel looked, he beheld a roll of a book in an outstretched hand. As the Lord spread it before him, he saw it was written within and without with "lamentations and mourning and woe." The Lord continued, "Eat that thou findest; eat this roll." Ezekiel obeyed, and it was in his "mouth as honey for sweetness."

Then said the Lord: "Son of man, go, get thee unto the house of Israel and speak with my words unto them. For thou art not sent to a people of a strange speech and of an

hard language but to the house of Israel . . . And go, get
thee to them of the captivity, unto the children of thy people,
and speak unto them and tell them, Thus saith the Lord God,
whether they will hear or whether they will forbear."

"The Spirit took me up," the narrative continues, "and I
heard behind me a voice of a great rushing, saying, Blessed be
the glory of the Lord from his place. I heard also the noise
of the wings of the living creatures that touched one another,
and the noise of the wheels over against them, and a noise of
a great rushing. So the Spirit lifted me up and took me away,
and I went in bitterness, in the heat of my spirit; but the
hand of the Lord was strong upon me."

## *Individual Responsibility, Ezek. 18, 36*

Again came the word of the Lord to Ezekiel: "What mean
ye that ye use this proverb concerning the land of Israel, saying, The fathers have eaten sour grapes, and the children's
teeth are set on edge? As I live, ye shall not have occasion
any more to use this proverb in Israel. Behold, all souls are
mine; as the soul of the father, so also the soul of the son is
mine: the soul that sinneth, it shall die. . .

"Yet say ye, Why? doth not the son bear the iniquity of
the father? When the son hath done that which is lawful
and right, and hath kept all my statutes, and hath done them,
he shall surely live. The soul that sinneth, it shall die. The
son shall not bear the iniquity of the father, neither shall the
father bear the iniquity of the son. The righteousness of the
righteous shall be upon him, and the wickedness of the wicked
shall be upon him.

"But if the wicked will turn from all his sins that he hath
committed, and keep all my statutes and do that which is
lawful and right, he shall surely live, he shall not die. All
his transgressions that he hath committed, they shall not be
mentioned unto him. In his righteousness that he hath done
he shall live. Have I any pleasure at all that the wicked

should die? and not that he should return from his ways and live?

"But when the righteous turneth away from his righteousness, and committeth iniquity and doeth according to all the abominations that the wicked man doeth, shall he live?  All his righteousness that he hath done shall not be mentioned. In his trespass that he hath trespassed, and in his sin that he hath sinned, in them shall he die.

"Yet ye say, The way of the Lord is not equal.  Hear now, O house of Israel, Is not my way equal? are not your ways unequal?  When a righteous man turneth away from his righteousness, and committeth iniquity and dieth in them, for his iniquity that he hath done shall he die.  Again, when the wicked man turneth away from his wickedness that he hath committed, and doeth that which is lawful and right, he shall save his soul alive . . .

"Then will I sprinkle clean water upon you and ye shall be clean; from all your filthiness and from all your idols will I cleanse you.  A new heart also will I give you, and a new spirit will I put within you; and I will take away the stony heart out of your flesh and I will give you an heart of flesh. And I will put my spirit within you, and cause you to walk in my statutes, and ye shall keep my judgments and do them. And ye shall dwell in the land that I gave to your fathers; and ye shall be my people and I will be your God."

·

## Faithless Shepherds, Ezek. 34

Once more the word of the Lord came to Ezekiel: "Woe be to the shepherds of Israel that do feed themselves!  Should not the shepherds feed the flocks? . . . As I live, surely because my flock became a prey, and my flock became meat to every beast of the field, because there was no shepherd, neither did my shepherds search for my flock, but the shepherds fed themselves and fed not my flock; therefore I am against the shepherds, and I will require my flock at their hand and cause them to cease from feeding the flock. Neither shall the shepherds feed themselves any more; for I will deliver my flock from their mouth, that they may not be meat for them.

"I, even I, will both search my sheep and seek them out. As a shepherd seeketh out his flock in the day that he is among his sheep that are scattered, so will I seek out my sheep and will deliver them out of all places where they have been scattered in the cloudy and dark day. And I will bring them out from the people and gather them from the countries, and will bring them to their own land and feed them upon the mountains of Israel by the rivers and in all the inhabited places of the country . . .

"Seemeth it a small thing unto you to have eaten up the good pasture, but ye must tread down with your feet the residue of your pastures? and to have drunk of the deep waters but ye must foul the residue with your feet? And as for my flock they eat that which ye have trodden with your feet, and they drink that which ye have fouled with your feet.

"Therefore I, even I, will judge between the fat cattle and between the lean cattle. Because ye have thrust with side and with shoulder, and pushed all the diseased with your horns, till ye have scattered them abroad; therefore will I save my flock, and they shall no more be a prey, and I will judge between cattle and cattle. And I will set up one shepherd over them, and he shall feed them, even my servant David; he shall feed them and he shall be their shepherd. And I the Lord will be their God, and my servant David a prince among them; I the Lord have spoken it."

# Later Minor Prophets

## Nahum

Nahum the Elkoshite was a contemporary of Jeremiah. He foresaw the doom of Nineveh: "Behold, I am against thee," saith the Lord of hosts, "and I will burn her chariots in the smoke, and the sword shall devour thy young lions; and I will cut off thy prey from the earth, and the voice of thy messengers shall no more be heard. . . And it shall come to pass that all they that look upon thee shall flee from thee and say: Nineveh is laid waste; who will bemoan her? whence shall I seek comforters for thee?

"All thy strongholds shall be like fig trees with the first ripe figs; if they be shaken they shall even fall into the mouth of the eater. . . Thy shepherds slumber, O king of Assyria; thy nobles shall dwell in the dust; thy people is scattered upon the mountains and no man gathereth them. There is no healing of thy bruise; thy wound is grievous. All that hear the bruit of thee shall clap the hands over thee, for upon whom hath not thy wickedness passed continually?"

## Zephaniah

Zephaniah was a descendant of Hezekiah. He prophesied in Judah in the days of Josiah, foreseeing practically universal destruction because of the sins of the people. Moab, Ammon, Ethiopia, Assyria were to be annihilated. "And the coast shall be for the remnant of the house of Judah; they shall feed thereupon. In the houses of Ashkelon shall they lie down in the evening. For the Lord their God shall visit them and turn away their captivity."

## *Habakkuk*

During the reign of Jehoiakim, Assyria was on the decline and Babylon was in the ascendancy. This was the period of Habakkuk. "O Lord, how long shall I cry," he exclaimed, "and thou wilt not hear! even cry out unto thee of violence, and thou wilt not save! Why dost thou show me iniquity and cause me to behold grievance? For spoiling and violence are before me; and there are that raise up strife and contention. Therefore the law is slacked and judgment doth never go forth. . .

"Thou art of purer eyes than to behold evil, and canst not look on iniquity. Wherefore lookest thou upon them that deal treacherously and holdest thy tongue when the wicked devoureth the man that is more righteous than he? . . . But the Lord is in his holy temple; let all the earth keep silence before him."

## *Obadiah*

Obadiah inveighed against Edom, the land of Esau, and thereby revived the ancient strife between Esau and Jacob: "Though thou exalt thyself as the eagle and though thou set thy nest among the stars, thence will I bring thee down, saith the Lord. . . For thy violence against thy brother Jacob, shame shall cover thee and thou shalt be cut off forever . . .

"For the day of the Lord is near upon all the heathen: as

thou hast done, it shall be done unto thee; thy reward shall
return upon thine own head . . . And the house of Jacob
shall be a fire, and the house of Joseph a flame, and the house
of Esau for stubble, and they shall kindle in them and devour
them; and there shall not be any remaining of the house of
Esau."

## Zechariah

The prophet Zechariah in the second year of Darius urged
the exiles to return to Jerusalem and rebuild the temple.
After their arrival he, with Haggai, exhorted them to proceed
with the work. He was a man of visions. He saw a rider on
a red horse, four chariots, a flying roll, two olive trees by a
golden candlestick. The word of the Lord came to him for
Zerubbabel, who was rebuilding the temple:

"Not by might, nor by power, but by my spirit. Who art
thou, O great mountain? Before Zerubbabel thou shalt become a plain; and he shall bring forth the headstone thereof
with shoutings, crying, Grace, grace unto it. The hands of
Zerubbabel have laid the foundation of this house; his hands
shall also finish it; and thou shalt know that the Lord of
hosts hath sent me unto you. For who hath despised the day
of small things? For they shall rejoice, and shall see the
plummet in the hand of Zerubbabel with those seven (lamps
of the candlestick); they are the eyes of the Lord, which run
to and fro through the whole earth."

## Haggai

Nearly twenty years had elapsed after the return of the
exiles to Jerusalem, and the temple was still unfinished.
Then arose the prophet Haggai. His message was not a de-
nunciation of the evils of the time, but an exhortation to

Zerubbabel and Joshua to hasten the work of construction. "Thus saith the Lord," he proclaimed, "go up to the mountain and bring wood and build the house, and I will take pleasure in it and I will be glorified.

"He looked for much and lo it came to little; and when ye brought it home, I did blow upon it. Why? Because of mine house that is waste, and ye run every man unto his own house. Therefore the heaven over you is stayed from dew and the earth is stayed from her fruit. And I called for a drought upon the land and upon the mountains and upon the corn and upon the new wine and upon the oil and upon that which the ground bringeth forth and upon men and upon cattle and upon all the labor of the hands. . .

"Yet now be strong, O Zerubbabel, and be strong, O Joshua, and be strong, all ye people of the land and work, for I am with you . . . The glory of this latter house shall be greater than of the former; and in this place will I give peace."

## Jonah

The word of the Lord came unto Jonah, saying: "Arise, go to Nineveh, that great city, and cry against it; for their wickedness is come up before me." But Jonah, thinking to escape the presence of the Lord, fled to Joppa, where he took a ship to Tarshish.

The Lord then raised a mighty tempest. The frightened mariners cried every man unto his god; while Jonah was below fast asleep. The shipmaster demanded: "What meanest thou, O sleeper? Arise, call upon thy God, if so be that God will think upon us, that we perish not."

The men said to each other, "Let us cast lots, that we may know for whose cause this evil is upon us." The lot fell upon Jonah. When he told them his story, they asked what they should do to quiet the storm. "Take me up and cast me forth into the sea," he replied, "so shall the sea be calm unto you; for I know that for my sake this great tempest is upon you."

When they threw him overboard, the sea "ceased from her raging." Meanwhile "the Lord had prepared a great fish to swallow up Jonah." Then out of the fish he prayed to the Lord: "I am cast out of thy sight; yet I will look again toward thy holy temple. The waters compassed me about, even to the soul; the depth closed me round about, the weeds were wrapped about my head. I went down to the bottoms of the mountains; the earth with her bars was about me forever; yet hast thou brought up my life from corruption, O Lord my God. When my soul fainted within me I remembered the Lord; and my prayer came in unto thee, into thine holy temple."

After three days the Lord spoke to the fish and it threw Jonah out upon the dry land. Proceeding to Nineveh, he entered the city and cried, "Yet forty days, and Nineveh shall be overthrown." His prophecy proclaimed, he went out and sat on the east side to see what would become of the city.

But the people believed God. They put on sackcloth. They fasted, both they and their flocks. When God saw them depart from their evil way he relented. But Jonah was grieved at the turn of events. Whereupon the Lord caused a gourd to spring up and shade him. The next morning, however, the Lord prepared a worm to eat the gourd till it withered. Then arose a vehement east wind. The sun beat down relentlessly. Jonah faltered, "It is better for me to die than to live."

"Doest thou well to be angry for the gourd?" asked the Lord. Jonah replied, "I do well to be angry, even unto death." Then said the Lord: "Thou hast had pity on the gourd, for the which thou hast not labored, neither madest it grow; which came up in a night and perished in a night: and should not I spare Nineveh, that great city, wherein are more than sixscore thousand persons that cannot discern between their right hand and their left hand; and also much cattle?"

## Malachi

Malachi may have been a contemporary of Ezra and Nehemiah, because he condemned some of the practices they condemned, namely, the taking of foreign wives and the profaning of temple worship. He also pronounced against sorcerers, perjurers, and oppressors of the widow and the fatherless.

"Thus saith the Lord of hosts," he warned, "I will send my messenger and he shall prepare the way before me; and the Lord, whom ye seek, shall suddenly come to his temple . . . And he shall sit as a refiner and purifier of silver; and he shall purify the sons of Levi and purge them as gold and silver, that they may offer unto the Lord an offering in righteousness.

"Then shall the offering of Judah and Jerusalem be pleasant unto the Lord, as in the days of old and as in former years . . . For I am the Lord, I change not . . . Return unto me and I will return unto you . . . Bring ye all the tithes into the storehouse, that there may be meat in mine house, and prove me now herewith if I will not open you the windows of heaven and pour you out a blessing that there shall not be room enough to receive it . . .

"For behold, the day cometh that shall burn as an oven, and all the proud, yea, and all that do wickedly shall be stubble; and the day that cometh shall burn them up, that it shall leave them neither root nor branch. But unto you that fear my name shall the Sun of righteousness arise with healing in his wings; and ye shall go forth and grow up as calves of the stall."

# Proverbs

## Forget Not My Law, Prov. 3

Every people has its wise sayings. Those of the Hebrew race have been assembled in The Book of Proverbs. Commonly ascribed to Solomon, they evidently represent the wisdom of various men of various periods. Chapter three starts out:

"My son, forget not my law, but let thine heart keep my commandments; for length of days and long life and peace shall they add to thee. Let not mercy and truth forsake thee, bind them about thy neck, write them upon the table of thine heart; so shalt thou find favor and good understanding in the sight of God and man.

"Trust in the Lord with all thine heart, and lean not unto thine own understanding. In all thy ways acknowledge him and he shall direct thy paths.

"Be not wise in thine own eyes, fear the Lord and depart from evil. It shall be health to thy navel and marrow to thy bones. Honor the Lord with thy substance, and with the firstfruits of all thine increase; so shall thy barns be filled with plenty, and thy presses shall burst out with new wine.

"My son, despise not the chastening of the Lord, neither be weary of his correction; for whom the Lord loveth he correcteth, even as a father the son in whom he delighteth.

"Happy is the man that findeth wisdom, and the man that

getteth understanding; for the merchandise of it is better than the merchandise of silver, and the gain thereof than fine gold. She is more precious than rubies, and all the things thou canst desire are not to be compared unto her.   Length of days is in her right hand, and in her left hand riches and honor.

"Her ways are ways of pleasantness, and all her paths are peace.   She is a tree of life to them that lay hold upon her, and happy is every one that retaineth her.   The Lord by wisdom hath founded the earth, by understanding hath he established the heavens.   By his knowledge the depths are broken up, and the clouds drop down the dew.

"My son, let not them depart from thine eyes, keep sound wisdom and discretion; so shall they be life unto thy soul and grace to thy neck.   Then shalt thou walk in thy way safely and thy foot shall not stumble.   When thou liest down thou shalt not be afraid, yea, thou shalt lie down and thy sleep shall be sweet.   Be not afraid of sudden fear, neither of the desolation of the wicked, when it cometh.   For the Lord shall be thy confidence and shall keep thy foot from being taken."

## *Antiquity of Wisdom, Prov. 8*

"Doth not wisdom cry? and understanding put forth her voice?   She standeth in the top of high places, by the way in the places of the paths.   She crieth at the gates, at the entry of the city, at the coming in at the doors: Unto you, O men, I call; and my voice is to the sons of man . . .

"The Lord possessed me in the beginning of his way, before his works of old.   I was set up from everlasting, from the beginning, or ever the earth was.   When there were no depths I was brought forth, when there were no fountains abounding with water.   Before the mountains were settled, before the hills, was I brought forth, while as yet he had not made the earth nor the fields nor the highest part of the dust of the world.

"When he prepared the heavens I was there, when he set

compass upon the face of the depth, when he established
the clouds above, when he strengthened the fountains of the
deep, when he gave to the sea his decree that the waters
should not pass his commandment, when he appointed the
foundations of the earth, then I was by him as one brought up
with him and I was daily his delight, rejoicing always before
him, rejoicing in the habitable part of his earth, and my de-
lights were with the sons of men."

## Miscellaneous Maxims, Prov. 4-29

Go to the ant, thou sluggard, consider her ways
and be wise; which having no guide, overseer or ruler,
provideth her meat in the summer and gathereth her
food in the harvest.

How long wilt thou sleep, O sluggard? when wilt
thou arise out of thy sleep? Yet a little sleep, a little
slumber, a little folding of the hands to sleep. So
shall thy poverty come as one that travelleth and thy
want as an armed man.

A soft answer turneth away wrath, but grievous
words stir up anger.

A word fitly spoken is like apples of gold in pictures
of silver.

As an earring of gold and an ornament of fine gold,
so is a wise reprover upon an obedient ear.

He that is slow to anger is better than the mighty,
and he that ruleth his spirit than he that taketh a city.

A merry heart doeth good like a medicine, but a
broken spirit drieth the bones.

Commit thy works unto the Lord, and thy
thoughts shall be established.

When a man's ways please the Lord, He maketh
even his enemies to be at peace with him.

Fret not thyself because of evil men, neither be
thou envious at the wicked; for there shall be no re-

ward to the evil man, the candle of the wicked shall be put out.

If thine enemy be hungry give him bread to eat, and if he be thirsty give him water to drink; for thou shalt heap coals of fire upon his head, and the Lord shall reward thee.

Pride goeth before destruction, and an haughty spirit before a fall.

Where no wood is, there the fire goeth out; so where there is no talebearer, the strife ceaseth.

Whoso diggeth a pit shall fall therein; and he that rolleth a stone, it will return upon him.

The wicked flee when no man pursueth, but the righteous are bold as a lion.

Where there is no vision the people perish; but he that keepeth the law, happy is he.

Look not thou upon the wine when it is red, when it giveth his color in the cup, when it moveth itself aright. At the last it biteth like a serpent and stingeth like an adder.

# Ecclesiastes

## Vanity of Vanities, Eccl. 1

The Book of Ecclesiastes has various moods. Generally accredited, like Proverbs, to Solomon, it almost certainly is the product of a much later time, probably the second century B. C. It opens:

"Vanity of vanities, saith the preacher, vanity of vanities; all is vanity. What profit hath a man of all his labor which he taketh under the sun? One generation passeth away, and another generation cometh, but the earth abideth forever. The sun also ariseth, and the sun goeth down and hasteth to his place where he arose.

"The wind goeth toward the south, and turneth about unto the north; it whirleth about continually, and the wind returneth again according to his circuits. All the rivers run into the sea, yet the sea is not full; unto the place from whence the rivers come, thither they return again.

"All things are full of labor, man cannot utter it; the eye is not satisfied with seeing nor the ear filled with hearing. The thing that hath been, it is that which shall be; and that which is done is that which shall be done; and there is no new thing under the sun . . . There is no remembrance of former things, neither shall there be any remembrance of things that are to come with those that shall come after. . .

"I communed with mine own heart, saying, Lo, I am come

to great estate and have gotten more wisdom than all they that have been before me in Jerusalem; yea, my heart had great experience of wisdom and knowledge. And I gave my heart to know wisdom, and to know madness and folly; I perceived that this also is vexation of spirit. For in much wisdom is much grief; and he that increaseth knowledge increaseth sorrow."

## Sage Reflections, Eccl. 3, 11

"To every thing there is a season, and a time to every purpose under the heaven: A time to be born and a time to die, a time to plant and a time to pluck up that which is planted, a time to kill and a time to heal, a time to break down and a time to build up, a time to weep and a time to laugh, a time to mourn and a time to dance, a time to cast away stones and a time to gather stones together, a time to embrace and a time to refrain from embracing, a time to get and a time to lose, a time to keep and a time to cast away, a time to rend and a time to sew, a time to keep silence and a time to speak, a time to love and a time to hate, a time of war and a time of peace.

"I know that whatsoever God doeth, it shall be forever. Nothing can be put to it nor anything taken from it. And God doeth it that men should fear before him. That which hath been is now, and that which is to be hath already been, and God requireth that which is past. . .

"Cast thy bread upon the waters, for thou shalt find it after many days . . . In the morning sow thy seed, and in the evening withhold not thine hand; for thou knowest not whether shall prosper, either this or that, or whether they both shall be alike good . . .

"Let us hear the conclusion of the whole matter: Fear God and keep his commandments, for this is the whole duty of man."

## Remember Thy Creator, Eccl. 11, 12

Remember now thy Creator in the days of thy youth,
While the evil days come not
Nor the years draw nigh when thou shalt say,
I have no pleasure in them;
While the sun or the light
Or the moon or the stars be not darkened,
Nor the clouds return after the rain;
In the day when the keepers of the house shall trem-
ble,
And the strong men shall bow themselves,
And the grinders cease because they are few,
And those that look out of the windows be darkened,
And the doors shall be shut in the streets;
When the sound of the grinding is low,
And he shall rise up at the voice of the bird,
And all the daughters of music shall be brought low;
Also when they shall be afraid of that which is high,
And fears shall be in the way,
And the almond tree shall flourish,
And the grasshopper shall be a burden,
And desire shall fail:
Because man goeth to his long home
And the mourners go about the streets:
Or ever the silver cord be loosed,
Or the golden bowl be broken,
Or the pitcher be broken at the fountain,
Or the wheel broken at the cistern.
Then shall the dust return to the earth as it was,
And the spirit shall return unto God who gave it.

# Job

*Enter Satan, Job 1, 2*

One of the oldest volumes of the Bible, and one of the most majestic poems in world literature, is the Book of Job. The author is unknown. The question, "Why does the good man suffer?" is the theme.

There was a day, so the argument begins, when the sons of God presented themselves before the Lord, and Satan appeared with them. When the Lord asked whence he came, Satan answered, "From going to and fro in the earth, and from walking up and down in it."

"Hast thou considered my servant Job, that there is none like him in the earth, a perfect and an upright man?" continued the Lord. "Doth Job fear God for nought?" rejoined Satan. "Thou hast blessed the work of his hands, and his substance is increased in the land. But put forth thine hand now, and touch all that he hath, and he will curse thee to thy face."

Thereupon the Lord put Job's possessions into Satan's power. Presently word came to Job that disasters had overtaken his flocks, his servants, and even his sons. He fell upon the ground, crying: "The Lord gave, and the Lord hath taken away; blessed be the name of the Lord."

Again the sons of God came before the Lord, Satan with them. The Lord asked Satan if he had observed that Job still held fast his integrity. Satan answered: "Skin for skin,

172

yea, all that a man hath will he give for his life. But put forth thine hand now and touch his bone and his flesh, and he will curse thee to thy face." "Behold, he is in thine hand," replied the Lord, "but save his life."

So went Satan forth and smote Job with sickness from the sole of his foot to the crown of his head. Then declared his wife, "Dost thou still retain thine integrity? curse God and die." "What, shall we receive good at the hand of God and shall we not receive evil?" he rejoined.

## The Three Friends, Job 3-5

Now came three of Job's friends, Eliphaz and Bildad and Zophar, to comfort him. For seven days they sat and spoke not a word, for they saw that his grief was very great.

After this Job cursed his day and lamented that ever he had been born. "For now," he cried, "should I have lain still and been quiet, I should have slept; then had I been at rest with kings and counselors of the earth . . . There the wicked cease from troubling; and there the weary be at rest . . . Why is light given to a man whose way is hid, and whom God hath hedged in? For my sighing cometh before I eat, and my roarings are poured out like the waters. For the thing which I greatly feared is come upon me."

Eliphaz answered: "Thou hast instructed many and thou hast strengthened the weak hands . . . But now it is come upon thee, and thou faintest . . . Remember, I pray thee, who ever perished, being innocent? or where were the righteous cut off? Even as I have seen, they that plow iniquity and sow wickedness reap the same."

Continuing, Eliphaz added: "Although affliction cometh not forth of the dust, neither doth trouble spring out of the ground; yet man is born unto trouble as the sparks fly upward. I would seek unto God, and unto God would I commit my cause; which doeth great things and unsearchable, marvelous things without number."

## Job Justifies Himself, Job 6-13

Job, insisting upon his righteousness, declared: "Teach me, and I will hold my tongue; and cause me to understand wherein I have erred. How forcible are right words! But what doth your arguing reprove?

"I am made to possess months of vanity, and wearisome nights are appointed to me . . . My days are swifter than a weaver's shuttle, and are spent without hope . . . Therefore I will not refrain my mouth; I will speak in the anguish of my spirit; I will complain in the bitterness of my soul."

"How long shall the words of thy mouth be like a strong wind?" exclaimed Bildad. "Can the rush grow up without mire? can the flag grow without water? Whilst it is yet in his greenness, and not cut down, it withereth before any other herb. So are the paths of all that forget God; and the hypocrite's hope shall perish."

All this Job admitted, yet could not see how to plead his cause with God. "If I justify myself," he argued, "mine own mouth shall condemn me; if I say, I am perfect, it shall also prove me perverse . . . Are not my days few? cease then and let me alone, that I may take comfort a little before I go whence I shall not return, even to the land of darkness and the shadow of death."

"Should a man full of talk be justified?" cried Zophar. "But oh that God would speak and open his lips against thee; and that he would show thee the secrets of wisdom . . . If iniquity be in thine hand, put it far away, and let not wickedness dwell in thy tabernacles. For then shalt thou lift up thy face without spot, yea, thou shalt be steadfast and shalt not fear; because thou shalt forget thy misery, and remember it as waters that pass away: and thine age shall be clearer than the noonday; thou shalt shine forth, thou shalt be as the morning . . . Also thou shalt lie down, and none shall make thee afraid."

"No doubt but ye are the people, and wisdom shall die with

you," retorted Job. "Who knoweth not in all these that the hand of the Lord hath wrought this? in whose hand is the soul of every living thing, and the breath of all mankind.

"Though He slay me, yet will I trust in him; but I will maintain mine own ways before him . . . Wherefore hidest thou thy face, and holdest me for thine enemy? Wilt thou break a leaf driven to and fro? and wilt thou pursue the dry stubble?"

## *Shall He Live Again, Job* 14-31

"Man that is born of a woman is of few days, and full of trouble. He cometh forth like a flower and is cut down; he fleeth also as a shadow, and continueth not. And dost thou open thine eyes upon such an one and bringest me into judgment with thee?

"If a man die, shall he live again? All the days of my appointed time will I wait till my change come. Thou shalt call, and I will answer thee: thou wilt have a desire to the work of thine hands. . . For I know that my Redeemer liveth, and that he shall stand at the latter day upon the earth . . . in my flesh shall I see God."

Here Eliphaz counseled: "Acquaint now thyself with Him, and be at peace; thereby good shall come unto thee. Receive, I pray thee, the law from his mouth, and lay up his words in thine heart. If thou return to the Almighty, thou shalt be built up, thou shalt put away iniquity far from thy tabernacles. Then shalt thou lay up gold as dust . . . Thou shalt also decree a thing, and it shall be established unto thee: and the light shall shine upon thy ways."

"Miserable comforters are ye all," ejaculated Job. "Even today is my complaint bitter; my stroke is heavier than my groaning. Oh that I knew where I might find Him! that I might come even to his seat! I would order my cause before Him and fill my mouth with arguments.

"Oh that I were as in months past, as in the days when God preserved me; when his candle shined upon my head, and when by his light I walked through darkness.

"When I went out to the gate through the city, when I prepared my seat in the street, the young men saw me and hid themselves, and the aged arose and stood up . . . Unto me men gave ear, and waited, and kept silence at my counsel . . . But now they that are younger than I have me in derision, whose fathers I would have disdained to have set with the dogs of my flock . . . I am a brother to dragons and a companion to owls . . .

"Doth not He see my ways and count all my steps? If I have walked with vanity, or if my foot hath hasted to deceit, let me be weighed in an even balance that God may know mine integrity . . . Oh that one would hear me! behold, my desire is that the Almighty would answer me, and that mine adversary had written a book."

### Elihu Argues, Job 32-37

The three men now ceased to argue, which gave Elihu, who had been listening, a chance to enter the debate. "I am young," he began, "and ye are very old; wherefore I was afraid and durst not show you mine opinion. I said, Days should speak, and multitude of years should teach wisdom. But there is a spirit in man; and the inspiration of the Almighty giveth them understanding . . . The Spirit of God hath made me, and the breath of the Almighty hath given me life."

He pointed out to Job that God has different ways of addressing himself to men, to warn them and draw them back from danger. One is by dreams and visions. Another is by chastisement through pain and sickness; then a messenger, one among a thousand, comes to their deliverance, and their flesh becomes fresher than a child's and they return to the days of their youth.

"Lo, all these things worketh God oftentimes with man," explained Elihu, "to bring back his soul from the pit, to be enlightened with the light of the living."

Turning to the three wise men he proceeded: "Hear my words . . . For the ear trieth words as the mouth tasteth meat . . . What man is like Job, who drinketh up scorning like water? . . . For he hath said, It profiteth a man nothing that he should delight himself with God.

"Job hath spoken without knowledge, and his words were without wisdom. My desire is that Job may be tried unto the end because of his answers for wicked men. For he addeth rebellion unto his sin, he clappeth his hands among us, and multiplieth his words against God."

Addressing himself again to Job, Elihu asked: "Thinkest thou this to be right, that thou saidst, My righteousness is more than God's? . . . Dost thou know the balancings of the clouds, the wondrous works of Him which is perfect in knowledge? How thy garments are warm, when He quieteth the earth by the south wind? Hast thou with Him spread out the sky, which is strong and as a molten looking-glass? . . .

"Touching the Almighty, we cannot find him out; he is excellent in power and in judgment and in plenty of justice; he will not afflict. Men do therefore fear him. He respecteth not any that are wise of heart."

## The Lord Speaks, Job 38-42

Then the Lord answered Job out of the whirlwind, saying: "Who is this that darkeneth counsel by words without knowledge? Gird up now thy loins like a man; for I will demand of thee, and answer thou me.

"Where wast thou when I laid the foundations of the earth? declare, if thou hast understanding. Who hath laid the measures thereof, if thou knowest? or who hath stretched the line upon it? Whereupon are the foundations thereof fastened? or who laid the cornerstone thereof; when the morning stars sang together, and all the sons of God shouted for joy? Or who shut up the sea with doors . . . and said, Hitherto shalt thou come, but no further; and here shall thy proud waves be stayed?

"Have the gates of death been opened unto thee? or hast thou seen the doors of the shadow of death . . . Where is the way where light dwelleth? and as for darkness, where is the place thereof?

"Canst thou bind the sweet influences of Pleiades, or loose the bands of Orion? Canst thou bring forth Mazzaroth in his season? or canst thou guide Arcturus with his sons?

"Who hath put wisdom in the inward parts? or who hath given understanding to the heart? . . . Who provideth for the raven his food? . . . Doth the hawk fly by thy wisdom, and stretch her wings toward the south? Doth the eagle mount up at thy command, and make her nest on high?"

"Behold, I am vile," confessed Job, "what shall I answer thee? I will lay mine hand upon my mouth. Once have I spoken; but I will not answer: yea, twice; but I will proceed no further . . . I know that thou canst do everything, and that no thought can be withholden from thee.

"Who is he that hideth counsel without knowledge? Therefore have I uttered that I understood not; things too wonderful for me, which I knew not. Hear, I beseech thee, and I will speak. I will demand of thee and declare thou unto me. I have heard of thee by the hearing of the ear; but now mine eye seeth thee. Wherefore I abhor myself and repent in dust and ashes."

The Lord now said to Eliphaz: "My wrath is kindled against thee, and against thy two friends; for ye have not spoken of me the thing that is right, as my servant Job hath. Therefore, lest I deal with you after your folly, take unto you now seven bullocks and seven rams, and go to my servant Job, and offer up for yourselves a burnt offering; and my servant Job shall pray for you, for him will I accept."

They did as commanded. "And the Lord turned the captivity of Job, when he prayed for his friends; also the Lord gave Job twice as much as he had before."

# *Lamentations*

The Book of Lamentations, often called "The Lamentations of Jeremiah," comprises five poems, which picture the sorrows of the Hebrews during their exile in Babylon following the overthrow of Jerusalem. Chapter three, having reference to the anger of the Lord, contains these lines:

> I am the man that hath seen affliction by the rod of
>    his wrath.
> He hath led me and brought me into darkness but
>    not into light.
> Surely against me is he turned; he turneth his hand
>    against me all the day.
> My flesh and my skin hath he made old; he hath
>    broken my bones.
> He hath builded against me and compassed me with
>    gall and travail.
> He hath set me in dark places as they that be dead
>    of old.
> He hath hedged me about that I cannot get out; he
>    hath made my chain heavy.
> Also when I cry and shout, he shutteth out my prayer.
> He hath inclosed my ways with hewn stone, he hath
>    made my paths crooked.

*It is of the Lord's mercies that we are not consumed,
    because his compassions fail not.*

*They are new every morning; great is thy faithful-
    ness.*

*The Lord is my portion, saith my soul; therefore
    will I hope in him.*

*The Lord is good unto them that wait for him, to
    the soul that seeketh him.*

*It is good that a man should both hope and quietly
    wait for the salvation of the Lord.*

*It is good for a man that he bear the yoke in his
    youth.*

*He sitteth alone and keepeth silence, because he
    hath borne it upon him.*

*He putteth his mouth in the dust, if so be there
    may be hope.*

*He giveth his cheek to him that smiteth him; he is
    filled full with reproach.*


*We have transgressed and rebelled; thou hast not
    pardoned.*

*Thou hast covered with anger and persecuted us;
    thou hast slain, thou hast not pitied.*

*Thou hast covered thyself with a cloud, that our
    prayer should not pass through.*

*Thou hast made us as the offscouring and refuse in
    the midst of the people.*

*All our enemies have opened their mouths against us.*

*Fear and a snare is come upon us, desolation and
    destruction.*

*Mine eye runneth down with rivers of water for the
    destruction of the daughter of my people.*

*Mine eye trickleth down, and ceaseth not, without
    any intermission,*

*Till the Lord look down and behold from heaven.*

# The Book of Psalms

*The Upright Man, Psalm 1*

The Psalms, one hundred and fifty in number, were composed at different times over a period of centuries, some apparently to meet special occasions. They were not put in final form, it is thought. until a century or two before Christ. Number one follows:

> Blessed is the man that walketh not in the counsel
>     of the ungodly,
> Nor standeth in the way of sinners,
> Nor sitteth in the seat of the scornful.
> But his delight is in the law of the Lord,
> And in his law doth he meditate day and night.
> And he shall be like a tree planted by the rivers of
>     water,
> That bringeth forth his fruit in his season,
> His leaf also shall not wither, and whatsoever he
>     doeth shall prosper.
>
> The ungodly are not so, but are like the chaff which
>     the wind driveth away.
> Therefore the ungodly shall not stand in the judg-
>     ment,

Nor sinners in the congregation of the righteous.
For the Lord knoweth the way of the righteous,
But the way of the ungodly shall perish.


## Consider Thy Heavens, Psalm 8

O Lord our Lord,
How excellent is thy name in all the earth!
Who hast set thy glory above the heavens.
Out of the mouth of babes and sucklings
Hast thou ordained strength because of thine ene-
     mies,
That thou mightest still the enemy and the avenger.
When I consider thy heavens, the work of thy fin-
     gers,
The moon and the stars, which thou hast ordained;
What is man, that thou art mindful of him?
And the son of man, that thou visitest him?
For thou hast made him a little lower than the
     angels,
And hast crowned him with glory and honor.
Thou madest him to have dominion
Over the works of thy hands;
Thou hast put all things under his feet.


## Meditations of the Heart, Psalm 19

The heavens declare the glory of God,
And the firmament showeth his handiwork.
Day unto day uttereth speech,
And night unto night showeth knowledge.
There is no speech nor language
Where their voice is not heard.

The law of the Lord is perfect, converting the soul;
The testimony of the Lord is sure, making wise the
     simple.
The statutes of the Lord are right, rejoicing the
     heart;
The commandment of the Lord is pure, enlighten-
     ing the eyes.
The fear of the Lord is clean, enduring for ever;
The judgments of the Lord are true and righteous
     altogether.
More to be desired are they than gold, yea, than
     much fine gold;
Sweeter also than honey and the honeycomb.

Moreover by them is thy servant warned;
And in keeping of them there is great reward.
Who can understand his errors?
Cleanse thou me from secret faults.
Keep back thy servant also from presumptuous sins,
Let them not have dominion over me;
Then shall I be upright,
And I shall be innocent from the great transgression.
Let the words of my mouth and the meditation of
     my heart
Be acceptable in thy sight, O Lord, my strength and
     my redeemer.


## Still Waters, Psalm 23

The Lord is my shepherd; I shall not want.
He maketh me to lie down in green pastures;
He leadeth me beside the still waters.
He restoreth my soul;
He leadeth me in the paths of righteousness for his
     name's sake.
Yea, though I walk through the valley of the shadow
     of death,

I will fear no evil, for thou art with me;
Thy rod and thy staff they comfort me.
Thou preparest a table before me in the presence of
          mine enemies;
Thou anointest my head with oil; my cup runneth
          over.
Surely goodness and mercy shall follow me all the
          days of my life,
And I will dwell in the house of the Lord for ever.


## He Spake and It Was Done, Psalm 33

Let all the earth fear the Lord;
Let all the inhabitants of the world stand in awe of
          him.
For he spake, and it was done;
He commanded, and it stood fast.
The Lord bringeth the counsel of the heathen to
          naught;
He maketh the devices of the people of none effect.
The counsel of the Lord standeth for ever;
The thoughts of his heart to all generations.
Blessed is the nation whose God is the Lord;
And the people whom he hath chosen for his own
          inheritance.


The Lord looketh from heaven;
He beholdeth all the sons of men.
From the place of his habitation he looketh
Upon all the inhabitants of the earth.
He fashioneth their hearts alike;
He considereth all their works.
There is no king saved by the multitude of a host;
A mighty man is not delivered by much strength.
An horse is a vain thing for safety;
Neither shall he deliver any by his great strength.

Behold, the eye of the Lord is upon them that fear
him,
Upon them that hope in his mercy,
To deliver their soul from death
And to keep them alive in famine.
Our soul waiteth for the Lord;
He is our help and our shield.
For our heart shall rejoice in him,
Because we have trusted in his holy name.
Let thy mercy, O Lord, be upon us,
According as we hope in thee.

## The Fountain of Life, Psalm 36

The transgression of the wicked saith within my
heart
That there is no fear of God before his eyes.
For he flattereth himself in his own eyes
Until his iniquity be found to be hateful.
The words of his mouth are iniquity and deceit;
He hath left off to be wise and to do good.
He deviseth mischief upon his bed;
He setteth himself in a way that is not good;
He abhorreth not evil.

Thy mercy, O Lord, is in the heavens,
And thy faithfulness reacheth unto the clouds.
Thy righteousness is like the great mountains;
Thy judgments are a great deep:
O Lord, thou preservest man and beast.
How excellent is thy loving-kindness, O God!
Therefore the children of men put their trust
Under the shadow of thy wings.
They shall be abundantly satisfied with the fatness
of thy house;
And thou shalt make them drink of the river of thy
pleasures.

For with thee is the fountain of life;
In thy light shall we see light.


## Mark the Perfect Man, Psalm 37

Commit thy way unto the Lord, trust also in him,
And he shall bring it to pass.
And he shall bring forth thy righteousness as the
        light,
And thy judgment as the noonday.
The steps of a good man are ordered by the Lord;
And he delighteth in his way.
Though he fall, he shall not be utterly cast down;
For the Lord upholdeth him with his hand.
I have been young, and now am old;
Yet have I not seen the righteous forsaken nor his
        seed begging bread.
I have seen the wicked in great power
And spreading himself like a green bay tree.
Yet he passed away and lo he was not;
Yea, I sought him but he could not be found.
Mark the perfect man, and behold the upright;
For the end of that man is peace.


## Why Art Thou Cast Down, Psalm 42

As the hart panteth after the water brooks,
So panteth my soul after thee, O God.
My soul thirsteth for God, for the living God;
When shall I come and appear before God?
My tears have been my meat day and night,
While they continually say unto me, Where is thy
        God?
When I remember these things, I pour out my soul
        in me.

Why art thou cast down, O my soul?
And why art thou disquieted in me?
Hope thou in God,
For I shall yet praise him for the help of his counte-
      nance.
O my God, my soul is cast down within me:
Therefore will I remember thee from the land of
      Jordan
And of the Hermonites, from the hill Mizar.
Deep calleth unto deep at the noise of thy water-
      spouts;
All thy waves and thy billows are gone over me.
Yet the Lord will command his loving-kindness in
      the daytime,
And in the night his song shall be with me,
And my prayer unto the God of my life.


## Be Still and Know, Psalm 46

God is our refuge and strength,
A very present help in trouble.
Therefore will not we fear, though the earth be re-
      moved,
And though the mountains be carried into the midst
      of the sea,
Though the waters thereof roar and be troubled,
Though the mountains shake with the swelling
      thereof.

There is a river the streams whereof shall make glad
      the city of God,
The holy place of the tabernacles of the Most High.
God is in the midst of her; she shall not be moved;
God shall help her, and that right early.
The heathen raged, the kingdoms were moved;

He uttered his voice, the earth melted.
The Lord of hosts is with us;
The God of Jacob is our refuge.

Come, behold the works of the Lord,
What desolations he hath made in the earth.
He maketh wars to cease unto the end of the earth;
He breaketh the bow and cutteth the spear in sun-
    der;
He burneth the chariot in the fire.
Be still, and know that I am God;
I will be exalted among the heathen,
I will be exalted in the earth.
The Lord of hosts is with us;
The God of Jacob is our refuge.


*Truth in the Inward Parts, Psalm 51*

Have mercy upon me, O God, according to thy lov-
    ing-kindness;
According unto the multitude of thy tender mercies
Blot out my transgressions.
Wash me throughly from mine iniquity,
And cleanse me from my sin.
For I acknowledge my transgressions;
And my sin is ever before me.
Against thee, thee only, have I sinned,
And done this evil in thy sight;
That thou mightest be justified when thou speakest,
And be clear when thou judgest.
Behold, I was shapen in iniquity;
And in sin did my mother conceive me.
Behold, thou desirest truth in the inward parts;
And in the hidden part thou shalt make me to know
    wisdom.

Purge me with hyssop, and I shall be clean;
Wash me, and I shall be whiter than snow.
Make me to hear joy and gladness,
That the bones which thou hast broken may rejoice.
Hide thy face from my sins
And blot out all mine iniquities.
Create in me a clean heart, O God,
And renew a right spirit within me.
For thou desirest not sacrifice; else would I give it:
Thou delightest not in burnt offering.
The sacrifices of God are a broken spirit;
A broken and a contrite heart, O God, thou wilt not
    despise.


## The Beauty of the Lord, Psalm 90

Lord, thou hast been our dwelling place in all gen-
    erations.
Before the mountains were brought forth,
Or ever thou hadst formed the earth and the world,
Even from everlasting to everlasting, thou art God.
Thou turnest man to destruction;
And sayest, Return, ye children of men.
For a thousand years in thy sight
Are but as yesterday when it is past,
And as a watch in the night.

The days of our years are threescore years and ten;
And if by reason of strength they be fourscore years,
Yet is their strength labor and sorrow,
For it is soon cut off and we fly away.
Who knoweth the power of thine anger?
Even according to thy fear, so is thy wrath.
So teach us to number our days,
That we may apply our hearts unto wisdom.

Return, O Lord, how long?
And let it repent thee concerning thy servants.
O satisfy us early with thy mercy,
That we may rejoice and be glad all our days.
Make us glad according to the days
Wherein thou hast afflicted us,
And the years wherein we have seen evil.
Let thy work appear unto thy servants,
And thy glory unto their children.
And let the beauty of the Lord our God be upon us;
And establish thou the work of our hands upon us,
Yea, the work of our hands establish thou it.

### The Shadow of the Almighty, Psalm 91

He that dwelleth in the secret place of the Most
    High
Shall abide under the shadow of the Almighty.
I will say of the Lord,
He is my refuge and my fortress; my God, in him
    will I trust.

Surely he shall deliver thee from the snare of the
    fowler,
And from the noisome pestilence.
He shall cover thee with his feathers,
And under his wings shalt thou trust;
His truth shall be thy shield and buckler.
Thou shalt not be afraid for the terror by night,
Nor for the arrow that flieth by day,
Nor for the pestilence that walketh in darkness,
Nor for the destruction that wasteth at noonday.
A thousand shall fall at thy side,
And ten thousand at thy right hand;
But it shall not come nigh thee.
Only with thine eyes shalt thou behold

And see the reward of the wicked.
Because thou hast made the Lord, which is my
            refuge,
Even the Most High, thy habitation,
There shall no evil befall thee,
Neither shall any plague come nigh thy dwelling.
For he shall give his angels charge over thee,
To keep thee in all thy ways.
They shall bear thee up in their hands,
Lest thou dash thy foot against a stone.
Thou shalt tread upon the lion and adder;
The young lion and the dragon shalt thou trample
            under feet.

Because he hath set his love upon me, therefore will
            I deliver him;
I will set him on high, because he hath known my
            name.
He shall call upon me, and I will answer him;
I will be with him in trouble;
I will deliver him and honor him.
With long life will I satisfy him,
And show him my salvation.


## He Sent His Word, Psalm 107

Oh that men would praise the Lord for his goodness,
And for his wonderful works to the children of men!
For he satisfieth the longing soul,
And filleth the hungry soul with goodness.
Such as sit in darkness and in the shadow of death,
Being bound in affliction and iron;
Because they rebelled against the words of God,
And contemned the counsel of the Most High:
Therefore he brought down their heart with labor;
They fell down, and there was none to help.

Then they cried unto the Lord in their trouble,
And he saved them out of their distresses.
He brought them out of darkness and the shadow of
      death,
And brake their bands in sunder.
He sent his word, and healed them,
And delivered them from their destructions.

They that go down to the sea in ships,
That do business in great waters;
These see the works of the Lord,
And his wonders in the deep.
For he commandeth, and raiseth the stormy wind,
Which lifteth up the waves thereof.
They mount up to the heaven,
They go down again to the depths;
Their soul is melted because of trouble.
They reel to and fro, and stagger like a drunken man,
And are at their wit's end.
Then they cry unto the Lord in their trouble,
And he bringeth them out of their distresses.
He maketh the storm a calm,
So that the waves thereof are still.
Then are they glad because they be quiet;
So he bringeth them unto their desired haven.

*The Lord Thy Keeper, Psalm 121*

I will lift up mine eyes unto the hills.
From whence cometh my help?
My help cometh from the Lord,
Which made heaven and earth.
He will not suffer thy foot to be moved;
He that keepeth thee will not slumber.
Behold, he that keepeth Israel

Shall neither slumber nor sleep.
The Lord is thy keeper;
The Lord is thy shade upon thy right hand.
The sun shall not smite thee by day,
Nor the moon by night.
The Lord shall preserve thee from all evil:
He shall preserve thy soul.
The Lord shall preserve thy going out and thy com-
     ing in
From this time forth, and even forevermore.

## The Divine Immanence, Psalm 139

O Lord, thou hast searched me and known me.
Thou knowest my downsitting and mine uprising;
Thou understandest my thought afar off.
Thou compassest my path and my lying down,
And art acquainted with all my ways.
For there is not a word in my tongue,
But lo, O Lord, thou knowest it altogether.
Thou hast beset me behind and before,
And laid thine hand upon me.
Such knowledge is too wonderful for me;
It is high, I cannot attain unto it.

Whither shall I go from thy Spirit?
Or whither shall I flee from thy presence?
If I ascend up into heaven, thou art there;
If I make my bed in hell, behold, thou art there;
If I take the wings of the morning,
And dwell in the uttermost parts of the sea,
Even there shall thy hand lead me,
And thy right hand shall hold me.
If I say, Surely the darkness shall cover me,
Even the night shall be light about me.

Yea, the darkness hideth not from thee,
But the night shineth as the day;
The darkness and the light are both alike to thee.

I will praise thee,
For I am fearfully and wonderfully made;
Marvelous are thy works,
And that my soul knoweth right well.
My substance was not hid from thee
When I was made in secret
And curiously wrought in the lowest parts of the
        earth.
Thine eyes did see my substance, yet being unper-
        fect;
And in thy book all my members were written,
Which in continuance were fashioned
When as yet there was none of them.
Search me, O God, and know my heart,
Try me and know my thoughts;
And see if there be any wicked way in me,
And lead me in the way everlasting.

# Between the Testaments

## Apochryphal Writings

We have now come to the end of the Old Testament. Between it and the New lie four centuries, whose events are not recorded in the King James version of the Bible. History was made during that period, of course. The field of literature was productive; but its books, except Ecclesiastes and the final compilation of the Psalms, are not classified by Protestants as canonical or authoritative.

Among the Apochryphal volumes of the time is "The Wisdom of Solomon." Written by an Alexandrian Jew a century or so before Christ, it makes a definite pronouncement of immortality. Hebrews had long thought of their nation as permanent. With their nation disintegrated, they began to recognize the permanence of individual man.

After the rebuilding of the wall in the days of Ezra and Nehemiah, referred to in previous pages, the Persian Empire succumbed to Alexander the Great in his world conquest (333 B. C.). Thereby were Greek rule and culture extended throughout Asia Minor and Egypt.

## Greek and Roman Conquests

Alexander, when he came into the possession of Palestine, founded Greek settlements there. Indeed he built Greek cities all about the eastern Mediterranean and invited the Hebrews to emigrate to them. Great numbers accepted the invitation. And so "The Dispersion," begun with deportations to Assyria and Babylon, was extended. With the scattering of the people there came about three Jewish centers: Alexandria, Babylon, Jerusalem.

In former times the Hebrews, on occasion, had turned to the gods of neighboring nations. Now they felt the attraction of Greek culture—games, theaters, art, literature. Just what impression Greek thought made on Jewish is difficult to say, but it could hardly have been insignificant. In Alexandria the Old Testament was translated into Greek two centuries before Christ. The translation, which in course of time became the Bible of the early Christians, met an immediate need. For Greek had already made itself the everyday language of the better classes. It was the language of business and of government. Hebrew was forgotten save by the rabbis and scholars. Aramaic had taken its place with the common people. If the Jews found it difficult to sing their songs while in exile, they found it next to impossible to preserve their native tongue.

Alexander did not live to realize his hope of a world united in one language and culture. When his empire was divided, following his death, Palestine was awarded to Egypt. Syria naturally coveted the territory. After long contention between Egypt and Syria, Palestine was finally allotted to the latter (198 B. C.).

Alexander and the Ptolemies, in dealing with the Hebrews, pursued a liberal even a generous policy. Syrian rule however was rigorous, and under Antiochus Epiphanes became tyrannical. He set about ruthlessly to extirpate Judaism. Fierce revolts followed. Led by Mattathias in the beginning,

hey were continued by his five sons until the Syrians were
lriven out of Palestine.  One of the sons, a notable military
eader, was called Judas Maccabeus.  From this the heroic
amily became known as "Maccabees."  The history of the
period is told in the important Apochryphal books, I and II
Maccabees.

All went well for a time with the revived Hebrew nation.
Difficulties began when John Hyrcanus, grandson of Mattathias, was on the throne.  He waged relentless wars on his
neighbors in order to restore the former boundaries of Palestine.  He forced Judaism upon the conquered races.  In sub-
duing the Samaritans he destroyed their temple.  Domestic
strife between rival leaders followed his reign.

Out of the stress of the times arose three contentious sects
or parties: Pharisees, Sadducees, Essenes.  The Pharisees
were narrow observers of the letter of Scripture.  The Sadducees were more interested in politics than in formal religion.
The Essenes, few in number, mystic and ascetic, looked for
the spiritual kingdom.  Pharisee and Sadducee disputed with
each other, while the Essene labored against them both.

At this juncture Pompey, the Roman general, then on a
campaign in Syria, descended upon Jerusalem (63 B. C.).
So insufferable had internal discord become that his intrusion
was almost welcome.  Impatient with turbulence and sedi-
tion, the Romans ruled with iron hand.  Some thirty years
passed, when Caesar appointed Herod king of the Jews.  A
good soldier, a capable administrator, a builder such as the
country had never seen, he nevertheless developed tendencies
in private and in public life which were better untold.

The temple having been looted during the turmoil, Herod,
as part of his extraordinary building program, erected a mag-
nificent new house of worship for the Jews, their third and
last.  But they could not be placated.  The unrest continued.
Revolutionists called Zealots plotted and terrorized.  Into
this seething world was Jesus of Nazareth ushered (6 or 5
B. C.).

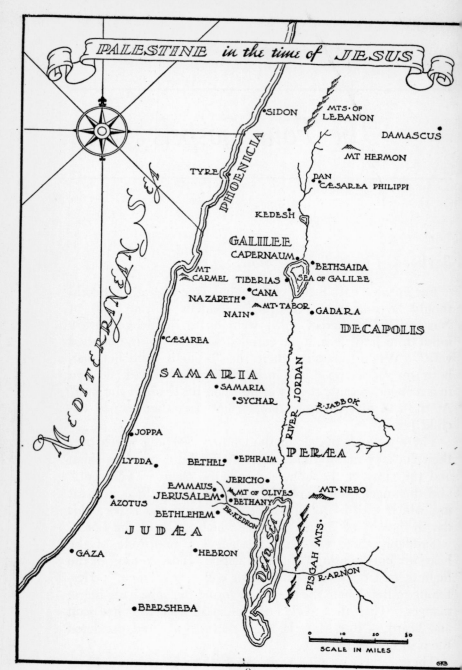

PALESTINE *in the time of* JESUS

MEDITERRANEAN SEA

MTS·OF LEBANON

DAMASCUS

SIDON

MT HERMON

PHOENICIA

DAN
CÆSAREA PHILIPPI

TYRE

KEDESH

GALILEE

CAPERNAUM

BETHSAIDA

MT
CARMEL  TIBERIAS  SEA OF GALILEE

CANA

NAZARETH

MT·TABOR  GADARA

NAIN

DECAPOLIS

CÆSAREA

RIVER JORDAN

SAMARIA

SAMARIA

SYCHAR

R·JABBOK

JOPPA

PERÆA

LYDDA

BETHEL  EPHRAIM

EMMAUS  JERICHO

JERUSALEM  MT OF OLIVES  MT·NEBO

BETHANY

AZOTUS  BETHLEHEM  BR·KEDRON

JUDÆA

DEAD SEA

PISGAH MTS·

GAZA  HEBRON

R·ARNON

BEERSHEBA

0    10    20    30
SCALE IN MILES

GKB

198

# The Four Gospels

## Boyhood of Jesus, Luke 2, Matt. 2, John 1

For in these days Rome sent out a decree that all the world should be numbered. Joseph, a resident of the town of Nazareth in southern Galilee, went up to Bethlehem, a few miles from Jerusalem, to be enrolled with Mary "his espoused wife." While they were there she "brought forth her first-born son and wrapped him in swaddling clothes and laid him in a manger, because there was no room for them in the inn." At the end of the conventional eight days they named the child Jesus.

There were shepherds in the country, keeping watch over their flock by night. The angel of the Lord came to them and the glory of the Lord shone round them. "Fear not," said the angel, "for behold, I bring you good tidings of great joy, which shall be to all people. For unto you is born this day in the city of David, a Savior, which is Christ the Lord."

Suddenly there was with the angel a multitude of the heavenly host praising God and saying: "Glory to God in the highest, and on earth peace, good will toward men." Hastening to Bethlehem the shepherds found the babe lying in the manger. Then they made known abroad what they had seen and heard. "But Mary kept all these things and pondered them in her heart."

There came wise men from the East to Jerusalem, asking:

"Where is he that is born King of the Jews? for we have seen his star in the East and are come to worship him." Herod, with all Jerusalem, was troubled. He therefore demanded of the scribes and chief priests where Christ should be born. "In Bethlehem of Judaea," he was told, "for thus it is written by the prophet." Inquiring of the wise men what time the star appeared, he sent them to Bethlehem, saying: "Go and search diligently for the young child; and when ye have found him, bring me word again that I may come and worship him also."

The star went before them on their way till it came and stood over the place where the child was. When they entered the house and saw him with his mother, they fell down and worshipped and presented him with gifts—gold, frankincense, myrrh. Warned of God in a dream that they should not return to Herod, they departed to their own country by another route.

Herod, exceedingly wroth that he had been mocked by the wise men, ordered the destruction of all male children in the vicinity under two years of age. "Arise and take the young child and his mother and flee into Egypt," said the Lord to Joseph in a dream. They fled at night and remained in Egypt several months until the death of Herod. Returning to Galilee, they took up their abode in their native town of Nazareth. "And the child grew and waxed strong in spirit, filled with wisdom; and the grace of God was upon him.'

So "in the beginning was the Word and the Word was with God and the Word was God . . . All things were made by him; and without him was not anything made that was made. In him was life; and the life was the light of men . . . And the Word was made flesh and dwelt among us; and we beheld his glory, the glory as of the only begotten of the Father, full of grace and truth . . . For the law was given by Moses, but grace and truth came by Jesus Christ."

When Jesus was twelve years of age his parents took him with them to the feast of the passover in Jerusalem. On their way home, after a day's journey, they missed him and turned

back to the city looking for him.   At the end of three days
they found him in the temple, "sitting in the midst of the
doctors, both hearing them and asking them questions.   And
all that heard him were astonished at his understanding and
answers."

The parents were amazed when they saw him, his mother
exclaiming, "Son, why hast thou thus dealt with us?   Behold,
thy father and I have sought thee sorrowing."   He answered,
"How is it that ye sought me?   Wist ye not that I must be
about my Father's business?"   Then "he went down with
them and came to Nazareth and was subject unto them; but
his mother kept all these sayings in her heart.   And Jesus increased in wisdom and stature, and in favor with God and
man."

Nazareth was an orderly village in the uplands to the west
of the Sea of Galilee.   Little changed it reposes today among
the noiseless hills.   Cana and Capernaum, old-time neighbors
on the north, are gone.   Sychar, on the way south to Jerusalem, has taken the new name Nablus.

From the summits back of Nazareth Jesus, as a boy, could
look out on the blue waters of the Mediterranean.   He could
count the ships and name the towns along the coast.   Not
far distant ran the highway from Egypt to Damascus and
thence on to the mysterious East.   The crawling caravans and
the tramping armies must have been familiar sights.   Along
this route had Abraham "looked for a city which hath foundations," and by it, farther south, had Joseph's jealous brothers
bargained with the Ishmaelites for his purchase.

## Baptism, John 1, Luke 1-4, Matt. 2-4, Mark 1

For the next eighteen years Jesus' biographers—Matthew,
Mark, Luke, John—make no mention of him.   Not until he
was around the age of thirty do they resume their narrative.
He then went down to the River Jordan where his cousin
John, six months older, was preaching and baptizing.   For

one day while Zacharias the priest was burning incense in the temple, the angel Gabriel appeared to him, saying: "Thy wife Elizabeth shall bear thee a son and thou shalt call his name John. And thou shalt have joy and gladness and many shall rejoice at his birth."

Zacharias asked: "Whereby shall I know this? for I am an old man and my wife well stricken in years." The angel answered: "Thou shalt be dumb and not able to speak until the day that these things shall be performed, because thou believest not my words." When it was time to name the child, because the promise was fulfilled, Zacharias called for a table and wrote, "His name is John." Then was his tongue loosed.

The child waxed strong in spirit. As he grew up he wore camel's hair garments with a leather girdle. His food was locusts and wild honey. He lived in the deserts until he appeared in the role of teacher by the Jordan. When priests from Jerusalem then demanded who he was, he admitted that he was not the Christ or even Elijah, but the voice of one crying in the wilderness, "Make straight the way of the Lord as said the prophet Isaiah." "Why baptizest thou then?" they asked. "I baptize with water," he answered, "but there standeth one among you, whom ye know not. He it is who coming after me is preferred before me, whose shoe latchet I am not worthy to unloose . . . He will baptize you with the Holy Ghost."

When Jesus presented himself for baptism, John hesitated, saying, "I have need to be baptized of thee and comest thou to me?" "Suffer it to be so now," answered Jesus, "for thus it becometh us to fulfil all righteousness." As he came up out of the water the heaven was opened and the Holy Ghost descended in a bodily shape like a dove upon him; and a voice came from heaven, saying, "Thou art my beloved Son; in thee I am well pleased."

Now was Jesus led up by the spirit into the wilderness. After long fasting he became hungry and uncertain. Then suggested the devil to him, "If thou be the Son of God, command this stone that it be made bread." He answered,

"It is written, Man shall not live by bread alone but by every word of God."

Next the devil took Jesus up into a high mountain and showed him all the kingdoms of the world. "If thou," he invited, "wilt worship me all shall be thine." "Get thee behind me, Satan," cried Jesus, "for it is written, Thou shalt worship the Lord thy God, and him only shalt thou serve."

Still persisting, the devil set Jesus on a pinnacle of the temple and argued, "If thou be the Son of God, cast thyself down from hence, for it is written, He shall give his angels charge over thee." Jesus rejoined, "It is said, Thou shalt not tempt the Lord thy God." The devil then departed for a season.

### Return to Galilee, John 1, 2, Luke 4

After these events by the Jordan, Jesus returned to Galilee. In Nazareth he entered the synagogue on the sabbath, and, standing up to read, opened the book of Isaiah where it is written: "The Spirit of the Lord is upon me, because he hath anointed me to preach the gospel to the poor; he hath sent me to heal the broken hearted, to preach deliverance to the captives and recovering of sight to the blind, to set at liberty them that are bruised, to preach the acceptable year of the Lord." As he sat down the eyes of all that were in the synagogue were fastened on him, and he said, "This day is this Scripture fulfilled in your ears." They all wondered at his gracious words and asked, "Is not this Joseph's son?"

In the neighboring village of Cana was a marriage. Jesus and his disciples were invited. His mother, also there, presently exclaimed, "They have no wine!" "Mine hour is not yet come," he replied. Soon, however, he directed the servants to fill stone jars with water and then draw out and bear to the governor of the feast. The governor, when he tasted the draft, remarked to the bridegroom: "Every man at the beginning doth set forth good wine; and when men have well drunk, then that which is worse; but thou hast kept the good wine until now."

## Visit to Jerusalem, John 2, 3

After this Jesus went to Capernaum at the head of the Sea of Galilee, his mother, brothers, and disciples accompanying him. But before long, the passover being at hand, he went up to Jerusalem. In the temple he found traders in cattle, sheep, and doves. Changers of money were also there. Making a scourge of small cords, he drove them all out. He poured out the changers' money and overthrew their tables. To those who sold doves he commanded, "Take these things hence; make not my Father's house an house of merchandise." The Jews asked, "What sign showest thou unto us, seeing thou doest these things?" He answered, "Destroy this temple and in three days I will raise it up."

Many believed on him in Jerusalem as they saw the miracles he performed. But he did not commit himself to them, because he knew what was in man and needed not to be told.

A Pharisee named Nicodemus, a ruler of the Jews, came to Jesus by night, saying: "Rabbi, we know that thou art a teacher come from God, for no man can do these miracles that thou doest except God be with him." Jesus answered: "Except a man be born again . . . except a man be born of water and of the Spirit, he cannot enter into the kingdom of God. That which is born of the flesh is flesh; and that which is born of the Spirit is spirit. Marvel not that I said unto thee, Ye must be born again. The wind bloweth where it listeth, and thou hearest the sound thereof, but canst not tell whence it cometh and whither it goeth: so is every one that is born of the Spirit."

"How can these things be?" questioned Nicodemus. Jesus replied: "If I have told you earthly things and ye believe not, how shall ye believe if I tell you of heavenly things? And no man hath ascended up to heaven but he that came down from heaven, even the Son of man which is in heaven.

"And as Moses lifted up the serpent in the wilderness, even so must the Son of man be lifted up, that whosoever believeth in him should not perish but have eternal life.

"For God so loved the world that he gave his only begotten Son, that whosoever believeth in him should not perish but have everlasting life. For God sent not his Son into the world to condemn the world, but that the world through him might be saved."

## Back to Galilee, John 4

After a short stay in Jerusalem and vicinity, Jesus started back to Galilee. On the way he stopped one morning at Jacob's Well near Sychar in Samaria. While his disciples were in town buying food, a woman came to draw water. He asked her for a drink. "How is it," she inquired, "that thou being a Jew askest drink of me which am a woman of Samaria?" Jesus answered: "Whosoever drinketh of this water shall thirst again. But whosoever drinketh of the water that I shall give him shall never thirst; but the water that I shall give him shall be in him a well of water springing up into everlasting life."

"Sir, give me this water," she implored, "that I thirst not, neither come hither to draw." "Call thy husband," said Jesus. "I have no husband," she replied. "Thou hast well said," Jesus observed, "for thou hast had five husbands, and he whom thou now hast is not thy husband." "Sir, I perceive that thou art a prophet," said she.

"Our fathers," she continued, "worshipped in this mountain, and ye say that in Jerusalem is the place where men ought to worship." "Woman, believe me," Jesus replied, "the hour cometh when ye shall neither in this mountain nor yet at Jerusalem worship the Father. Ye worship ye know not what; we know what we worship, for salvation is of the Jews.

But the hour cometh and now is when the true worshippers shall worship the Father in spirit and in truth, for the Father seeketh such to worship him. God is Spirit; and they that worship him must worship him in spirit and in truth."

The woman replied, "I know that Messias cometh, which is called Christ; when he is come he will tell us all things." "I that speak unto thee am he," said Jesus. Leaving her waterpot, the woman went into town and said to the men, "Come, see a man which told me all things that ever I did; is not this the Christ?" The people then came out to see Jesus.

Meanwhile his disciples, having returned, entreated him to eat. But he explained: "I have meat to eat that ye know not of . . . My meat is to do the will of Him that sent me and to finish His work. Say not ye, There are yet four months and then cometh harvest? Lift up your eyes and look on the fields, for they are white already to harvest. And he that reapeth receiveth wages and gathereth fruit unto life eternal, that both he that soweth and he that reapeth may rejoice together. And herein is that saying true, One soweth and another reapeth."

Many of the Samaritans believed on Jesus because of the woman's statement, "He told me all that ever I did." They therefore persuaded him to tarry with them. Whereupon many more believed because of his own words. But after two days he resumed his journey. In Cana, where the water had been made wine, a certain nobleman whose son was sick at Capernaum besought Jesus to heal him. He exclaimed, "Except ye see signs and wonders ye will not believe."

"Sir, come down ere my child die," he pleaded. Jesus said to him, "Go thy way, thy son liveth." The man believed and departed. As he was going down his servants met him and reported, "Thy son liveth." When he inquired the hour that the boy began to improve, they answered, "Yesterday at the seventh hour the fever left him." It was the same hour when Jesus declared, "Thy son liveth." Then the man believed and his whole house.

## Around Capernaum, Mark 1, 2; Matt. 8; Luke 5

Proceeding to Capernaum Jesus entered the synagogue on the sabbath day to teach. They were astonished at his doctrine, for he taught them as one that had authority and not as the scribes. Presently a man with an unclean spirit cried out: "Let us alone; what have we to do with thee, thou Jesus of Nazareth? Art thou come to destroy us? I know thee who thou art, the Holy One of God."

"Hold thy peace and come out of him," commanded Jesus. The spirit tore the man and cried with a loud voice and came out. The people were amazed and questioned among themselves, "What thing is this? what new doctrine is this? for with authority commandeth he even the unclean spirits and they do obey him."

One day while Jesus was teaching by the Lake of Gennesaret, generally known as the Sea of Galilee, his audience so pressed upon him that he stepped into a ship and asked the owner, Simon Peter, to thrust out a little from the land. Then he sat down and taught the people from the ship.

His discourse over, Jesus said to Simon, "Launch out into the deep and let down your nets for a draught." "Master, we have toiled all the night and have taken nothing," Simon replied, "nevertheless at thy word I will let down the net." Such a multitude of fishes were caught that the net broke. Therefore Simon beckoned to his partners James and John, the sons of Zebedee, who were in another ship. They came and both ships were so filled that they began to sink.

"Depart from me," Simon exclaimed, "for I am a sinful man, O Lord." "Fear not; henceforth thou shalt catch men," Jesus answered. When they had brought their ships to land, they forsook all and followed him.

Before long Jesus was back in Capernaum. When the people discovered where he was stopping, they gathered about the house. A man sick with the palsy was carried by his friends. Since they could not get near Jesus because of the crowd, they went upon the roof, opened it, and let him down, bed and

all, into the midst before Jesus. He, noting their faith, said
to the man, "Son, thy sins be forgiven thee."

Observing that the scribes questioned his right to forgive
sins, Jesus exclaimed: "Why reason ye these things in your
hearts? Whether is it easier to say to the sick of the palsy,
Thy sins be forgiven thee; or to say, Arise and take up thy bed
and walk? But that ye may know that the Son of man hath
power on earth to forgive sins . . . I say unto thee, Arise
and take up thy bed and go thy way into thine house." The
man stood up and strode forth before them all. They were
amazed and glorified God, saying, "We never saw it on this
fashion."

In Capernaum a centurion appealed to Jesus, "Lord, my
servant lieth at home sick of the palsy, grievously tormented."
"I will come and heal him," responded Jesus. "Lord, I am
not worthy that thou shouldest come under my roof," answered the centurion, "but speak the word only and my servant shall be healed. For I am a man under authority, having
soldiers under me. And I say to this man, Go, and he goeth;
and to another, Come, and he cometh; and to my servant,
Do this, and he doeth it."

To those who followed, Jesus declared: "I have not found
so great faith, no, not in Israel." Turning to the centurion
he added, "Go thy way; and as thou hast believed, so be it
done unto thee." The servant was healed in the same hour.


## By Sea of Tiberias, Matt. 8; Mark 9; Luke 6

Such crowds gathered about that Jesus decided to cross to
the other side of the Tiberias. His disciples followed him
into the ship and they launched forth. A storm sprang up
directly, which covered the boat with waves. He was asleep
in the hinder part on a pillow. Awaking him they cried,
"Master, carest thou not that we perish?" Whereupon he
arose, rebuked the wind, and said to the sea, "Peace, be still."
The storm ceased and there was a great calm. "Why are ye

so fearful?" he asked, "how is it that ye have no faith?" The men marveled, exclaiming, "What manner of man is this, that even the wind and the sea obey him!"

Coming to the opposite shore in the country of the Gadarenes, Jesus was met by a man "with an unclean spirit, who had his dwelling among the tombs; and no man could bind him, no, not with chains." He cried with a loud voice, "What have I to do with thee, Jesus, thou Son of the most high God? I adjure thee by God that thou torment me not." For Jesus had said, "Come out of the man, thou unclean spirit . . . What is thy name?" He answered, "My name is Legion, for we are many."

Nearby was a herd of swine feeding. The devils requested that they might go into them. Jesus gave them leave; and the unclean spirits went out and entered the swine, and the herd ran violently down a steep place into the sea. The swineherds at once spread the news and soon the people of the neighborhood began to gather. When they learned the fate of the swine, and found the man sitting and clothed and in his right mind, they were afraid and entreated Jesus to depart from their coasts. As Jesus got into the boat to recross the water, the man asked to go along; but Jesus said to him, "Go home to thy friends and tell them how great things the Lord hath done for thee."

The people were all waiting for Jesus when he got back to his own side of the sea and gladly received him. Leaving them, after a time, and walking along the shore, he met Matthew, who sat at the receipt of custom. "Follow me," he said. Matthew did so; and prepared him a great feast in his own house.

A large company of publicans sat down with them. "Why eateth your master with publicans and sinners?" asked the Pharisees of the disciples. When Jesus heard their questioning he said to them: "They that be whole need not a physician, but they that are sick. But go ye and learn what this meaneth, I will have mercy and not sacrifice, for I am not come to call the righteous but sinners to repentance."

Then came the disciples of John, asking, "Why do we and

the Pharisees fast oft but thy disciples fast not?" Jesus an
swered: "Can the children of the bridechamber mourn as long
as the bridegroom is with them? But the days will come
when the bridegroom shall be taken from them, and then
shall they fast."

As he went through the cornfields one sabbath "his disci
ples plucked the ears of corn and did eat, rubbing them in
their hands." Certain of the Pharisees asked, "Why do ye
that which is not lawful to do on the sabbath days?" Jesus
answering said: "Have ye not read so much as this, what
David did when himself was an hungered and they which
were with him, how he went into the house of God and did
take and eat the shewbread, and gave also to them that were
with him, which it is not lawful to eat but for the priests
alone?" Then he added, "The Son of man is Lord also of
the sabbath."

On another sabbath, when he entered the synagogue to
teach, he observed a man in the congregation whose right
hand was withered. The scribes and Pharisees watched to
see if he would heal on the sabbath, that "they might find an
accusation against him." Knowing their thoughts, Jesus said
to the man, "Rise up and stand forth in the midst." He did
so. Then Jesus asked them, "Is it lawful on the sabbath days
to do good or to do evil? to save life or to destroy it?" And
looking round about upon them all, he said to the man,
"Stretch forth thy hand." The man obeyed and his hand
was restored whole as the other. Then were they filled with
madness and consulted with one another how they might
destroy Jesus.


## Sermon on the Mount, Matt. 5-7

In those days it came to pass that he went out into a
mountain and continued all night in prayer. When it was
day he called his disciples; and of them he chose twelve and
named them apostles: Simon, also called Peter; Andrew his
brother; James and John, sons of Zebedee; Philip and Bar-

holomew, the latter probably also known as Nathanael; Matthew the publican; Thomas the twin; James the son of Alpheus; Simon the Zealot; Judas the brother of James; and Judas Iscariot.

Jesus then taught them the Beatitudes:

> Blessed are the poor in spirit; for theirs is the king-
> dom of heaven.
> Blessed are they that mourn; for they shall be com-
> forted.
> Blessed are the meek; for they shall inherit the earth.
> Blessed are they which do hunger and thirst after
> righteousness; for they shall be filled.
> Blessed are the merciful; for they shall obtain mercy.
> Blessed are the pure in heart; for they shall see God.
> Blessed are the peacemakers; for they shall be called
> the children of God.
> Blessed are they which are persecuted for righteous-
> ness' sake; for theirs is the kingdom of heaven.
> Blessed are ye when men shall revile you and per-
> secute you, and shall say all manner of evil
> against you falsely for my sake. Rejoice and
> be exceeding glad, for great is your reward in
> heaven: for so persecuted they the prophets
> which were before you.

Continuing his discourse, which has come to be known as The Sermon on the Mount, he instructed them:

"Ye have heard that it hath been said, An eye for an eye and a tooth for a tooth; but I say unto you that ye resist not evil, but whosoever shall smite thee on thy right cheek turn to him the other also. And if any man will sue thee at the law, and take away thy coat, let him have thy cloak also. And whosoever shall compel thee to go a mile, go with him twain. Give to him that asketh thee, and from him that would borrow of thee turn not thou away.

"Ye have heard that it hath been said, Thou shalt love thy neighbor and hate thine enemy. But I say unto you, Love

your enemies, bless them that curse you, do good to them tha
hate you, and pray for them which despitefully use you an
persecute you; that ye may be the children of your Fathe
which is in heaven. For he maketh his sun to rise on the evi
and on the good, and sendeth rain on the just and on the un
just. For if ye love them which love you, what reward have
ye? do not even the publicans the same? And if ye salute
your brethren only, what do ye more than others? do not even
the publicans so? Be ye therefore perfect, even as your
Father which is in heaven is perfect. . .

"When thou prayest enter into thy closet, and when thou
hast shut thy door, pray to thy Father which is in secret, and
thy Father which seeth in secret shall reward thee openly . . .
For your Father knoweth what things ye have need of before
ye ask him. After this manner therefore pray ye:

> Our Father which art in heaven, hallowed be thy
> name. Thy kingdom come. Thy will be done in
> earth as it is in heaven. Give us this day our daily
> bread. And forgive us our debts as we forgive our
> debtors. And lead us not into temptation but de-
> liver us from evil. For thine is the kingdom and the
> power and the glory forever. Amen.

"Lay not up for yourselves treasures upon earth, where moth
and rust doth corrupt and where thieves break through and
steal, but lay up for yourselves treasures in heaven, where
neither moth nor rust doth corrupt and where thieves do
not break through nor steal, for where your treasure is there
will your heart be also.

"The light of the body is the eye. If therefore thine eye
be single, thy whole body shall be full of light; but if thine
eye be evil, thy whole body shall be full of darkness. If
therefore the light that is in thee be darkness, how great is
that darkness.

"No man can serve two masters; for either he will hate the
one and love the other, or else he will hold to the one and
despise the other. Ye cannot serve God and mammon.

Therefore I say unto you, Take no thought for your life, what ye shall eat or what ye shall drink; nor yet for your body, what ye shall put on. Is not the life more than meat and the body than raiment?

"Behold the fowls of the air; for they sow not, neither do they reap nor gather into barns, yet your heavenly Father feedeth them. Are ye not much better than they?

"Which of you by taking thought can add one cubit unto his stature? And why take ye thought for raiment? Consider the lilies of the field, how they grow; they toil not, neither do they spin, and yet I say unto you that even Solomon in all his glory was not arrayed like one of these. Wherefore if God so clothe the grass of the field which today is and tomorrow is cast into the oven, shall he not much more clothe you, O ye of little faith?

"Therefore take no thought, saying, What shall we eat? or what shall we drink? or wherewithal shall we be clothed? For after all these things do the Gentiles seek. For your heavenly Father knoweth that ye have need of all these things. But seek ye first the kingdom of God, and his righteousness; and all these things shall be added unto you. Take therefore no thought for the morrow, for the morrow shall take thought for the things of itself. Sufficient unto the day is the evil thereof . . .

"Ask, and it shall be given you; seek, and ye shall find; knock, and it shall be opened unto you. For every one that asketh receiveth, and he that seeketh findeth, and to him that knocketh it shall be opened. Or what man is there of you, whom if his son ask bread, will he give him a stone? Or if he ask a fish, will he give him a serpent? If ye then, being evil, know how to give good gifts unto your children, how much more shall your Father which is in heaven give good things to them that ask him?

"Therefore all things whatsoever ye would that men should do to you, do ye even so to them; for this is the law and the prophets . . . Therefore whosoever heareth these sayings of mine, and doeth them, I will liken him unto a wise man which built his house upon a rock. And the rain descended and the

floods came and the winds blew and beat upon that house
and it fell not, for it was founded upon a rock.

"And every one that heareth these sayings of mine, and
doeth them not, shall be likened unto a foolish man which
built his house upon the sand. And the rain descended and
the floods came and the winds blew and beat upon that house
and it fell, and great was the fall of it."

√ *Teachings Tested, Mark 3, 6, Luke 8, Matt. 9*

The multitude so pressed upon Jesus and the disciples that
they could not "so much as eat bread." And when his friends
heard of it, they went out to lay hold of him; for they said,
"He is beside himself." Scribes from Jerusalem declared,
"He hath Beelzebub, and by the prince of the devils casteth
he out devils." "How can Satan cast out Satan?" rejoined
Jesus; "and if a kingdom be divided against itself that kingdom
cannot stand."

Next his mother and his brethren came, and, standing without, called for him. When told of their presence he asked,
"Who is my mother or my brethren?" Stretching forth his
hand toward his disciples, he exclaimed: "Behold my mother
and my brethren! For whosoever shall do the will of my
Father which is in heaven, the same is my brother and sister
and mother."

While Jesus was thus speaking there came a ruler of the
synagogue, named Jairus. "And he fell down at Jesus' feet
and besought him that he would come into his house, for he
had one only daughter about twelve years of age, and she lay
a dying." As Jesus and his disciples followed Jairus, a woman
who had an issue of blood twelve years, and had spent all her
living on physicians, came behind and touched the hem of
his garment; for within herself she said, "If I may but touch
his garment I shall be whole." Turning about Jesus declared,
"Daughter, be of good comfort; thy faith hath made thee
whole." The woman was well from that hour.

Word now came from the ruler's house, "Thy daughter is dead; trouble not the master." Jesus assured them, "Fear not; believe only and she shall be made whole." On reaching the house he permitted no one to go in with him except Peter, James, John, and the parents. They all wept and bewailed. "Weep not; she is not dead but sleepeth," he said. "And they laughed him to scorn, knowing that she was dead." Putting them all out, he took the girl by the hand and called, "Maid, arise." Then "her spirit came again and she arose straightway; and he commanded to give her meat." He charged the astonished parents to tell no one.

Going to his native place he taught in the synagogue on the sabbath. Those who heard him were astonished, asking: "From whence hath this man these things? and what wisdom is this which is given unto him that even such mighty works are wrought by his hands? Is not this the carpenter, the son of Mary, the brother of James and Joses and of Juda and Simon? and are not his sisters here with us?"

They were offended at him. Then he remarked, "A prophet is not without honor, but in his own country and among his own kin and in his own house." He could there do no mighty works, "save that he laid his hands upon a few sick folk and healed them. And he marveled because of their unbelief."

As he went about the villages and cities with the twelve, preaching and showing the glad tidings of the kingdom of God, certain women, who had been healed of evil spirits and infirmities, ministered unto him of their substance. Among them were "Mary called Magdalene, out of whom went seven devils," Joanna, the wife of Herod's steward, and Susanna. This was the first appearance of Mary of Magdala. She and the mother of Jesus and the sister of Lazarus were the three great Marys of the period. Associated from the start with important women supporters, she was not only present at the crucifixion and burial, but was the first to recognize Jesus after the resurrection. Apart from the events here mentioned the Bible makes no reference to her.

## Parables in Galilee, Matt. 13; Luke 8

Afterwards, as Jesus sat by the seaside, such crowds gathered that he went into a ship and sat while the people stood on the shore. Speaking to them in parables, he said: "A sower went forth to sow; and when he sowed, some seeds fell by the wayside, and the fowls came and devoured them up. Some fell upon stony places where they had not much earth, and forthwith they sprang up because they had no deepness of earth; and when the sun was up they were scorched, and because they had no root they withered away. And some fell among thorns, and the thorns sprang up and choked them.

"But other fell into good ground and brought forth fruit, some an hundredfold, some sixtyfold, some thirtyfold. Who hath ears to hear, let him hear." And the disciples came and inquired, "Why speakest thou unto them in parables?" He answered: "Because it is given unto you to know the mysteries of the kingdom of heaven, but to them it is not given. For whosoever hath, to him shall be given, and he shall have more abundance; but whosoever hath not, from him shall be taken away even that he hath."

Another parable he put forth: "The kingdom of heaven is likened unto a man which sowed good seed in his field. But while men slept his enemy came and sowed tares among the wheat and went his way. But when the blade was sprung up and brought forth fruit, then appeared the tares also. So the servants of the householder came and said unto him, Sir, didst not thou sow good seed in thy field? whence then hath it tares? He said unto them, An enemy hath done this.

"The servants said unto him, Wilt thou then that we go and gather them up? But he said, Nay, lest while ye gather up the tares ye root up also the wheat with them. Let both grow together until the harvest; and in the time of harvest I will say to the reapers, Gather ye together first the tares and bind them in bundles to burn them, but gather the wheat into my barn."

*In Jerusalem, John 5*

After this Jesus went up to Jerusalem to a feast. By the sheep market in the city was a pool called, in the Hebrew tongue, Bethesda, having five porches. "In these lay a great multitude of impotent folk, of blind, halt, withered, waiting for the moving of the water. For an angel went down at a certain season into the pool and troubled the water. Whosoever then first after the troubling of the water stepped in was made whole of whatsoever disease he had."

One invalid had been helpless thirty-eight years. When Jesus saw him and knew that he had been infirm a long time, he asked, "Wilt thou be made whole?" "Sir, I have no man, when the water is troubled, to put me into the pool," he replied, "but while I am coming another steppeth down before me." "Rise, take up thy bed and walk," said Jesus. Immediately was the man restored. And on the same day was the sabbath.

As he departed he told the Jews that it was Jesus who had healed him. They, because Jesus had done these things on the sabbath, persecuted and sought to slay him. But Jesus contended, "My Father worketh hitherto and I work." They sought the more to kill him, because he had not only broken the sabbath but claimed that God was his father.

Then declared Jesus: "The Son can do nothing of himself but what he seeth the Father do, for what things soever He doeth these also doeth the Son likewise. For the Father loveth the Son and showeth him all things that himself doeth, and He will show him greater works than these that ye may marvel. For as the Father raiseth up the dead and quickeneth them, even so the Son quickeneth whom he will.

"For the Father judgeth no man but hath committed all judgment unto the Son, that all men should honor the Son even as they honor the Father. He that honoreth not the Son honoreth not the Father which hath sent him . . . He that heareth my word and believeth on Him that sent me hath everlasting life and shall not come into condemnation but is passed from death unto life . . . The hour is coming and now is when the dead shall hear the voice of the Son of God; and they that hear shall live. For as the Father hath life in himself, so hath he given to the Son to have life in himself, and hath given him authority to execute judgment also because he is the Son of man."

## John the Baptist, John 1, 3; Matt. 11, 14

Herod the tetrarch, hearing of the fame of Jesus, remarked to his men, "This is John the Baptist; he is risen from the dead." Because some time before, John had censured Herod for taking his brother's wife Herodias. "It is not lawful for thee to have her," John declared. Therefore Herod laid hold of him and put him in prison.

Learning there of the works of Jesus, John sent two of his disciples to inquire, "Art thou he that should come or do we look for another?" Jesus answered: "Go and show John again those things which ye do hear and see. The blind receive their sight and the lame walk, the lepers are cleansed and the deaf hear, the dead are raised up and the poor have the gospel preached to them."

Turning to the people, as the messengers departed, Jesus said: "All the prophets and the law prophesied until John. And if ye will receive it, this is Elijah which was for to come. He that hath ears to hear let him hear. But whereunto shall I liken this generation? It is like unto children sitting in the markets and calling unto their fellows and saying, We have piped unto you, and ye have not danced; we have mourned unto you, and ye have not lamented. For John came neither eating nor drinking, and they say, He hath a devil. The Son of man came eating and drinking, and they say, Behold a man gluttonous and a winebibber, a friend of publicans and sinners. But wisdom is justified of her children."

Severe as any Essene was John when he exclaimed to the Pharisees and Sadducees who had come to him by the Jordan: "O generation of vipers, who hath warned you to flee from the wrath to come?" But he rose to the pinnacle of magnanimity in joyously announcing to those who would compare him with Jesus: "He must increase but I must decrease."

At the celebration of Herod's birthday the daughter of Herodias charmed him with her dancing. Whereupon he promised, with an oath, to give her whatsoever she desired. Instructed by her mother, she asked for the life of John the Baptist. Herod was sorry, but "for the oath's sake and them which sat with him at meat," he commanded John to be executed.


## In the Northland, Matt. 14, Mark 7, Luke 9, John 6

When Jesus heard of the tragedy he departed by ship to a desert place. There the people came to him from out of the towns. When he saw them he was moved with compassion and healed their sick. But in the evening his disciples said to him: "This is a desert place and the time is now past; send the multitude away that they may go into the villages and buy themselves victuals."

He replied, "They need not depart; give ye them to eat." They answered, "We have here but five loaves and two fishes." "Bring them hither to me," he said. Then he commanded the people to sit down on the grass; and, taking the loaves and fishes "and looking up to heaven, he blessed and brake and gave to his disciples, and the disciples to the multitude. And they did all eat and were filled; and they took up of the fragments that remained twelve baskets full. And they that had eaten were about five thousand men, beside women and children."

Perceiving that they would make him king by force, he sent the people away and constrained his disciples to get into a ship and go before him to the other side. He then went up into a mountain to pray; and when the evening was come he was there alone. But the ship was in the midst of the sea, tossed with waves. In the fourth watch of the night Jesus went to the disciples, walking on the water. When they saw him they were troubled, exclaiming, "It is a spirit!"

"Be of good cheer," he assured them, "it is I, be not afraid." "Lord, if it be thou," Peter answered, "bid me come unto thee." "Come," he replied. Peter, stepping down out of the ship, walked on the water toward Jesus; but when he saw the wind boisterous he was afraid, and, beginning to sink, he cried, "Lord, save me." Jesus stretched forth his hand and caught him, saying, "O thou of little faith, wherefore didst thou doubt?" When they reached the ship the wind ceased; and immediately the ship was at the land whither they went.

Going now to the coasts of Tyre and Sidon, Jesus was met by a Greek woman, a Syrophœnician by nation, whose young daughter had an unclean spirit. She besought Jesus that he would cast the devil forth. But he said to her, "Let the children first be filled, for it is not meet to take the children's bread and to cast it unto the dogs." "Yes, Lord," she answered, "yet the dogs under the table eat of the children's crumbs." "For this saying go thy way," he replied, "the devil is gone out of thy daughter." When she arrived at her house she found the girl well.

Jesus now returned from the Mediterranean country to the shores of Galilee. There multitudes came to him "having with them those that were lame, blind, dumb, maimed, and many others, and cast them down at Jesus' feet; and he healed them. Insomuch that the multitude wondered when they saw the dumb to speak, the maimed to be whole, the lame to walk, and the blind to see; and they glorified the God of Israel."

Feeding the people, who had now been without food for three days, he took ship and proceeded to the coasts of Magdala. The Pharisees and Sadducees asked for a sign from heaven. He answered: "When it is evening ye say, It will be fair weather for the sky is red; and in the morning, It will be foul weather today for the sky is red and lowering. O ye hypocrites, ye can discern the face of the sky, but can ye not discern the signs of the times? There shall be no sign given

this wicked generation but the sign of the prophet Jonah."
He then left.


## The Transfiguration, Matt. 16, Luke 9, Mark 9

Going north into the country about Caesarea Philippi, he
asked his disciples, "Whom do men say that I the Son of man
am?" They answered: "Some say that thou art John the
Baptist; some, Elijah; and others, Jeremiah or one of the
prophets." But he persisted, "Whom say ye that I am?"
Simon Peter answered, "Thou art the Christ, the Son of the
living God." "Blessed art thou, Simon Barjona," replied
Jesus, "for flesh and blood hath not revealed it unto thee, but
my Father which is in heaven."

He added: "Thou art Peter, and upon this rock I will build
my church; and the gates of hell shall not prevail against it."
Then he instructed the disciples to "tell no man that he was
Jesus the Christ." From this time forth he began to show
his disciples that he must go to Jerusalem, suffer many things
of the elders and chief priests and scribes, be killed, and be
raised the third day.

A week afterward Jesus took Peter and John and James
farther north into a high mountain, and was transfigured before them. "The fashion of his countenance was altered and
his raiment was white and glistering. And behold, there
talked with him two men, Moses and Elijah, who appeared in
glory and spoke of his decease which he should accomplish at
Jerusalem. But Peter and they that were with him were
heavy with sleep; and when they were awake, they saw his
glory and the two men that stood with him."

"Master," said Peter, "it is good for us to be here; and let
us make three tabernacles, one for thee and one for Moses
and one for Elijah." While he was speaking a cloud over-
shadowed them, and out of it a voice proclaimed: "This is
my beloved Son; hear him." When the voice ceased Jesus
and his disciples were alone.

The next day, as Jesus came down from the mountain, he
was met by many people.  One of the multitude implored:
"Master, I have brought unto thee my son, which hath a
dumb spirit.  And wheresoever he taketh him, he teareth him
. . . I spake to thy disciples that they should cast him out;
and they could not."

"O faithless generation," reproved Jesus, "how long shall I
be with you? how long shall I suffer you?  Bring him unto
me."  When Jesus saw the boy, straightway the spirit tore
him; and he fell on the ground.  Then Jesus asked the father,
"How long is it ago since this came unto him?"  The father
answered: "Of a child.  And ofttimes it hath cast him into
the fire and into the waters to destroy him; but if thou canst
do any thing, have compassion on us and help us."

"If thou canst believe," assured Jesus, "all things are pos-
sible to him that believeth."  Straightway the father cried
out: "Lord, I believe; help thou mine unbelief."

The people came running together; and when Jesus saw
them, he rebuked the evil spirit, saying: "Thou dumb and
deaf spirit, I charge thee, come out of him and enter no more
into him."  The spirit cried and rent him and came out.

When Jesus entered the house, his disciples asked him pri-
vately, "Why could not we cast him out?"  He replied, "This
kind can come forth by nothing, but by prayer and fasting."

## The Bread of Life, John 6, Luke 9

Now arose a reasoning as to which of them should be greatest.  Perceiving their thought Jesus took a child and set him
by him.  Then he remarked: "Whosoever shall receive this
child in my name receiveth me; and whosoever shall receive
me receiveth Him that sent me; for he that is least among
you all, the same shall be great."

John here reported, "Master, we saw one casting out devils
in thy name, and we forbade him because he followeth not

with us." Jesus replied, "Forbid him not, for he that is not against us is for us."

The Jews murmured, as Jesus discoursed in the synagogue at Capernaum, because he said, "I am the bread which came down from heaven." "Is not this Jesus, the son of Joseph, whose father and mother we know?" they asked. "How is it then that he saith, I came down from heaven."

"No man can come to me," Jesus continued, "except the Father, which hath sent me, draw him; and I will raise him up at the last day. It is written in the prophets, And they shall be all taught of God. Every man therefore that hath heard, and hath learned of the Father, cometh unto me. Not that any man hath seen the Father, save he which is of God, he hath seen the Father.

"He that believeth on me hath everlasting life. I am that bread of life. Your fathers did eat manna in the wilderness, and are dead. This is the bread which cometh down from heaven, that a man may eat thereof and not die." Many therefore of his disciples said, "This is an hard saying; who can hear it?"

"Doth this offend you?" Jesus asked. "What and if ye shall see the Son of man ascend up where he was before? It is the Spirit that quickeneth; the flesh profiteth nothing. The words that I speak unto you, they are spirit and they are life."

## Departure to Jerusalem, Luke 9-17

Jesus now deciding to go to Jerusalem, sent messengers ahead to a village in Samaria to make ready for him. But the Samaritans, when they saw "his face was as though he would go to Jerusalem," would not receive him. Then asked James and John, "Lord, wilt thou that we command fire to come down from heaven and consume them even as Elijah did?" But he turned and rebuked them, saying: "Ye know not what manner of spirit ye are of. For the Son of man is not come to destroy men's lives but to save them." And they went to another village.

As they continued their journey a certain man declared, "Lord, I will follow thee whithersoever thou goest." "Foxes have holes and birds of the air have nests," Jesus answered, "but the Son of man hath not where to lay his head." Another declared, "Lord, I will follow thee, but let me first go bid them farewell which are at home at my house." "No man, having put his hand to the plow, and looking back," Jesus replied, "is fit for the kingdom of God."

As he approached one of the villages he was accosted by ten lepers standing afar off. Lifting up their voices they cried, "Jesus, Master, have mercy on us." "Go show yourselves unto the priests," he directed. As they went their way they were cleansed. And one of them, when he saw that he was healed, turned back and with a loud voice glorified God and fell at Jesus' feet, giving thanks. And he was a Samaritan. Jesus asked: "Were there not ten cleansed? but where are the nine? There are not found that returned to give glory to God, save this stranger."

## The Kingdom of Heaven, Luke 17

When asked by the Pharisees when the kingdom of God should come, he answered: "The kingdom of God cometh not with observation. Neither shall they say, Lo here! or lo there! for behold the kingdom of God is within you." To his disciples he said: "The days will come when ye shall desire to see one of the days of the Son of man, and ye shall not see it. And they shall say to you, See here or see there. Go not after them nor follow them.

"For as the lightning, that lighteneth out of the one part under heaven, shineth unto the other part under heaven, so shall also the Son of man be in his day. But first must he suffer many things and be rejected of this generation.

"And as it was in the days of Noah, so shall it be also in the days of the Son of man. They did eat, they drank, they married wives, they were given in marriage until the day that Noah entered into the ark, and the flood came and destroyed them all.

"Likewise also as it was in the days of Lot. They did eat, they drank, they bought, they sold, they planted, they builded; but the same day that Lot went out of Sodom it rained fire and brimstone from heaven and destroyed them all. Even thus shall it be in the day when the Son of man is revealed. In that day he which shall be upon the housetop, and his stuff in the house, let him not come down to take it away; and he that is in the field, let him likewise not return back. Remember Lot's wife.

"Whosoever shall seek to save his life shall lose it; and whosoever shall lose his life shall preserve it. I tell you in that night there shall be two men in one bed; the one shall be taken and the other shall be left. Two women shall be grinding together; the one shall be taken and the other left. . .

"Two men went up into the temple to pray, the one a Pharisee and the other a publican. The Pharisee stood and prayed thus with himself: God, I thank thee, that I am not as other men are—extortioners, unjust, or even as this publican. I fast twice in the week; I give tithes of all that I possess. And the publican, standing afar off, would not lift up so much as his eyes unto heaven, but smote upon his breast, saying, God be merciful to me a sinner. I tell you, this man went down to his house justified rather than the other."

## The Seventy Disciples, Luke 10

And it came to pass that the Lord appointed seventy other disciples, and sent them "two and two before his face into every city and place whither he himself would come." He said to them: "The harvest truly is great but the laborers are few; pray ye therefore the Lord of the harvest that he would send forth laborers into his harvest . . . Salute no man by the

way . . . Heal the sick . . . He that heareth you heareth me
and he that despiseth you despiseth me; and he that despisetl
me despiseth Him that sent me."

The seventy returned with joy, saying, "Lord, even th
devils are subject unto us through thy name." He answered
"I beheld Satan as lightning fall from heaven.   Behold, I giv
unto you power to tread on serpents and scorpions, and ove
all the power of the enemy; and nothing shall by any mean
hurt you.   Notwithstanding in this rejoice not, that the spirit
are subject unto you, but rather rejoice because your name
are written in heaven."

Jesus was elated in that hour and said: "I thank thee, C
Father, Lord of heaven and earth, that thou hast hid thes
things from the wise and prudent and hast revealed them unt
babes."   Turning to his disciples, he added: "Blessed are th
eyes which see the things that ye see; for I tell you that many
prophets and kings have desired to see those things which ye
see, and have not seen them, and to hear those things which
ye hear, and have not heard them."


## The Good Samaritan, Luke 10

Then a lawyer stood up to ask, "Master, what shall I do to
inherit eternal life?"   "What is written in the law? how read-
est thou?" asked Jesus.   He answered: "Thou shalt love the
Lord thy God with all thy heart and with all thy soul and with
all thy strength and with all thy mind; and thy neighbor as
thyself."   Jesus replied, "Thou hast answered right; this do
and thou shalt live."   But the lawyer, desiring to justify himself, asked, "Who is my neighbor?"   Answering him Jesus
said:

"A certain man went down from Jerusalem to Jericho and
fell among robbers, which stripped him of his raiment and
wounded him and departed, leaving him half dead.   And by
chance there came down a certain priest that way; and when
he saw him he passed by on the other side.   And likewise a

Levite, when he was at the place, came and looked on him and passed by on the other side. But a certain Samaritan, as he journeyed, came where he was; and when he saw him he had compassion on him and went to him and bound up his wounds, pouring in oil and wine, and set him on his own beast and brought him to an inn and took care of him.

"And on the morrow when he departed, he took out two pence and gave them to the host and said unto him, Take care of him, and whatsoever thou spendest more, when I come again, I will repay thee. Which now of these three, thinkest thou, was neighbor unto him that fell among the robbers?" The lawyer replied, "He that showed mercy on him." "Go, and do thou likewise," said Jesus.

As they went it came to pass that Jesus entered a certain village where a woman named Martha received him into her house. Her sister Mary "sat at Jesus' feet and heard his word. But Martha was cumbered about much serving." She therefore came to Jesus and asked: "Lord, dost thou not care that my sister hath left me to serve alone? Bid her therefore that she help me." "Martha, Martha," he answered, "thou art careful and troubled about many things. But one thing is needful; and Mary hath chosen that good part, which shall not be taken away from her."

While discoursing at another place, Jesus was invited by one of the Pharisees to dinner. When they sat down the Pharisee marveled that his guest had not first washed. Jesus rejoined: "Now do ye Pharisees make clean the outside of the cup and the platter, but your inward part is full of ravening and wickedness . . . Woe unto you, Pharisees! For ye tithe mint and rue and all manner of herbs, and pass over judgment and the love of God. These ought ye to have done and not to leave the other undone."

Then said a lawyer to him, "Master, thus saying thou reproachest us also." Jesus replied: "Woe unto you also, ye lawyers! For ye lade men with burdens grievous to be borne and ye yourselves touch not the burdens with one of your fingers . . . Ye build the sepulchers of the prophets and your fathers killed them . . . Ye have taken away the key of

knowledge. Ye entered not in yourselves, and them that were
entering in ye hindered."


## Parables in Judea, Luke 12-15, Matt. 22

Jesus spoke a parable of a rich man whose ground brought
forth plentifully, and who thought within himself: "What
shall I do because I have no room where to bestow my fruits?
. . . I will pull down my barns and build greater; and there
will I bestow all my fruits and my goods. And I will say to
my soul, Soul, thou hast much goods laid up for many years;
take thine ease, eat, drink, and be merry." But God said:
"Thou fool, this night thy soul shall be required of thee; then
whose shall those things be which thou hast provided?"

Then drew near publicans and sinners to hear Jesus. But
the scribes and Pharisees murmured, "This man receiveth sinners and eateth with them." So Jesus spoke this parable:
"What man of you, having an hundred sheep, if he lose one
of them doth not leave the ninety and nine in the wilderness,
and go after that which is lost until he find it? And when he
hath found it, he layeth it on his shoulders, rejoicing. And
when he cometh home, he calleth together his friends and
neighbors, saying unto them, Rejoice with me, for I have
found my sheep which was lost. I say unto you that likewise
joy shall be in heaven over one sinner that repenteth, more
than over ninety and nine just persons which need no repentance."

Again he said: "Either what woman, having ten pieces of
silver, if she lose one piece, doth not light a candle and sweep
the house and seek diligently till she find it? And when she
hath found it she calleth her friends and her neighbors together, saying, Rejoice with me for I have found the piece
which I had lost. Likewise, I say unto you, there is joy in the
presence of the angels of God over one sinner that repenteth."

Then he spoke a parable of a man who had two sons. The

younger persuaded the father to give him his inheritance. A few days later he departed to a far country, where he wasted his substance in riotous living. Coming to himself he resolved, in his distress, to return home. When yet afar off his father ran to embrace him. "Father," he confessed, "I have sinned against heaven and before thee, and am no more worthy to be called thy son." But the father brought him the best robe, put a ring on his hand and shoes on his feet, and said, "Let us eat and be merry."

The elder son, coming in from the field, was angry when he learned what was taking place and would not enter the house. In answer to the parent's entreaty he said: "Lo, these many years do I serve thee, neither transgressed I at any time thy commandment, and yet thou never gavest me a kid that I might make merry with my friends." "Son," replied the father, "thou art ever with me and all that I have is thine. It was meet that we should make merry and be glad; for this thy brother was dead and is alive again, and was lost and is found."

Pharisees desiring to entangle Jesus asked, "Is it lawful to give tribute unto Caesar?" Perceiving their purpose he replied, "Why tempt ye me, ye hypocrites? Show me the tribute money." They brought him a penny. "Whose is this image and superscription?" he asked. "Caesar's," they answered. Then said he, "Render therefore unto Caesar the things which are Caesar's, and unto God the things that are God's."

## Immortality, Luke 16, John 8, Matt. 22

One day while teaching, Jesus told of a rich man who was clothed in fine raiment and fared sumptuously, and of a beggar named Lazarus who lay at the gate to be fed with the crumbs from the rich man's table. And it came to pass that the beggar died and was carried by the angels into Abraham's bosom. The rich man also died and was buried; and in hell he lifted up his eyes, being in torment, and saw Abraham afar off and Lazarus in his bosom.

He cried: "Father Abraham, have mercy on me and send Lazarus that he may dip the tip of his finger in water and cool my tongue." Abraham replied: "Son, remember that thou in thy lifetime receivedst thy good things, and likewise Lazarus evil things, but now he is comforted and thou art tormented. And beside all this, between us and you there is a great gulf fixed; so that they which would pass from hence to you cannot, neither can they pass to us that would come from thence."

Then prayed the rich man: "Father, that thou wouldest send him to my father's house, for I have five brethren, that he may testify unto them lest they also come into this place of torment." Abraham answered, "They have Moses and the prophets; let them hear them." And he said, "Nay, father Abraham, but if one went unto them from the dead they will repent." "If they hear not Moses and the prophets, neither will they be persuaded though one rose from the dead," replied Abraham.

Sadducees, who believed not in the resurrection, came with the question: "Master, Moses said, If a man die, having no children, his brother shall marry his wife and raise up seed unto his brother. Now there were with us seven brethren. And the first, when he had married a wife, deceased and, having no issue, left his wife unto his brother. Likewise the second and also the third unto the seventh. And last of all the woman died also. Therefore in the resurrection whose wife shall she be of the seven? for they all had her."

Jesus answered: "Ye do err, not knowing the Scriptures nor the power of God. For in the resurrection they neither marry nor are given in marriage, but are as the angels of God in heaven. But as touching the resurrection of the dead, have ye not read that which was spoken unto you by God, saying, I am the God of Abraham and the God of Isaac and the God of Jacob? God is not the God of the dead but of the living."

Speaking with those Jews who believed on him, Jesus remarked: "If ye continue in my word then are ye my disciples indeed; and ye shall know the truth, and the truth shall make you free." They answered: "We be Abraham's seed and were never in bondage to any man." Jesus rejoined: "I know that ye are Abraham's seed, but ye seek to kill me because my word hath no place in you. I speak that which I have seen with my Father, and ye do that which ye have seen with your father." Then said they, "We have one Father, even God." "Ye are of your father the devil," Jesus replied, "and the lusts of your father ye will do. He was a murderer from the beginning, and abode not in the truth because there is no truth in him. When he speaketh a lie he speaketh of his own, for he is a liar and the father of it."

The Jews answered, "Say we not well that thou art a Samaritan and hast a devil?" "I have not a devil," Jesus protested, "but I honor my Father and ye do dishonor me . . . Verily, verily, I say unto you, If a man keep my saying he shall never see death." They replied: "Now we know that thou hast a devil. Abraham is dead and the prophets, and thou sayest, If a man keep my saying he shall never taste of death. Art thou greater than our father Abraham . . . Whom makest thou thyself?"

"Your father Abraham," asserted Jesus, "rejoiced to see my day; and he saw it and was glad." They argued, "Thou art not yet fifty years old, and hast thou seen Abraham?" He answered, "Verily, verily, I say unto you, Before Abraham was, I am." Then they took up "stones to cast at him, but Jesus hid himself and went out of the temple, going through the midst of them and so passed by."


## Around Jericho, Luke 13, 18, 19; John 9

As Jesus approached Jericho a blind man sat by the wayside begging. Hearing the crowd pass by he asked what it meant. He was told that Jesus of Nazareth was going by. He cried, "Jesus, thou son of David, have mercy on me." Those who went ahead rebuked him, but he cried the more, "Thou son

of David, have mercy on me." Jesus stopped and directed
the man to be brought to him; and when he came near he
asked him, "What wilt thou that I shall do unto thee?" He
answered, "Lord, that I may receive my sight." "Receive thy
sight," said Jesus, "thy faith hath saved thee." And immediately the man's vision was restored and he followed Jesus
glorifying God; and all the people, when they saw it, gave
praise to God.

Jesus now entered and passed through Jericho. Zacchaeus,
who was the chief among the publicans, tried to see Jesus but
could not for the press because he was small of stature. He
therefore ran before and climbed up into a sycamore tree.
When Jesus came to the place he looked up and called,
"Zacchaeus, make haste and come down, for today I must
abide at thy house."

He hurried down and Jesus received him joyfully. But
when the people saw it they all murmured because he had
become the guest of a sinner. Zacchaeus stood and avowed:
"Lord, the half of my goods I give to the poor; and if I have
taken any thing from any man by false accusation, I restore
him fourfold." "This day is salvation come to this house,"
announced Jesus, "forsomuch as he also is a son of Abraham."

Journeying on the sabbath day, Jesus saw a man blind from
birth. His disciples asked, "Master, who did sin, this man or
his parents, that he was born blind?" "Neither hath this
man sinned nor his parents," he answered, "but that the works
of God should be made manifest in him." Jesus then
anointed the eyes of the man with clay and directed him to
go wash in the pool of Siloam. "He went his way therefore
and washed, and came seeing."

Pharisees asked the man how he had been cured. When
he told them they said, "This man is not of God because he
keepeth not the sabbath day." But others asked, "How can
a man that is a sinner do such miracles?" Calling the man
again the Jews said to him, "Give God the praise; we know
that this man is a sinner." He replied: "Whether he be a
sinner or no, I know not; one thing I know, that, whereas I
was blind, now I see."

There came other Pharisees warning Jesus, "Get thee out and depart hence, for Herod will kill thee." "Go ye and tell that fox," deliberated Jesus, "behold, I cast out devils and I do cures today and tomorrow, and the third day I shall be perfected. Nevertheless I must walk today and tomorrow and the day following, for it cannot be that a prophet perish out of Jerusalem.

"O Jerusalem, Jerusalem, which killest the prophets and stonest them that are sent unto thee, how often would I have gathered thy children together as a hen doth gather her brood under her wings, and ye would not! Behold, your house is left unto you desolate; and verily I say unto you, Ye shall not see me until the time come when ye shall say, Blessed is he that cometh in the name of the Lord."

## In Bethany and Jerusalem, John 10-12

It was now winter in Jerusalem and the feast of the dedication was being observed. As Jesus walked in the temple in Solomon's porch, the Jews came about to ask: "How long dost thou make us to doubt? If thou be the Christ, tell us plainly." "I told you and ye believed not," he insisted, "the works that I do in my Father's name, they bear witness of me. But ye believe not, because ye are not of my sheep, as I said unto you. My sheep hear my voice and I know them and they follow me. And I give unto them eternal life; and they shall never perish, neither shall any man pluck them out of my hand.

"My Father, which gave them me, is greater than all; and no man is able to pluck them out of my Father's hand. I and my Father are one." Then the Jews took up stones to cast at him. He answered: "Many good works have I showed you from my Father, for which of those works do ye stone me?" They replied: "For a good work we stone thee not, but for blasphemy, and because that thou, being a man, makest thyself God."

He rejoined: "Is it not written in your law, I said, Ye are gods? If he called them gods unto whom the word of God came, and the Scripture cannot be broken, say ye of him whom the Father hath sanctified and sent into the world, Thou blasphemest, because I said, I am the Son of God? If I do not the works of my Father, believe me not. But if I do, though ye believe not me, believe the works, that ye may know and believe that the Father is in me and I in him."

## Raising of Lazarus, John 11

Therefore they sought again to take him; but he escaped out of their hand, and went away beyond Jordan and abode where John at first baptized. Word came to him there from Mary and Martha that their brother Lazarus of Bethany, a town close to Jerusalem, was sick. After two days he said to his disciples, "Our friend Lazarus sleepeth; but I go that I may awake him." They replied, "Lord, if he sleep he shall do well." Then said Jesus plainly, "Lazarus is dead."

As soon as Martha heard that Jesus was coming she went to meet him, but Mary sat still in the house. Then said Martha to him: "Lord, if thou hadst been here, my brother had not died. But I know that even now whatsoever thou wilt ask of God God will give it thee." "Thy brother shall rise again," he said. "I know that he shall rise again in the resurrection at the last day," she replied. "I am the resurrection and the life," he answered, "he that believeth in me, though he were dead, yet shall he live; and whosoever liveth and believeth in me shall never die. Believest thou this?" "Yea, Lord," she said, "I believe that thou art the Christ, the Son of God, which should come into the world."

After that she summoned her sister Mary, saying, "The Master is come and calleth for thee." Mary arose and went quickly. Falling down at Jesus' feet, she cried, "Lord, if thou hadst been here my brother had not died." When Jesus saw her weeping, and the people who came with her also weeping,

he groaned in the spirit and was troubled. "Where have ye
laid him?" he asked. "Lord, come and see," they answered.
"Jesus wept." Then said the people, "Behold how he loved
him!" And some of them asked, "Could not this man,
which opened the eyes of the blind, have caused that even this
man should not have died?"

Jesus now came to the grave. It was a cave and a stone lay
upon it. "Take ye away the stone," he said. "He hath been
dead four days," interposed Martha. "Said I not unto thee
that if thou wouldest believe, thou shouldest see the glory of
God?" responded Jesus. They removed the stone; and Jesus
lifted up his eyes and said: "Father, I thank thee that thou
hast heard me; and I knew that thou hearest me always, but
because of the people which stand by I said it that they may
believe that thou hast sent me." Then he cried in a loud
voice, "Lazarus, come forth."

Thereupon he that was dead came forth, bound hand and
foot with graveclothes; and his face was bound about with a
napkin. "Loose him and let him go," said Jesus.

## Lazarus' Sister Anoints Jesus, John 12; Matt. 26; Mark 14

Many of the Jews now believed in Jesus, but others proceeded to the Pharisees to tell them what things he had done.
From that day forth, accordingly, "they took counsel together
for to put him to death. Jesus therefore walked no more
openly among the Jews; but went thence unto a country near
to the wilderness into a city called Ephraim, and there continued with his disciples."

A week before the passover, however, Jesus returned to
Bethany. There Simon the leper made him a supper.
Lazarus was one of them that sat at the table. His sister
Martha served. Then took their sister Mary "a pound of
ointment of spikenard, very costly, and anointed the feet of
Jesus, and wiped his feet with her hair; and the house was
filled with the odor of the ointment." "Why was not this

ointment sold for three hundred pence and given to the poor?" protested Judas Iscariot. "Let her alone," rejoined Jesus. "Against the day of my burying hath she kept this; for the poor always ye have with you, but me ye have not always."

The next day many people, when they learned Jesus was coming to Jerusalem, took branches of palm trees and went forth to meet him, crying: "Hosanna, blessed is the King of Israel that cometh in the name of the Lord." Therefore the Pharisees reasoned among themselves, "Perceive ye how ye prevail nothing? Behold, the world is gone after him."

Certain Greeks who had come up to worship at the feast asked to see Jesus. He answered: "The hour is come that the Son of man should be glorified. Verily, verily, I say unto you, Except a corn of wheat fall into the ground and die, it abideth alone; but if it die, it bringeth forth much fruit. He that loveth his life shall lose it; and he that hateth his life in this world shall keep it unto life eternal."

## Last Supper, Mark 14; John 13, 14, 17

The first day of unleavened bread the disciples asked Jesus where they should eat the passover. He instructed two of them: "Go ye into the city, and there shall meet you a man bearing a pitcher of water. Follow him. And wheresoever he shall go in, say ye to the goodman of the house, The master saith, Where is the guestchamber where I shall eat the passover with my disciples? And he will show you a large upper room furnished and prepared. There make ready for us." They did as directed, and in the evening he came with the twelve.

During the supper he remarked, "One of you shall betray me." They began to be sorrowful and looked at one another doubting of whom he spoke. John, who was close to him, asked, "Who is it?" He answered, "He it is to whom I shall give a sop when I have dipped it." When he had dipped the sop, he turned to Judas Iscariot, and gave it to him.

As they ate he took bread, blessed and broke it, and gave to them, saying, "Take, eat; this is my body." And he took the cup, and when he had given thanks, gave it to them; and they all drank of it. "This is my blood of the new testament," he explained, "which is shed for many. Verily I say unto you, I will drink no more of the fruit of the vine until that day that I drink it new in the kingdom of God."

Judas having gone out, Jesus proceeded: "Little children, yet a little while I am with you . . . A new commandment I give unto you, That ye love one another; as I have loved you, that ye also love one another. By this shall all men know that ye are my disciples, if ye have love one to another . . . Greater love hath no man than this, that a man lay down his life for his friends . . .

"Let not your heart be troubled; ye believe in God, believe also in me. In my Father's house are many mansions. If it were not so, I would have told you. I go to prepare a place for you. And if I go and prepare a place for you, I will come again and receive you unto myself, that where I am there ye may be also. And whither I go ye know, and the way ye know."

"Lord," interrupted Thomas, "we know not whither thou goest, and how can we know the way?" "I am the way, the truth, and the life," answered Jesus, "no man cometh unto the Father but by me. If ye had known me, ye should have known my Father also; and henceforth ye know him and have seen him."

"Lord," insisted Philip, "show us the Father and it sufficeth us." "Have I been so long time with you," responded Jesus, "and yet hast thou not known me, Philip? He that hath seen me hath seen the Father; and how sayest thou then, Show us the Father? Believest thou not that I am in the Father and the Father in me? The words that I speak unto you I speak not of myself; but the Father that dwelleth in me he doeth the works.

"Believe me that I am in the Father, and the Father in me; or else believe me for the very works' sake. Verily, verily, I say unto you, He that believeth on me the works that I do shall he do also, and greater works than these shall he do, because I go unto my Father. And whatsoever ye shall ask in my name, that will I do, that the Father may be glorified in the Son. If ye shall ask anything in my name, I will do it.

"If ye love me keep my commandments. And I will pray the Father, and he shall give you another Comforter, that he may abide with you forever; even the Spirit of truth, whom the world cannot receive, because it seeth him not, neither knoweth him; but ye know him, for he dwelleth with you and shall be in you. I will not leave you comfortless; I will come to you. Yet a little while and the world seeth me no more; but ye see me. Because I live, ye shall live also.

"These things have I spoken unto you, being yet present with you. But the Comforter, which is the Holy Ghost, whom the Father will send in my name, he shall teach you all things, and bring all things to your remembrance, whatsoever I have said unto you. Peace I leave with you, my peace I give unto you; not as the world giveth, give I unto you. Let not your heart be troubled, neither let it be afraid . . .

"Father, the hour is come; glorify thy Son that thy Son also may glorify thee: as thou hast given him power over all flesh, that he should give eternal life to as many as thou hast given him. And this is life eternal, that they might know thee the only true God, and Jesus Christ whom thou hast sent. I have glorified thee on the earth; I have finished the work which thou gavest me to do. And now, O Father, glorify thou me with thine own self with the glory which I had with thee before the world was.

"I have manifested thy name unto the men which thou gavest me . . . I pray not that thou shouldest take them out of the world, but that thou shouldest keep them from the evil. They are not of the world, even as I am not of the world. Sanctify them through thy truth: thy word is truth . . . Father, I will that they also, whom thou hast given me, be with me where I am, that they may behold my glory which thou hast given me; for thou lovedst me before the foundation of the world."

## Seizure in Garden, John 18, Luke 22

Supper over they went down the hill, crossed the Brook Kedron, and entered the garden of Gethsemane at the foot of the Mount of Olives. There Jesus withdrew a stone's cast from the disciples and prayed: "Father, if thou be willing, remove this cup from me; nevertheless not my will but thine be done." Then, "being in an agony, he prayed more earnestly; and his sweat was as it were great drops of blood falling down to the ground." When he arose and came to his disciples, he found them sleeping. "Why sleep ye?" he exclaimed, "rise and pray, lest ye enter into temptation."

At this moment came a band of men and officers from the chief priests and Pharisees, with torches and weapons, Judas leading the way. When the disciples saw what would follow, they asked, "Lord, shall we smite with the sword?" And Peter drew his sword and cut off the right ear of the servant of the high priest. "Suffer ye thus far," interceded Jesus; and he touched the ear and healed it.

Then they seized Jesus and took him to the house of the high priest. Those who held him, blindfolded him and struck him in the face, saying, "Prophesy, who is it that smote thee?" As soon as it was day the elders, scribes, and chief priests came together and led Jesus into their council. They asked, "Art thou the Christ?" He answered: "If I tell you ye will not believe; and if I also ask you ye will not answer me nor let me go. Hereafter shall the Son of man sit on the right hand of the power of God." "Art thou then the Son of God?" they asked. "Ye say that I am," he replied. Then said they, "What need we any further witness? For we ourselves have heard of his own mouth."

## Before Pilate, John 19, Luke 23

Then they all rose up and led him to Pilate the governor. "We found this fellow perverting the nation and forbidding to give tribute to Caesar, saying that he himself is Christ a King," they charged. Pilate asked, "Art thou the King of the Jews?" "Thou sayest that I am a king," Jesus answered. "To this end was I born, and for this cause came I into the world, that I should bear witness unto the truth. Every one that is of the truth heareth my voice." "What is truth?" asked Pilate. Then to the Jews he said: "I find in him no fault at all. But ye have a custom that I should release unto you one at the passover; will ye therefore that I release unto you the King of the Jews?" They all cried, "Not this man, but Barabbas." Now Barabbas was a robber who lay "bound with them that had made insurrection."

Herod, tetrarch of Galilee, was in Jerusalem at the time. Pilate, now learning that Jesus was a Galilean and therefore under Herod's jurisdiction, sent Jesus to him. Herod was delighted, for he had long desired to see Jesus and witness some miracle by him. But Jesus would answer him not a word. Whereupon Herod with his men of war set him at naught, arrayed him in a gorgeous robe, and sent him again to Pilate.

Pilate then took Jesus and scourged him. The soldiers platted a crown of thorns and put it on his head, saying, "Hail, King of the Jews!" Again Pilate went out and said to the accusers, "Behold, I bring him forth to you that ye may know that I find no fault in him." Then came Jesus, wearing the crown of thorns and the purple robe; and Pilate said to them, "Behold the man." "Crucify him, crucify him!" they shouted. "Take ye him and crucify him," Pilate yielded, "for I find no fault in him."

## The Crucifixion, John 19, Mark 15, Luke 23

Reentering the judgment hall Pilate asked Jesus, "Whence art thou?" Jesus made no answer. "Speakest thou not unto me?" urged Pilate. "Knowest thou not that I have power to crucify thee, and have power to release thee?" "Thou couldest have no power at all against me, except it were given thee from above," replied Jesus.

Thenceforth Pilate sought to release him, but the Jews cried: "If thou let this man go, thou art not Caesar's friend; whosoever maketh himself a king speaketh against Caesar." Pilate then delivered Jesus to them to be crucified, and they led him away to a place called Golgotha, that is, the place of a skull. There they crucified him with a robber on either side. "Father, forgive them," said Jesus, "for they know not what they do."

One of the robbers railed at Jesus, "If thou be Christ save thyself and us." But the other rebuked him: "Dost not thou fear God, seeing thou art in the same condemnation? And we indeed justly, for we receive the due reward of our deeds; but this man hath done nothing amiss." "Jesus," he implored, "remember me when thou comest into thy kingdom." "Today," answered Jesus, "shalt thou be with me in paradise."

Standing by the cross were his mother, her sister, Mary the wife of Cleophas, and Mary Magdalene. When Jesus saw his mother, and John nearby, he said to her, "Behold thy son!" To John he said, "Behold thy mother!" From that hour the disciple took her into his own home.

After this, Jesus knowing that all things were accomplished, said, "I thirst." A sponge filled with vinegar was put to his mouth. "It is finished," he breathed. He bowed his head and gave up the ghost.

The centurion standing by exclaimed, "Certainly this was a righteous man." Joseph of Arimathea, a disciple of Jesus, having secretly gained permission from Pilate, came and took the body. There came also Nicodemus, who brought a mixture of myrrh and aloes. They wound the body in linen clothes with the spices "as the manner of the Jews is to bury" and placed it in a new sepulcher in the garden close by. This was Friday evening.

## The Resurrection, Mark 16, John 20, Luke 24

The next day, Saturday, was the sabbath. Sunday morning, while it was still dark, Mary Magdalene and other women came to the tomb with spices to anoint him. They found the stone rolled away from the door of the sepulcher. Entering, they saw a young man clothed in a long white garment, who said to them: "Be not affrighted. Ye seek Jesus of Nazareth, which was crucified. He is risen; he is not here. Behold the place where they laid him." They went out quickly and fled, for they trembled and were amazed.

Mary Magdalene ran to Peter and John, exclaiming, "They have taken away the Lord out of the sepulcher, and we know not where they have laid him!" Running to the sepulcher, and stepping inside, they saw the linen clothes lying on the floor, and the napkin, which had been about his head, folded up by itself. Then they returned to their homes.

But Mary Magdalene remained. Glancing into the sepulcher, she saw two angels in white sitting. "Why weepest thou?" they asked. "Because they have taken away my Lord, and I know not where they have laid him," she answered. Then, turning about, she saw Jesus standing but knew not that it was he. "Why weepest thou?" Jesus asked, "whom seekest thou?" She, taking him for the gardener, replied: "Sir, if thou have borne him hence, tell me where thou hast laid him, and I will take him away."

"Mary!" he said. She turned and cried, "Rabboni!" which is to say, Teacher. "Touch me not," he cautioned, "for I am not yet ascended to my Father; but go to my brethren and say unto them, I ascend unto my Father, and your Father; and to my God, and your God." She went then and told the disciples what she had seen and heard.

That same day two of the disciples went to Emmaus, a village seven or eight miles from Jerusalem. On the way Jesus drew near and went with them, "but their eyes were holden that they should not know him." He asked them what they were reasoning about, and they told him of the

happenings of the past few days. He said to them: "O foolish men, and slow of heart to believe all that the prophets
have spoken! Ought not Christ to have suffered these things
and to enter into his glory?"

Then, beginning with Moses and the prophets, he expounded to them in all the Scriptures the things concerning
himself. As they drew nigh their destination, he made as
though he would go farther. But they invited him to tarry
with them, for the day was far spent. While they sat at meat
he broke bread and blessed it and gave to them. "And their
eyes were opened, and they knew him; and he vanished out
of their sight." Then said they to one another: "Did not our
heart burn within us while he talked with us by the way, and
while he opened to us the Scriptures?"

The same hour the two rose up and returned to Jerusalem,
where they found the eleven, who exclaimed: "The Lord is
risen indeed and hath appeared to Simon!" Then the two
related what had happened to them on their journey to Emmaus.

While they were thus speaking Jesus stood in their midst
and said to them, "Peace be unto you." But they were ter-
rified, supposing that they had seen a spirit. "Why are ye
troubled?" he asked. "Behold my hands and my feet, that
it is I myself. Handle me and see, for a spirit hath not flesh
and bones as ye see me have." And while they wondered and
believed not for joy, he asked, "Have ye here any meat?"
They gave him a piece of a broiled fish and of a honeycomb.
"He took it and did eat before them . . . Then opened he
their understanding, that they might understand the Scriptures."

But Thomas was not there; and when he was told that Jesus
had been seen, he would not believe. A week later the disciples were once more assembled. This time Thomas was
with them. Again came Jesus, the doors being shut, and
stood in the midst. "Peace be unto you," he said. Then to
Thomas he added: "Reach hither thy finger and behold my
hands, and reach hither thy hand and thrust it into my side;
and be not faithless but believing." "My Lord and my God!"

exclaimed Thomas. Jesus replied: "Thomas, because thou hast seen me thou hast believed; blessed are they that have not seen and yet have believed."

After these things Jesus showed himself to his disciples at the Sea of Tiberias. For Peter had said to the others, "I go a fishing"; and they had replied, "We also go with thee." They went forth immediately but that night caught nothing. In the morning Jesus stood on the shore, but they did not recognize him. "Children, have ye any meat?" he asked. They answered, "No." He said, "Cast the net on the right side of the ship and ye shall find." When they did so they were not able to draw the net for the multitude of fishes. "It is the Lord!" exclaimed John to Peter. When they came to land they saw bread and a fire of coals with fish laid thereon. "Come and dine," he invited. "And none of the disciples durst ask him, Who art thou? knowing that it was the Lord."


### The Ascension, Mark 16, Luke 24, Acts 1

Jesus was seen "of above five hundred brethren at once," following the resurrection, writes Paul in his first epistle to the Corinthians, "and last of all he was seen of me also as of one born out of due time." And Luke, who now takes up our narrative in his "Acts of the Apostles," records that Jesus, after his ordeal, showed himself alive to his disciples through a period of forty days. Further, on one occasion as he ate with them, he instructed them to wait in Jerusalem "for the promise of the Father."

When therefore they came together at their last meeting they asked, "Lord, wilt thou at this time restore again the kingdom to Israel?" He answered: "It is not for you to know the times or the seasons which the Father hath put in his own power. But ye shall receive power after that the Holy Ghost is come upon you; and ye shall be witnesses unto me both in

Jerusalem and in all Judea and in Samaria and unto the uttermost part of the earth."

When he had thus spoken, "while they beheld, he was taken up, and a cloud received him out of their sight. And while they looked steadfastly toward heaven as he went up, behold, two men stood by them in white apparel," who said: "Ye men of Galilee, why stand ye gazing up into heaven? This same Jesus, which is taken up from you into heaven, shall so come in like manner as ye have seen him go." They then returned from the Mount of Olives to Jerusalem. There they gathered in the upper chamber where they were accustomed to meet, and, with the women and Jesus' mother and brothers, prayed.

Three years had passed since Jesus, doubtful and hungry in the hills back from the Jordan, reasoned out what it means to be the Son of God, and resolved what he would do with his awakened powers. The world was at his feet. He could exploit it. He could rule it. Ambition argued all this. He chose to bear witness to the truth.

# Acts of the Apostles

## Peter, Stephen, and Philip, Acts 1-8

The disciples now numbered about one hundred and twenty. One of their first acts was to select Matthias to take the place of Judas Iscariot. On the day of Pentecost, the harvest feast, suddenly there came a sound from heaven of a rushing mighty wind, which filled the house where they were sitting. Cloven tongues as of fire appeared and rested on them. Filled with the Holy Ghost, they spoke in divers languages as the Spirit gave them utterance.

There were in Jerusalem at the time devout Jews from every nation under heaven. When they heard what was going on, they gathered in wonder asking: "Are not all these which speak Galileans? How hear we every man in his own tongue, wherein we were born?"

Some said, mockingly, "These men are full of new wine." But Peter, standing up with the eleven, declared: "This is what was spoken by the prophet Joel: It shall come to pass in the latter days, saith the Lord, I will pour out of my Spirit upon all flesh; and your sons and your daughters shall prophesy and your young men shall see visions and your old men shall dream dreams." Peter's exhortation, which followed, was gladly received and people were baptized to the number of three thousand.

A man lame from birth, who each day begged at the gate of the temple, observing Peter and John about to enter, asked

246

alms. "Silver and gold have I none," said Peter, "but such as I have give I thee. In the name of Jesus Christ of Nazareth rise up and walk." Immediately his limbs received strength and he stood up and went into the temple with them. Sick folk were brought in from the cities round about and they were healed every one.

The high priest and the Sadducees, filled with indignation, thrust the apostles into the common jail. But the angel of the Lord by night opened the doors and said, "Speak in the temple to the people all the words of this life." They did so in the morning; and when officers came to fetch them from the prison, they found no man within. Gamaliel here counseled, "Refrain from these men and let them alone . . . lest haply ye be found even to fight against God." So they beat the apostles, commanded them to speak no more in the name of Jesus, and let them go.

Stephen, full of faith and power, did wonders and miracles among the people. His disputants, when he charged them with betraying the Just One, stopped their ears and rushed upon him, laying down their clothes at the feet of a young Pharisee, Saul of Tarsus. As Stephen expired under the shower of missiles hurled by the mob, he prayed, "Lord, lay not this sin to their charge."

Unrelenting persecution, in which Saul entered house after house and haled men and women to prison, followed the tragedy, scattering the disciples throughout Judea and Samaria, even to Phoenicia, Cyprus, and Antioch. Philip therefore preached in the city of Samaria. The people, impressed by the many healings which he performed, gave heed to his doctrine. On his way south to Gaza he saw an Ethiopian, who had been to Jerusalem to worship, in his chariot reading Isaiah.

When Philip asked if he understood the book, he replied, "How can I, except some man should guide me?" Philip interpreted the Scripture, and when they reached water baptized him. As they came up the Spirit of the Lord caught away Philip and he was found at Azotus. The Ethiopian went on his way rejoicing. Passing through Azotus Philip preached in all the cities till he came to Caesarea.

## Saul's Conversion, Acts 9

Saul, "breathing out threatenings and slaughter against the disciples," started for Damascus.  As he neared the city "suddenly there shined round about him a light from heaven," and a voice cried, "Saul, Saul, why persecutest thou me?"  He asked, "Who art thou, Lord?"  "I am Jesus whom thou persecutest," came the reply.  Trembling and astonished, Saul prayed, "What wilt thou have me to do?"  "Arise and go into the city and it shall be told thee," was the answer.

Those who were with Saul led him by the hand into Damascus, for he could not see.  Ananias, whom the Lord had instructed in a vision, came to him and said: "Brother Saul, the Lord, even Jesus, that appeared unto thee in the way as thou camest, hath sent me that thou mightest receive thy sight and be filled with the Holy Ghost."  Immediately there fell from Saul's eyes "as it had been scales," and he arose and was baptized.

Straightway he preached Christ in the synagogues of Damascus to the amazement of those who knew he had come with hostile intent.  The Jews having purposed to slay him, the disciples one night lowered him in a basket over the wall of the city.

His freedom gained, he retired to Arabia.  After a season he returned to Damascus and then went on to Jerusalem.  The disciples there were afraid of him at first.  But Barnabas spoke in his behalf and Peter entertained him for a fortnight.  James, the brother of the Lord, also talked with him.  Saul's preaching in Jerusalem soon brought him in danger.  The brethren therefore sent him to Tarsus.

## Gentiles Receive Gospel, Acts 10

Peter, as he passed throughout all quarters, restored a man in Lydda who had been sick of the palsy eight years.  Accord-

ingly the people of Lydda and Saron turned to the Lord.   In
Joppa a disciple named Tabitha, widely known for her good
deeds, had died.   Peter, who was still nearby at Lydda, was
sent for.   When he arrived he put the friends out of the
chamber and kneeled down and prayed.   Then turning to
the body he said, "Tabitha, arise."   She opened her eyes, and
when she saw Peter, sat up.   Many people therefore in Joppa
believed in the Lord.

Cornelius, a devout centurion of the Italian band in Caesarea, was instructed in a vision to send for Peter.   Meanwhile
Peter was admonished in a vision to call no man common or
unclean.   When Peter arrived in Caesarea, Cornelius told of
his vision.   Thereupon Peter remarked, "I perceive that God
is no respecter of persons, but in every nation he that feareth
Him and worketh righteousness is accepted."

As Peter preached to Cornelius and his friends, "the Holy
Ghost fell on all."   The disciples were astonished "because
that on the Gentiles also was poured out the gift of the Holy
Ghost, for they heard them speak with tongues and magnify
God."   When the brethren in Judaea heard that the Gentiles
had received the word of God, they contended with Peter.
But after he had explained the matter they held their peace.

Herod now vexed certain of the church.   He executed
James the brother of John.   Observing that this pleased the
Jews, he put Peter in prison.   But prayer without ceasing was
made for him, and that night an angel of the Lord led him
out to the street.   Going to Mark's house, he related what
had happened, much to the delight of the disciples there
gathered.   Soon he was on his way to another town.   In the
morning there was no small stir among the soldiers when they
could not find him.

## Paul, Barnabas, and Mark, Acts 11; Mark 14

The church at Jerusalem, learning that progress was being
made at Antioch, sent Barnabas there.   It was in Antioch that

the disciples were first called Christians. After a time Barnabas fetched Saul from Tarsus. The two labored successfully at Antioch for a year. Then they set out for the North, taking Mark with them. In most of the cities they found the Gentiles more receptive than the Jews. At Salamis, a city on the island of Cyprus, this provoked Saul (hereafter known as Paul) to say: "It was necessary that the word of God should first have been spoken to you; but seeing ye put it from you, and judge yourselves unworthy of everlasting life, lo we turn to the Gentiles."

Expelled from Cyprus, Paul and Barnabas visited Iconium. There they met with no little success for a time. But later, attacked by both Jews and Gentiles, they fled to Lystra and Derbe. At Lystra, a man lame from birth listened to Paul. Steadfastly beholding him, and perceiving that he had faith to be healed, Paul cried, "Stand upright on thy feet." In response the man leaped and walked. The people exclaimed, "The gods are come down to us in the likeness of men!" They would have offered sacrifices; but Paul protested, "We also are men of like passions with you."

Jews now came to Lystra from other towns where Paul had preached, and stirred up the people to stone him. He was drawn out of town apparently dead; but as the disciples stood around him he revived. Barnabas and he now preached from town to town until they got back to Antioch, where they narrated all that God had done with them, and how he had opened the door of faith to the Gentiles. A dispute having arisen over the necessity of Gentile converts observing Jewish rites, Paul and Barnabas went to Jerusalem to argue the matter. Paul and Peter set forth their experiences and James pleaded for tolerance. Accordingly concessions were made to the Gentiles.

After four years in Antioch Paul and Barnabas decided to revisit the northern cities. Barnabas desired to take Mark with them, but Paul would not have it, because in the middle of their first trip Mark had left them at Pamphylia. So sharp was their difference that they parted, Barnabas and Mark going to Cyprus, and Paul and Silas going northward on the mainland. "So were the churches established in the faith, and increased in number daily."

Sadly enough Paul saw no more of Barnabas. It is pleasant to note, however, that he afterward became reconciled to Mark; because, when nearing his end in Rome, he wrote Timothy: "Only Luke is with me. Take Mark and bring him with thee, for he is profitable to me for the ministry."

It is not unlikely that Mark was the "young man" who slipped out of the sheet he was wearing, and fled, when seized by the mob that memorable night in the garden. Too young to be numbered with the disciples, he must have been acquainted with them, for his mother's house was their rendezvous. That he saw Jesus on occasion cannot be doubted. At times he was with Peter, acting as the apostle's interpreter to Greek-speaking audiences. Thus was Mark equipped to be Jesus' first biographer.

## Timothy, Luke, Priscilla, Apollos, Acts 16-18

At Lystra Timothy, whose father was a Greek, joined Paul; and at Troas, near the Hellespont, the Greek physician Luke. A vision now appeared to Paul: "There stood a man of Macedonia and prayed him, Come over into Macedonia and help us." Loosing from Troas, they stopped at Philippi in Macedonia, where many women accepted the gospel. One of them, Lydia, invited Paul to abide in her house.

When Paul cast out a spirit of divination from a girl who had been a source of much profit to her masters, he and Silas were thrust into prison. At midnight they prayed and sang praises, and the doors swung open. The jailer, when he awoke, would have slain himself, supposing that the prisoners had fled. But Paul cried, "Do thyself no harm, for we are all here." "What must I do to be saved?" he implored. Then they spoke to him the word of the Lord, and he and all his house were baptized.

At Thessalonica, and again at Berea, the next towns visited, there was much tumult over Paul's preaching, and even danger to him, although many believed, both Jews and Greeks. Hence Paul hastened on to Athens. There he disputed with the Jews in the synagogue and with devout persons in the market. The Stoics and Epicureans took him to the Areopagus and invited him to explain his doctrines. "Ye men of Athens," he began, "I perceive that in all things ye are very religious; for as I passed by and beheld your devotions, I found an altar with this inscription, To The Unknown God. . .

"God . . . neither is worshipped with men's hands as though he needed anything, seeing he giveth to all life and breath and all things . . . that they should seek the Lord, if haply they might feel after him and find him, though he be not far from every one of us; for in him we live and move and have our being." When he spoke of the resurrection of Jesus, some of the Athenians mocked, while others said, "We will hear thee again of this matter."

Departing to Corinth, Paul took up his abode with Aquilla and his wife Priscilla, lately from Italy. Paul and Aquilla were of the same craft, tentmakers. Before long opposition from the Jews arose in the synagogue, as had been the case in other cities. Whereupon Paul exclaimed: "Your blood be upon your own heads; I am clean. From henceforth I will go unto the Gentiles." At the end of a year and a half the three went to Ephesus. Priscilla and Aquilla remained there, while Paul toured as far south as Caesarea.

An eloquent Alexandrian Jew named Apollos, knowing only the baptism of John, came to Ephesus. Aquilla and Priscilla, hearing him in the synagogue, expounded to him the way of God more perfectly. On Paul's return he found quite a group of John's disciples in Ephesus who had not heard of the Holy Ghost. When baptized in the name of the Lord Jesus, "they spoke with tongues and prophesied." Paul remained two years in the city, preaching in the school of Tyrannus when opposed in the synagogue.

## Closing Events of Tour, Acts 19

Strolling exorcists, in imitation of Paul, called the name of Christ Jesus over those who had evil spirits, saying, "We adjure you by Jesus whom Paul preacheth." When seven sons of Sceva, chief of the priests, did this to a man, the evil spirit in him answered, "Jesus I know, and Paul I know, but who are ye?" And the man leaped on them and drove them out of the house.

Fear fell on all when this became known to the Jews and Greeks at Ephesus; and many believed. Those who "used curious arts" brought their books together and burned them in public. "So mightily grew the word of God and prevailed."

Demetrius, a silversmith who made shrines for Diana, saw his business in jeopardy because of Paul's preaching that "they be no gods which are made with hands." Accordingly he incited the craftsmen to riot; and for a space of two hours they cried, "Great is Diana of the Ephesians!" Finally the town clerk established order by cautioning, "We are in danger to be called in question for this day's uproar."

. The tumult having subsided, Paul called the disciples together and proceeded to Macedonia. After encouraging the people there, he spent three months in Greece. About to sail for Syria, he learned that the Jews lay in wait for him. Therefore he parted from his disciples, passed through Macedonia again, and sailed from Philippi, joining them at Troas.

Here he stayed for a week. On the eve of his departure for Jerusalem, because he was hurrying to reach the Holy City by the day of Pentecost, he preached till midnight. A young man named Eutychus, who sat in a window, dropped to sleep, as Paul was long preaching, fell from the third loft, and was taken up dead. "Trouble not yourselves," cried Paul as he ran down to him, "for his life is in him." Returning upstairs, Paul talked on till break of day, and departed. Friends brought forth the young man alive, and were not a little comforted.

## Paul Under Arrest, Acts 20-28

At Tyre, and again at Caesarea, the disciples begged him not to go to Jerusalem. But as he would not be dissuaded, they said, "The will of the Lord be done." Violence breaking out in Jerusalem against him, he was rescued by the soldiers and carried up on the stairs of the castle for safety. From there he was permitted to speak. When the people observed that he spoke in Hebrew, they gave him better attention. "I am," he said, "a Jew, born in Tarsus, yet brought up in this city at the feet of Gamaliel and taught according to the perfect manner of the law of the fathers."

He told of meeting Jesus on the road to Damascus and of being sent by him to the Gentiles. At this the audience shouted, "Away with such a fellow from the earth, for it is not fit that he should live." As they cast off their clothes and threw dust in the air, the chief captain had Paul brought into the castle and ordered that he should be examined by scourging, to determine why they cried so against him; but he desisted when reminded that Paul was a Roman citizen.

The next day Paul was brought before the council. Observing that both Pharisees and Sadducees were present, he announced: "I am a Pharisee, the son of a Pharisee; of the hope and resurrection of the dead I am called in question." Promptly dissension arose between the two sects; and the chief captain, fearing lest Paul should be pulled to pieces, commanded the soldiers to take him into the castle. The following night the Lord stood by him and said: "Be of good cheer, Paul; for as thou hast testified of me in Jerusalem, so must thou bear witness also at Rome."

The Jews now conspired to slay him. Hence the chief captain sent him under guard to Felix, governor of Caesarea, where he was held for over two years. King Agrippa, while visiting Caesarea, directed Paul to be brought before him to speak in his own defense. "My manner of life from my youth," said Paul, "know all the Jews, who knew me from the beginning, if they would testify, that after the most straitest

sect of our religion I lived a Pharisee.   And now I stand and
am judged for the hope of the promise made of God unto our
fathers . . . For which hope's sake, King Agrippa, I am accused of the Jews.   Why should it be thought a thing in-
credible with you that God should raise the dead?"

Then Paul spoke of Jesus appearing to him on the road to
Damascus and appointing him to his service.   "Whereupon,
O King Agrippa, I was not disobedient unto the heavenly
vision."   At this point Festus, who had succeeded Felix, interrupted to say: "Paul, thou art beside thyself; much learning
doth make thee mad."   "I am not mad, most noble Festus,"
Paul replied, "but speak forth the words of truth and sober-
ness, for the king knoweth of these things . . . King Agrippa,
believest thou the prophets?   I know that thou believest."
Then said Agrippa to Paul, "Almost thou persuadest me to be
a Christian."   While to Festus he remarked, "This man
might have been set at liberty if he had not appealed unto
Caesar."

For when Festus had come into office and found Paul on
his hands, he asked him if he desired to be sent to Jerusalem
for trial.   "I stand at Caesar's judgment seat," answered Paul,
"where I ought to be judged.   To the Jews have I done no
wrong, as thou very well knowest . . . I appeal unto Caesar."
Then Festus, after he had conferred with the council, answered: "Hast thou appealed unto Caesar?   Unto Caesar
shalt thou go."

On the way to Rome a tempest pursued the ship for two
weeks and finally drove it upon the island of Melita.   Paul
heartened the passengers and crew during the ordeal and even
advised the captain what course to take.   Not a soul was lost.
They were three months on the island, waiting for transport.
The governor received Paul courteously, and Paul healed his
father.   As a result other sick people came and were cured.
So that when they departed, Paul and his friends were presented with such things as they needed.

On his arrival in Rome Paul was allowed to dwell by himself for a time with a soldier who guarded him.   Out of patience with the Jews whom he tried to teach the gospel, he

declared, "Be it known therefore unto you that the salvation of God is sent unto the Gentiles." For two years he dwelt in his own hired house, receiving and teaching all who came.

Here Luke's story ends abruptly. Quite likely he intended to write more. Maybe he did. But nothing further from his pen has come down to us. In due course Paul must have been released, because his writings indicate that he made still another trip to Greece and Asia Minor.

It is believed by many that he carried out his purpose, mentioned in his letter to the Romans, to visit Spain, and by some that he journeyed as far as Great Britain; but the evidence is not conclusive.

Brought to Rome a prisoner the second time, he was not accorded the privileges he enjoyed before. Both Peter and he, there is reason to believe, were martyred by Nero (65 to 68). He mentioned his impending execution in his last letter to Timothy.

# Letters of the Apostles

## Beginnings of New Testament

Christian literature begins with letters written by the apostles to friends and churches. Twenty-one in number they constitute one third of the New Testament. The four Gospels were written between the years 70 and 100, Mark first in Rome and John last in Ephesus, probably. The letters were produced twenty years earlier, that is, in the period between 50 and 70. (All dates here given are necessarily approximate only.)

Jesus had been gone scarcely more than ten years before the letters began to appear. Paul wrote the first ones from Corinth to the Thessalonians; John, who survived all his associates, wrote the last from Ephesus, perhaps as late as 100. The King James Bible, it will be observed, does not arrange the Epistles in the order of their production.

While the personal touch is not absent, doctrine and admonition are stressed. Some of the Epistles, indeed, are little else than sermons. They were calculated to instruct and encourage the churches in their early development and to warn against false teaching and resulting apostasy. Paul's messages to Titus and Philemon were personal notes, terse but intensely human. He instructed Titus, who was pastor or bishop at Crete, on the manner of conducting his office. And to Philemon he returned a runaway slave, Onesimus by name, with an appeal for mercy.

Though some have supposed that the Gospels were orig inally written in Aramaic, the great weight of scholarship in sists that they were penned in Greek. That the Epistles were Greek there is no doubt. Paul was by far the most prolific writer. Generally he dictated his messages though he alway. signed them. They were delivered by friends—Phoebe, Titus Timothy, Luke, and others. Toward the conclusion of his letter to the Galatians it is significant that he said, "Ye see how large a letter I have written unto you with mine own hand."

## Struggle for Good, Romans 7, 8

At the end of his second visit to Macedonia and Greece, Paul found himself at Corinth. For years he had hoped to visit Rome en route to Spain. Now was the way open be- cause there was a temporary lull in his work and the trip by way of Brindisi would not be long. He chose rather to go to Jerusalem to deliver in person contributions which he had gathered for needy Christians. But before starting out, fear- ful that he would never see the Imperial City, he sent his friends there a long letter, expounding the gospel and cau- tioning them against the dangers which experience had shown might confront them. He intrusted the letter to Phoebe. Having in thought his inner struggles, he wrote:

"The good that I would, I do not; but the evil which I would not, that I do. Now if I do that I would not, it is no more I that do it, but sin that dwelleth in me. I find then a law, that when I would do good, evil is present with me, for I delight in the law of God after the inward man; but I see another law in my members, warring against the law of my mind and bringing me into captivity to the law of sin which is in my members. O wretched man that I am! Who shall deliver me from the body of this death? I thank God through Jesus Christ our Lord. So then with the mind I myself serve the law of God; but with the flesh the law of sin.

"There is therefore now no condemnation to them which

re in Christ Jesus, who walk not after the flesh but after the Spirit. For the law of the Spirit of life in Christ Jesus hath made me free from the law of sin and death . . . To be carnally minded is death; but to be spiritually minded is life and peace . . . For as many as are led by the Spirit of God, they are the sons of God. For ye have not received the spirit of bondage again to fear; but ye have received the Spirit of adoption, whereby we cry, Abba, Father . . . For I reckon that the sufferings of this present time are not worthy to be compared with the glory which shall be revealed in us . . . Because the creature itself also shall be delivered from the bondage of corruption into the glorious liberty of the children of God."

Paul got to Italy after all, though in tragic fashion; for, in constant danger from the Jews after reaching Jerusalem, he was rescued by soldiers and held two years in Caesarea. Then, having appealed to Caesar, he was ordered to the Imperial City, a prisoner.


## Eye Hath Not Seen, I Corinthians 2

Before all this, while Paul was in Ephesus, he received a letter from Corinth raising questions of conduct and doctrine. News also came of serious dissensions in the church. There were followers of Paul, of Apollos, of Peter, of Christ. "Is Christ divided?" he asked, "was Paul crucified for you?"

In his replies to the Corinthians the apostle appears at his best, emphasizing those things which "eye hath not seen," the things which abide. Thus:

"And I, brethren, when I came to you, came not with excellency of speech or of wisdom, declaring unto you the testimony of God. For I determined not to know anything among you, save Jesus Christ, and him crucified.

"And I was with you in weakness and in fear and in much trembling. And my speech and my preaching was not with enticing words of man's wisdom, but in demonstration of the Spirit and of power; that your faith should not stand in the wisdom of men, but in the power of God.

"Howbeit we speak wisdom among them that are perfect,
yet not the wisdom of this world, nor of the princes of this
world, that come to naught. But we speak the wisdom of God
in a mystery, even the hidden wisdom, which God ordained
before the world unto our glory; which none of the princes
of this world knew, for had they known it they would not
have crucified the Lord of glory.

"But as it is written: Eye hath not seen nor ear heard,
neither have entered into the heart of man, the things which
God hath prepared for them that love him.

"But God hath revealed them unto us by his Spirit; for the
Spirit searcheth all things, yea, the deep things of God. For
what man knoweth the things of a man, save the spirit of
man which is in him? Even so the things of God knoweth
no man, but the Spirit of God.

"Now we have received, not the spirit of the world, but
the Spirit which is of God, that we might know the things
that are freely given to us of God. Which things also we
speak, not in the words which man's wisdom teacheth, but
which the Holy Ghost teacheth; comparing spiritual things
with spiritual.

"But the natural man receiveth not the things of the Spirit
of God, for they are foolishness unto him; neither can he
know them, because they are spiritually discerned. But he
that is spiritual judgeth all things, yet he himself is judged of
no man. For who hath known the mind of the Lord, that he
may instruct him? But we have the mind of Christ."

## All Things Are Yours, I Corinthians 3

"And I, brethren, could not speak unto you as unto spiritual but as unto carnal, even as unto babes in Christ. I have
fed you with milk, and not with meat; for hitherto ye were
not able to bear it, neither yet now are ye able. For ye are
yet carnal; for whereas there is among you envying and strife
and divisions, are ye not carnal and walk as men?

"For while one saith: I am of Paul; and another, I am of Apollos; are ye not carnal?   Who then is Paul, and who is Apollos, but ministers by whom ye believed, even as the Lord gave to every man?   I have planted, Apollos watered, but God gave the increase.   So then neither is he that planteth any thing, neither he that watereth, but God that giveth the increase.

"Now he that planteth and he that watereth are one; and every man shall receive his own reward according to his own labor.   For we are laborers together with God; ye are God's husbandry, ye are God's building.   According to the grace of God which is given unto me, as a wise master-builder, I have laid the foundation, and another buildeth thereon.   But let every man take heed how he buildeth thereupon.

"For other foundation can no man lay than that is laid, which is Jesus Christ.   Now if any man build upon this foundation gold, silver, precious stones, wood, hay, stubble, every man's work shall be made manifest; for the day shall declare it, because it shall be revealed by fire, and the fire shall try every man's work of what sort it is.   If any man's work abide which he hath built thereupon, he shall receive a reward. If any man's work shall be burned, he shall suffer loss; but he himself shall be saved, yet so as by fire.

"Know ye not that ye are the temple of God, and that the Spirit of God dwelleth in you?   If any man defile the temple of God, him shall God destroy; for the temple of God is holy, which temple ye are.

"Let no man deceive himself.   If any man among you seemeth to be wise in this world, let him become a fool, that he may be wise.   For the wisdom of this world is foolishness with God; for it is written, He taketh the wise in their own craftiness.   And again, The Lord knoweth the thoughts of the wise, that they are vain.

"Therefore let no man glory in men; for all things are yours, whether Paul or Apollos or Cephas or the world or life or death or things present or things to come; all are yours; and ye are Christ's; and Christ is God's."

## Charity, I Corinthians 13

"Though I speak with the tongues of men and of angels
and have not charity, I am become as sounding brass or a
tinkling cymbal.  And though I have the gift of prophecy
and understand all mysteries and all knowledge, and though
I have all faith so that I could remove mountains, and have
not charity, I am nothing.  And though I bestow all my good
to feed the poor, and though I give my body to be burned, and
have not charity, it profiteth me nothing.

"Charity suffereth long, and is kind; charity envieth not
charity vaunteth not itself, is not puffed up, doth not behave
itself unseemly, seeketh not her own, is not easily provoked
thinketh no evil; rejoiceth not in iniquity but rejoiceth in the
truth; beareth all things, believeth all things, hopeth all things,
endureth all things.  Charity never faileth: but whether there
be prophecies, they shall fail; whether there be tongues, they
shall cease; whether there be knowledge, it shall vanish away.

"For we know in part and we prophesy in part; but when
that which is perfect is come, then that which is in part shall
be done away.  When I was a child, I spake as a child, I understood as a child, I thought as a child; but when I became a
man, I put away childish things.  For now we see through a
glass, darkly, but then face to face; now I know in part, but
then shall I know even as also I am known.  And now abideth faith, hope, charity, these three; but the greatest of these
is charity."

## Resurrection, I Corinthians 15

Perhaps the letter Paul received from Corinth brought word
of an epidemic or a shipwreck, with the inquiry, "With what
body do they come in the resurrection?"  For wherever Paul
preached he made the continuity of individual life an outstanding theme; and his argument, which follows, has remained the solace of the Christian world to this day.

"If Christ be not risen," he wrote, "then is our preaching vain and your faith is also vain . . . For since by man came death, by man came also the resurrection of the dead. For as in Adam all die, even so in Christ shall all be made alive. If after the manner of men I have fought with beasts at Ephesus, what advantageth it me if the dead rise not? let us eat and drink, for tomorrow we die.

"But some man will say, How are the dead raised up? and with what body do they come? Thou foolish one, that which thou sowest is not quickened except it die. And that which thou sowest, thou sowest not that body that shall be, but bare grain, it may chance of wheat or of some other grain; but God giveth it a body as it hath pleased him, and to every seed his own body.

"All flesh is not the same flesh; but there is one kind of flesh of men, another flesh of beasts, another of fishes, and another of birds. There are also celestial bodies and bodies terrestrial; but the glory of the celestial is one, and the glory of the terrestrial is another. There is one glory of the sun and another glory of the moon and another glory of the stars; for one star differeth from another star in glory.

"So also is the resurrection of the dead. It is sown in corruption, it is raised in incorruption; it is sown in dishonor, it is raised in glory; it is sown in weakness, it is raised in power; it is sown a natural body, it is raised a spiritual body. There is a natural body and there is a spiritual body. And so it is written, The first man Adam was made a living soul; the last Adam was made a quickening spirit. Howbeit that was not first which is spiritual, but that which is natural; and afterward that which is spiritual.

"The first man is of the earth, earthy; the second man is the Lord from heaven. As is the earthy, such are they also that are earthy; and as is the heavenly, such are they also that are heavenly. And as we have borne the image of the earthy, we shall also bear the image of the heavenly. Now this I say, brethren, that flesh and blood cannot inherit the kingdom of God; neither doth corruption inherit incorruption.

"Behold, I show you a mystery: We shall not all sleep but

we shall all be changed in a moment, in the twinkling of an eye, at the last trump; for the trumpet shall sound and the dead shall be raised incorruptible and we shall be changed. For this corruptible must put on incorruption, and this mortal must put on immortality. So when this corruptible shall have put on incorruption, and this mortal shall have put on immortality, then shall be brought to pass the saying that is written, Death is swallowed up in victory."

## *Inward Man*, II Corinthians 4-12

"We are troubled on every side," Paul resumed in his next letter, "yet not distressed; we are perplexed, but not in despair; persecuted, but not forsaken; cast down but not destroyed . . . Though our outward man perish, yet the inward man is renewed day by day. For our light affliction, which is but for a moment, worketh for us a far more exceeding and eternal weight of glory while we look not at the things which are seen, but at the things which are not seen, for the things which are seen are temporal, but the things which are not seen are eternal.

"For we know that if our earthly house of this tabernacle were dissolved, we have a building of God, an house not made with hands, eternal in the heavens. For in this we groan, earnestly desiring to be clothed upon with our house which is from heaven; if so be that being clothed we shall not be found naked. For we that are in this tabernacle do groan, being burdened; not for that we would be unclothed, but clothed upon, that mortality might be swallowed up of life . . .

"What agreement hath the temple of God with idols? for ye are the temple of the living God; as God hath said, I will dwell in them and walk in them, and I will be their God and they shall be my people."

## Perils and Hardships, II Corinthians 11

"Would to God ye could bear with me a little in my folly . . . That which I speak, I speak it not after the Lord but as it were foolishly in this confidence of boasting. Seeing that many glory after the flesh, I will glory also . . . Are they Hebrews? So am I. Are they Israelites? So am I. Are they the seed of Abraham? So am I. Are they ministers of Christ? I am more; in labors more abundant, in stripes above measure, in prisons more frequent, in deaths oft.

"Of the Jews five times received I forty stripes save one. Thrice was I beaten with rods, once was I stoned, thrice I suffered shipwreck, a night and a day I have been in the deep; in journeyings often, in perils of waters, in perils of robbers, in perils by mine own countrymen, in perils by the heathen, in perils in the city, in perils in the wilderness, in perils in the sea, in perils among false brethren; in weariness and painfulness, in watchings often, in hunger and thirst, in fastings often, in cold and nakedness.

"Beside those things that are without, that which cometh upon me daily, the care of all the churches. Who is weak, and I am not weak? Who is offended, and I burn not? If I must needs glory, I will glory of the things which concern mine infirmities. The God and Father of our Lord Jesus Christ, which is blessed forevermore, knoweth that I lie not. In Damascus the governor under Aretas the king kept the city of the Damascenes with a garrison, desirous to apprehend me. And through a window in a basket was I let down by the wall, and escaped his hands."

## Visions and Revelations, II Corinthians 12, 13

"It is not expedient for me doubtless to glory. I will come to visions and revelations of the Lord. I knew a man in Christ above fourteen years ago (whether in the body, I cannot tell; or whether out of the body, I cannot tell: God knoweth) such a one caught up to the third heaven. And I knew such a man (whether in the body or out of the body, I cannot tell: God knoweth) how that he was caught up into paradise and heard unspeakable words, which it is not lawful for a man to utter.

"Of such a one will I glory; yet of myself I will not glory, but in mine infirmities. For though I would desire to glory, I shall not be a fool, for I will say the truth; but now I forbear, lest any man should think of me above that which he seeth me to be or that he heareth of me.

"And lest I should be exalted above measure through the abundance of the revelations, there was given to me a thorn in the flesh, the messenger of Satan to buffet me, lest I should be exalted above measure. For this thing I besought the Lord thrice, that it might depart from me. And he said unto me: My grace is sufficient for thee; for my strength is made perfect in weakness.

"Most gladly therefore will I rather glory in my infirmities, that the power of Christ may rest upon me. Therefore I take pleasure in infirmities, in reproaches, in necessities, in persecutions, in distresses for Christ's sake; for when I am weak, then am I strong.

"I am become a fool in glorying; ye have compelled me. For I ought to have been commended of you; for in nothing am I behind the very chiefest apostles, though I be nothing. Truly the signs of an apostle were wrought among you in all patience, in signs and wonders and mighty deeds. For what is it wherein ye were inferior to other churches, except it be that I myself was not burdensome to you? Forgive me this wrong . . .

"Finally, brethren, farewell. Be perfect, be of good comfort, be of one mind, live in peace; and the God of love and peace shall be with you . . . The grace of the Lord Jesus Christ, and the love of God, and the communion of the Holy Ghost, be with you all. Amen."

## *Tolerance and Steadfastness, Galatians* 3-6

Paul wrote most of his letters from Rome, while under guard or in prison. One of them, a document of unusual vigor, he addressed to the Galatians. He told them how he came to the gospel. He marveled that they had so soon departed from his instruction. "O foolish Galatians, who hath bewitched you?" he asked. Counseling tolerance, he observed: "There is neither Jew nor Greek, there is neither bond nor free, there is neither male nor female . . . Brethren, if a man be overtaken in a fault, ye which are spiritual restore such an one in the spirit of meekness, considering thyself lest thou also be tempted."

Urging them to hold their ground, he added: "Stand fast therefore in the liberty wherewith Christ hath made us free, and be not entangled again with the yoke of bondage . . . Ye have been called unto liberty; only use not liberty for an occasion to the flesh, but by love serve one another . . . Walk in the Spirit . . . The fruit of the Spirit is love, joy, peace, longsuffering, gentleness, goodness, faith, meekness, temperance: against such there is no law."

## *The Whole Armor, Ephesians* 4-6

Another stirring message from Rome the renowned apostle directed to the Ephesians. "I therefore, the prisoner of the Lord, beseech you that ye walk worthy of the vocation wherewith ye are called," he exhorted, "with all lowliness and meekness, with longsuffering, forbearing one another in love, endeavoring to keep the unity of the Spirit in the bond of peace. There is one body and one Spirit, even as ye are called in one hope of your calling; one Lord, one faith, one baptism, one God and Father of all, who is above all and through all and in you all . . .

"Finally, my brethren, be strong in the Lord and in the

power of his might.   Put on the whole armor of God, that ye may be able to stand against the wiles of the devil.   For we wrestle not against flesh and blood, but against principalities, against powers, against the rulers of the darkness of this world, against spiritual wickedness in high places.

"Wherefore take unto you the whole armor of God, that ye may be able to withstand in the evil day, and having done all, to stand.   Stand therefore, having your loins girt about with truth, and having on the breastplate of righteousness, and your feet shod with the preparation of the gospel of peace; above all, taking the shield of faith, wherewith ye shall be able to quench all the fiery darts of the wicked."

## Alertness and Fidelity, Colossians 2, 3

While writing to the Ephesians Paul also wrote to the Colossians, sending both letters by the same messenger, Tychicus. "Though I be absent in the flesh," he said, "yet am I with you in the spirit, joying and beholding your order and the steadfastness of your faith in Christ . . . Beware lest any man spoil you through philosophy and vain deceit, after the tradition of men, after the rudiments of the world, and not after Christ . . .

"Let no man beguile you of your reward in a voluntary humility and worshipping of angels, intruding into those things which he hath not seen, vainly puffed up by his fleshy mind . . . Set your affections on things above, not on things on the earth . . . Lie not one to another, seeing that ye have put off the old man with his deeds, and have put on the new man, which is renewed in knowledge after the image of Him that created him . . . Let your speech be always with grace, seasoned with salt, that ye may know how ye ought to answer every man."

## *Forgetting the Past, Philippians 1-4*

Paul of course had hours of depression while restrained in the Imperial City. In one of them he started his famous letter to the Philippians: "I am in a strait betwixt two, having a desire to depart and to be with Christ, which is far better; nevertheless to abide in the flesh is more needful for you."

Then in more hopeful mood he exclaimed: "Rejoice in the Lord alway; and again I say, Rejoice. Let your moderation be known unto all men . . . And the peace of God, which passeth all understanding, shall keep your hearts and minds through Christ Jesus.

"Let this mind be in you which was also in Christ Jesus . . . Brethren, I count not myself to have apprehended; but this one thing I do, forgetting those things which are behind, and reaching forth unto those things which are before, I press toward the mark for the prize of the high calling of God in Christ Jesus."

## *Second Coming of Christ, I and II Thessalonians*

The composition of the New Testament began (50 to 52) when Paul, on his first visit to Corinth, addressed a letter to the church in Thessalonica, which he had founded a few months before. Silas and Timothy had just come from there with encouraging news. Little he realized, as he wrote, that he was making Scripture.

In his first communication he featured the return of Jesus in visible form. "For the Lord himself shall descend from heaven with a shout," he said. In his second communication he cautioned the Thessalonians not to take his words too literally. "For that day shall not come except there come a falling away first, and that man of sin be revealed, the son of perdition, who opposeth and exalteth himself above all that is called God or that is worshipped; so that he as God sitteth in the temple of God, showing himself that he is God."

Pursuing the argument, he added: "But I would not have you to be ignorant, Brethren, concerning them which are asleep, that ye sorrow not, even as others which have no hope. For if we believe that Jesus died and rose again, even so them also which sleep in Jesus will God bring with him . . . Wherefore comfort one another with these words."

Turning to exhortation he wrote: "Rejoice evermore. Pray without ceasing. In everything give thanks. For this is the will of God in Christ Jesus concerning you. Quench not the Spirit. Despise not prophesyings. Prove all things; hold fast that which is good. Abstain from all appearance of evil. And the very God of peace sanctify you wholly; and I pray God your whole spirit and soul and body be preserved blameless unto the coming of our Lord Jesus Christ . . . Brethren, pray for us . . . I charge you by the Lord that this epistle be read unto all the holy brethren." So ends Paul's first epistle.

## The Good Fight, II Timothy

Fifteen years later came his last. It was a touching missive to Timothy, whom he called "my dearly beloved son." Not so long ago he had left Timothy at Ephesus. Now he greatly desired to see him, and quickly, for any day he might be sent to execution by Nero. Yet he still had hope, for he asked Timothy to bring his cloak, books, and precious parchments.

Courageous as ever he declared: "For God hath not given us the spirit of fear, but of power and of love and of a sound mind . . . Study to show thyself approved unto God, a workman that needeth not to be ashamed, rightly dividing the word of truth . . . Preach the word; be instant in season, out of season; reprove, rebuke, exhort with all longsuffering and doctrine. For the time will come when they will not endure sound doctrine; but after their own lusts shall they heap to themselves teachers having itching ears, and they shall turn away their ears from the truth and shall be turned unto fables. But watch thou in all things, endure afflictions, do the work of an evangelist, make full proof of thy ministry.

"For I am now ready to be offered, and the time of my departure is at hand. I have fought a good fight, I have finished my course, I have kept the faith. Henceforth there is laid up for me a crown of righteousness, which the Lord, the righteous judge, shall give me at that day; and not to me only, but unto all them also that love his appearing.

"Do thy diligence to come shortly unto me; for Demas hath forsaken me, having loved this present world, and is departed unto Thessalonica; Crescens to Galatia, Titus unto Dalmatia. Only Luke is with me. Take Mark and bring him with thee, for he is profitable to me for the ministry. And Tychicus have I sent to Ephesus. The cloak that I left at Troas with Carpus, when thou comest, bring with thee, and the books, but especially the parchments.

"Alexander the coppersmith did me much evil; the Lord reward him according to his works; of whom be thou ware also, for he hath greatly withstood our words. At my first answer no man stood with me, but all men forsook me. I pray God that it may not be laid to their charge. Notwithstanding the Lord stood with me and strengthened me; that by me the preaching might be fully known, and that all the Gentiles might hear. And I was delivered out of the mouth of the lion. And the Lord shall deliver me from every evil work, and will preserve me unto his heavenly kingdom: to whom be glory forever and ever. Amen.

"Salute Prisca and Aquilla and the household of Onesiphorus. Erastus abode at Corinth; but Trophimus have I left at Miletum sick. Do thy diligence to come before winter. Eubulus greeteth thee, and Pudens and Linus and Claudia and all the brethren. The Lord Jesus Christ be with thy spirit. Grace be with you. Amen."

Not long afterward Timothy himself must have been put under arrest, because the Book of Hebrews carries the news, "Know ye that our brother Timothy is set at liberty!"

## *Faith and Vigilance, Hebrews 2, 4, 7, 11*

Not a little uncertainty hovers about the authorship of the Epistle to the Hebrews. Still undetermined, it has been credited to various notables from Paul to Priscilla. It was intended, of course, for Hebrew Christians, but for just what church or group cannot be said with any degree of assurance. Some authorities believe that it was written about 70, when the fall of Jerusalem, invested by the Roman general Titus, was imminent. Thenceforth the church would radiate from Rome.

In literary form the book is an oration rather than an epistle, eloquent and persuasive. It argues the advantages Christianity offers over Judaism. To those falling away from the church, for in those perilous days apostasy was abroad, it warned, "How shall we escape if we neglect so great salvation?"

It exalts Jesus above all other teachers, "who is made, not after the law of a carnal commandment, but after the power of an endless life." Yet "we have not an high priest which cannot be touched with the feelings of our infirmities, but was in all points tempted like as we are, yet without sin."

Chapter eleven, defining and valuating faith, avers: "Now faith is the substance of things hoped for, the evidence of things not seen . . . Through faith we understand that the worlds were framed by the word of God, so that things which are seen were not made of things which do appear . . . By faith Enoch was translated that he should not see death; and was not found, because God had translated him . . . By faith Noah, being warned of God of things not seen as yet, moved with fear, prepared an ark to the saving of his house . . . By faith Abraham, when he was called to go out into a place which he should after receive for an inheritance, obeyed; and he went out not knowing whither he went . . .

"By faith Moses, when he was born, was hid three months

of his parents, because they saw he was a proper child, and they were not afraid of the king's commandment . . . By faith he forsook Egypt, not fearing the wrath of the king, for he endured as seeing Him who is invisible. . . By faith the walls of Jericho fell down after they were compassed about seven days. By faith Rahab perished not with them that believed not, when she had received the spies with peace.

"And what shall I more say? For the time would fail me to tell of Gideon and of Barak and of Samson and of Jephthah, of David also and Samuel and of the prophets; who through faith subdued kingdoms, wrought righteousness, obtained promises, stopped the mouths of lions, quenched the violence of fire, escaped the edge of the sword, out of weakness were made strong, waxed valiant in fight, turned to flight the armies of the aliens: women received their dead raised to life again."

## Pure Religion, James 1, 5

The James who wrote the Epistle bearing that name was probably the brother of Jesus. Not one of the twelve apostles, he was nevertheless a pillar of the early church in Jerusalem. His message is an incisive sermon, inculcating everyday virtues and putting deeds above words. His admonitions and practical wisdom are as much in point today as when first written.

"My brethren," he exhorted, "count it all joy when ye fall into divers temptations; knowing this, that the trying of your faith worketh patience. But let patience have her perfect work, that ye may be perfect and entire, wanting nothing.

"If any of you lack wisdom, let him ask of God, that giveth to all men liberally and upbraideth not, and it shall be given him. But let him ask in faith, nothing wavering; for he that wavereth is like a wave of the sea driven with the wind and tossed. For let not that man think that he shall receive anything of the Lord. A double minded man is unstable in all his ways. . .

"But be ye doers of the word, and not hearers only, deceiving your own selves. For if any be a hearer of the word, and not a doer, he is like unto a man beholding his natural face in a glass; for he beholdeth himself and goeth his way and straightway forgetteth what manner of man he was. But whoso looketh into the perfect law of liberty, and continueth therein, he being not a forgetful hearer but a doer of the work, this man shall be blessed in his deed.

"If any man among you seem to be religious, and bridleth not his tongue, but deceiveth his own heart, this man's religion is vain. Pure religion and undefiled before God and the Father is this, to visit the fatherless and widows in their affliction, and to keep himself unspotted from the world . . .

"Is any among you afflicted? let him pray. Is any merry? let him sing psalms. Is any sick among you? let him call for the elders of the church; and let them pray over him, anointing him with oil in the name of the Lord. And the prayer of faith shall save the sick, and the Lord shall raise him up; and if he have committed sins, they shall be forgiven him."


## Goodly Conversation, I Peter

The First Epistle of Peter, probably written from Rome, was directed to the Christians of Asia Minor. It cautioned and strengthened them against Nero's persecution. "Thou art Peter," the Lord had said to him, "and upon this rock will I build my church." Well was the prophecy fulfilled, because Peter became not only an outstanding disciple, but the leader of the early apostolic movement. Mark must have obtained from him, while the two were associated, much of the material for his Gospel. The impetuous disciple admonished:

"It is written, Be ye holy for I am holy. And if ye call on the Father, who without respect of persons judgeth according to every man's work, pass the time of your sojourning here in fear; forasmuch as ye know that ye were not redeemed with corruptible things, as silver and gold, from your vain conversation received by tradition from your fathers, but with the precious blood of Christ, as of a lamb without blemish and without spot; who verily was foreordained before the foundation of the world, but was manifest in these last times for you . . .

"Seeing ye have purified your souls in obeying the truth through the Spirit unto unfeigned love of the brethren, see that ye love one another with a pure heart fervently; being born again, not of corruptible seed but of incorruptible, by the word of God, which liveth and abideth forever . . .

"Submit yourselves to every ordinance of man for the Lord's sake; whether it be to the king as supreme or unto governors as unto them that are sent by him for the punishment of evildoers and for the praise of them that do well. For so is the will of God, that with well-doing ye may put to silence the ignorance of foolish men; as free, and not using your liberty for a cloak of maliciousness but as the servants of God.

"Honor all men. Love the brotherhood. Fear God. Honor the king. Servants, be subject to your masters with all fear; not only to the good and gentle but also to the froward. For this is thankworthy, if a man for conscience toward God endure grief, suffering wrongfully. For what glory is it if, when ye be buffeted for your faults, ye shall take it patiently? But if, when ye do well and suffer for it, ye take it patiently, this is acceptable with God . . .

"Be sober, be vigilant; because your adversary the devil, as a roaring lion, walketh about, seeking whom he may devour; whom resist steadfast in the faith, knowing that the same afflictions are accomplished in your brethren that are in the world. But the God of all grace, who hath called us unto his eternal glory by Christ Jesus, after that ye have suffered a while, make you perfect, stablish, strengthen, settle you. To Him be glory and dominion forever and ever."

### He First Loved Us, I John 1-4

Of the three letters contributed by John, the apostle of love, the first is by far the most important. "That which we have seen and heard declare we unto you," he writes, "that ye also may have fellowship with us; and truly our fellowship is with the Father and with his Son Jesus Christ. And these things write we unto you, that your joy may be full.

"This then is the message which we have heard of him, and declare unto you, that God is light and in him is no darkness at all . . . He that loveth his brother abideth in the light, and there is none occasion of stumbling in him. But he that hateth his brother is in darkness and walketh in darkness and knoweth not whither he goeth, because that darkness hath blinded his eyes . . .

"Love not the world, neither the things that are in the world; if any man love the world, the love of the Father is not in him. For all that is in the world, the lust of the flesh and the lust of the eyes and the pride of life, is not of the Father but is of the world. And the world passeth away, and the lust thereof; but he that doeth the will of God abideth forever . . .

"Behold, what manner of love the Father hath bestowed upon us, that we should be called the sons of God: therefore the world knoweth us not, because it knew him not. Beloved, now are we the sons of God; and it doth not yet appear what we shall be, but we know that when he shall appear we shall be like him, for we shall see him as he is. And every man that hath this hope in him purifieth himself, even as He is pure . . .

"Whosoever is born of God doth not commit sin; for His seed remaineth in him, and he cannot sin because he is born of God . . . Believe not every spirit, but try the spirits whether they are of God . . .

"Let us love one another; for love is of God, and every one that loveth is born of God and knoweth God. He that loveth not, knoweth not God, for God is love. In this was manifested the love of God toward us, because that God sent his only begotten Son into the world, that we might live through him . . .

"Beloved, if God so loved us, we ought also to love one another. No man hath seen God at any time. If we love one another, God dwelleth in us and his love is perfected in us . . . And we have known and believed the love that God hath to us. God is love; and he that dwelleth in love dwelleth in God, and God in him . . . There is no fear in love, but perfect love casteth out fear, because fear hath torment. He that feareth is not made perfect in love. We love Him, because He first loved us."

## Doxology, Jude

The last Epistle of the New Testament bears the name of Jude, that is, Judas, one of Jesus' brothers. It closes with the matchless doxology: "Now unto Him that is able to keep you from falling, and to present you faultless before the presence of His glory with exceeding joy, to the only wise God our Savior, be glory and majesty, dominion and power, both now and ever."

One is here reminded, naturally, of the strangely beautiful benediction from the sixth chapter of Numbers: "The Lord bless thee and keep thee; the Lord make his face shine upon thee and be gracious unto thee; the Lord lift up his countenance upon thee and give thee peace."

## Last Book of Bible

The last book of the Bible, The Revelation of John the Divine, is at hand. The author, as the opening sentence intimates, had been exiled, because of his advocacy of Christianity, to the small rocky island of Patmos, fifty miles out from Ephesus in the Aegean.

In the course of a century a person, if he lives that long, may, through growth and change, become three different individuals in point of temperament. Hence the same man may have been the author of the Gospel of John, the Epistles of John, and the Revelation of John, notwithstanding the widely divergent tone and quality of the three. But Bible scholars are not agreed that such is the case.

The gorgeous imagery of the Revelation or Apocalypse, intelligible enough, it may be supposed, to the harried Christians of the time for whose encouragement it was primarily intended, was meaningless to the Roman censor, and presumably was meant to be. Its unrestrained symbolism has been the despair of many an interpreter since. But no one questions that the splendor of the composition makes it a fitting conclusion to the Book of Books.

# The Revelation

"I John, who also am your brother and companion in tribulation and in the kingdom and patience of Jesus Christ, was in the isle that is called Patmos, for the word of God and for the testimony of Jesus Christ. I was in the Spirit on the Lord's day and heard behind me a great voice as of a trumpet . . . And I turned to see the voice that spake with me. And being turned, I saw seven golden candlesticks; and in the midst of the seven candlesticks one like unto the Son of man, clothed with a garment down to the foot and girt about the paps with a golden girdle.

"His head and his hairs were white like wool, as white as snow; and his eyes were as a flame of fire; and his feet like unto fine brass, as if they burned in a furnace; and his voice as the sound of many waters. And he had in his right hand seven stars; and out of his mouth went a sharp two edged sword; and his countenance was as the sun shineth in his strength.

"And when I saw him, I fell at his feet as dead. And he laid his right hand upon me, saying unto me, Fear not; I am the First and the Last. I am he that liveth, and was dead; and behold, I am alive forevermore, amen; and have the keys of hell and of death . . .

"After this I looked, and behold, a door was opened in

heaven. And the first voice which I heard was as it were of a trumpet talking with me; which said, Come up hither and I will show thee things which must be hereafter. And immediately I was in the Spirit; and behold, a throne was set in heaven and one sat on the throne.

"And round about the throne were four and twenty seats. And upon the seats I saw four and twenty elders sitting, clothed in white raiment; and they had on their heads crowns of gold. And out of the throne proceeded lightnings and thunderings and voices; and there were seven lamps of fire burning before the throne, which are the seven Spirits of God. And before the throne there was a sea of glass like unto crystal; and in the midst of the throne, and round about the throne, were four beasts full of eyes before and behind . . .

"And I saw in the right hand of him that sat on the throne a book written within and on the backside, sealed with seven seals. And I saw a strong angel proclaiming with a loud voice, Who is worthy to open the book and to loose the seals thereof? And no man in heaven nor in earth, neither under the earth, was able to open the book, neither to look thereon.

"And I wept much because no man was found worthy to open and to read the book, neither to look thereon. And one of the elders saith unto me, Weep not; behold, the Lion of the tribe of Juda, the Root of David, hath prevailed to open the book and to loose the seven seals thereof.

"And I beheld, and lo, in the midst of the throne and of the four beasts, and in the midst of the elders, stood a Lamb as it had been slain, having seven horns and seven eyes, which are the seven Spirits of God sent forth into all the earth. And he came and took the book out of the right hand of him that sat upon the throne."


## The Four Horsemen, Rev. 6

"And when he had taken the book, the four beasts and four and twenty elders fell down before the Lamb, having every

one of them harps and golden vials full of odors, which are
the prayers of saints. And they sang a new song, saying:
Thou art worthy to take the book and to open the seals
thereof, for thou wast slain and hast redeemed us to God by
thy blood out of every kindred and tongue and people and
nation, and hast made us unto our God kings and priests; and
we shall reign on the earth.

"And I saw when the Lamb opened one of the seals, and I
heard, as it were the noise of thunder, one of the four beasts
saying, Come and see. And I saw, and behold a white horse;
and he that sat on him had a bow, and a crown was given unto
him, and he went forth conquering and to conquer.

"And when he had opened the second seal, I heard the
second beast say, Come and see. And there went out another horse that was red; and power was given to him that sat
thereon to take peace from the earth, and that they should
kill one another, and there was given unto him a great sword.

"And when he had opened the third seal, I heard the third
beast say, Come and see. And I beheld, and lo a black horse;
and he that sat on him had a pair of balances in his hand.
And I heard a voice in the midst of the four beasts say, A
measure of wheat for a penny, and three measures of barley
for a penny; and see thou hurt not the oil and the wine.

"And when he had opened the fourth seal, I heard the voice
of the fourth beast say, Come and see. And I looked, and
behold a pale horse; and his name that sat on him was Death,
and Hell followed with him. And power was given unto
them over the fourth part of the earth to kill with sword and
with hunger and with death and with the beasts of the earth."

## *The Little Book, Rev. 10*

"And I saw another mighty angel come down from heaven,
clothed with a cloud; and a rainbow was upon his head, and
his face was as it were the sun, and his feet as pillars of fire;
and he had in his hand a little book open; and he set his right

foot upon the sea and his left foot on the earth, and cried with a loud voice as when a lion roareth; and when he had cried, seven thunders uttered their voices. And when the seven thunders had uttered their voices, I was about to write; and I heard a voice from heaven saying unto me, Seal up those things which the seven thunders uttered and write them not.

"And the angel which I saw stand upon the sea and upon the earth lifted up his hand to heaven, and sware by Him that liveth forever and ever, who created heaven and the things that therein are, and the earth and the things that therein are, and the sea and the things which are therein, that there should be time no longer; but in the days of the voice of the seventh angel, when he shall begin to sound, the mystery of God should be finished as he hath declared to his servants the prophets.

"And the voice which I heard from heaven spake unto me again and said, Go and take the little book which is open in the hand of the angel which standeth upon the sea and upon the earth. And I went unto the angel and said unto him, Give me the little book. And he said unto me, Take it and eat it up; and it shall make thy belly bitter, but it shall be in thy mouth sweet as honey. And I took the little book out of the angel's hand and ate it up, and it was in my mouth sweet as honey; and as soon as I had eaten it, my belly was bitter."

## War in Heaven, Rev. 12

"And there appeared a great wonder in heaven: A woman clothed with the sun and the moon under her feet, and upon her head a crown of twelve stars. And she being with child cried . . . to be delivered. And there appeared another wonder in heaven: A great red dragon, having seven heads and ten horns and seven crowns upon his heads. And his tail drew the third part of the stars of heaven and did cast them to the earth. And the dragon stood before the woman . . . to devour her child . . .

"And she brought forth a man child who was to rule all nations with a rod of iron. And her child was caught up unto God and to his throne. And the woman fled into the wilderness, where she hath a place prepared of God, that they should feed her there a thousand two hundred and threescore days.

"And there was war in heaven: Michael and his angels fought against the dragon; and the dragon fought and his angels, and prevailed not, neither was their place found any more in heaven. And the great dragon was cast out, that old serpent called the Devil and Satan, which deceiveth the whole world; he was cast out into the earth, and his angels were cast out with him.

"And I heard a loud voice saying in heaven: Now is come salvation and strength and the kingdom of our God and the power of his Christ; for the accuser of our brethren is cast down, which accused them before our God day and night.

"And they overcame him by the blood of the Lamb, and by the word of the testimony; and they loved not their lives unto the death. Therefore rejoice, ye heavens, and ye that dwell in them. Woe to the inhabiters of the earth and of the sea! For the devil is come down unto you, having great wrath, because he knoweth that he hath but a short time.

"And when the dragon saw that he was cast unto the earth, he persecuted the woman which brought forth the man child. And to the woman were given two wings of a great eagle, that she might fly into the wilderness, into her place, where she was nourished for a time and times and half a time from the face of the serpent.

"And the serpent cast out of his mouth water as a flood after the woman, that he might cause her to be carried away of the flood. And the earth helped the woman; and the earth opened her mouth and swallowed up the flood which the dragon cast out of his mouth. And the dragon was wroth with the woman and went to make war with the remnant of her seed, which keep the commandments of God and have the testimony of Jesus Christ."

## The Water of Life, Rev. 21, 22

"And I saw a new heaven and a new earth; for the first heaven and the first earth were passed away, and there was no more sea. And I John saw the holy city, new Jerusalem, coming down from God out of heaven, prepared as a bride adorned for her husband. And I heard a great voice out of heaven saying: Behold, the tabernacle of God is with men, and he will dwell with them, and they shall be his people, and God himself shall be with them and be their God. And God shall wipe away all tears from their eyes; and there shall be no more death, neither sorrow nor crying, neither shall there be any more pain: for the former things are passed away.

"And he that sat upon the throne said, Behold, I make all things new. And he said unto me, Write: for these words are true and faithful. And he said unto me: It is done. I am Alpha and Omega, the beginning and the end. I will give unto him that is athirst of the fountain of the water of life freely. He that overcometh shall inherit all things; and I will be his God and he shall be my son.

"And he showed me a pure river of water of life, clear as crystal, proceeding out of the throne of God and of the Lamb. In the midst of the street of it, and on either side of the river, was there the tree of life, which bare twelve manner of fruits and yielded her fruit every month; and the leaves of the tree were for the healing of the nations.

"And there shall be no more curse: but the throne of God and of the Lamb shall be in it; and his servants shall serve him: and they shall see his face; and his name shall be in their foreheads. And there shall be no night there; and they need no candle, neither light of the sun; for the Lord God giveth them light: and they shall reign forever and ever.

"Blessed are they that do his commandments, that they may have right to the tree of life and may enter in through the gates into the city. And the Spirit and the bride say, Come. And let him that heareth say, Come. And let him that is athirst come. And whosoever will, let him take the water of life freely."

# Index